WHEN MORE IS LESS

ASTRI SUHRKE

When More is Less

*The International Project
in Afghanistan*

Columbia University Press
New York

Columbia University Press
Publishers Since 1893
New York
cup.columbia.edu
© Astri Suhrke, 2011
All rights reserved

Library of Congress Cataloging-in-Publication Data

Suhrke, Astri.
  When more is less : the international project in Afghanistan / Astri Suhrke.
    p. cm.
  Includes bibliographical references and index.
  ISBN 978-0-231-70272-0 (cloth: alk. paper)
  ISBN 978-0-231-80066-2 (e-book)
  1. Nation-building—Afghanistan. 2. Peace-building—Afghanistan.
  3. Postwar reconstruction—Afghanistan. 4. Democratization—
  Afghanistan. 5. National security—Afghanistan. 6. Afghanistan—Politics
  and government—2001– I. Title.

  DS371.4.S85 2011
  958.104'71—dc23

                    2011029523

♾

Columbia University Press books are printed on permanent and durable acid-free paper. This book is printed on paper with recycled content.
Printed in India

c 10 9 8 7 6 5 4 3 2 1

References to Internet Web sites (URLs) were accurate at the time of writing. Neither the author nor Columbia University Press is responsible for URLs that may have expired or changed since the manuscript was prepared.

CONTENTS

PREFACE AND ACKNOWLEDGEMENTS

This book has been a long journey. It started on a flight from Delhi to Kabul in November 1987. The Ariana plane was packed with business-men, officials and what seemed to be ordinary traders, including a lime vendor from Delhi who had placed her huge net of brightly coloured fruit in the middle of the aisle. In the back of the plane was a group of Indian and foreign journalists, including myself, an academic equipped with a press card from the Norwegian daily *Arbeiderbladet*. We had been invited by the Afghan Ministry of Foreign Affairs to cover the upcoming *loya jirga*—a traditional Afghan grand assembly called by the king to consult on important matters of state. This *loya jirga* was called by President Najibullah to launch his policy of national unity and reconciliation as the Soviet Union prepared to withdraw its troops from Afghanistan.

It was my first and memorable introduction to the country. Subse-quently there were more visits, the next one less than a year later when the first Soviet troops were heading home. It was a bright and sunny day in May 1988. The tanks rolled out of Kabul towards the Salang Pass, their crews decorated with garlands of pink and blue plastic flowers. Bands were playing and schoolchildren lined the road waving Afghan flags. We followed them northwards (courtesy of the Afghan Ministry of Foreign Affairs and the Soviet military command), across the Amu Darya and into what was then still the Soviet Union. Here a huge ban-quet of rice and lamb was laid out under trees and more bands were playing. Returning to Kabul a year or so later, and again in 1990, I found the capital eerily quiet, but the streets were still perfectly safe—except for the odd incoming shell from the *mujahedin*—and the Kabu-lis politely answered my questions about their expectations of the future.

These early encounters with Afghanistan probably shaped much of my later work on the international involvement in the country. I wrote about my visits to Communist-controlled Afghanistan in a book published in Oslo called *Det Andre Afghanistan* (The Other Afghanistan), and subsequently followed events from a distance, not returning until July 2001, just before the US-led invasion. In the following years I frequently visited to do research or prepare reports commissioned by donor governments. The present book draws heavily on this work. Earlier versions of some sections have appeared in journals or working papers and been presented at seminars. The list of institutions and individuals to which I am indebted is therefore long.

The Chr. Michelsen Institute in Bergen provided generous support throughout in the form of time, other resources, a professional environment and splendid colleagues. The Norwegian Ministry of Foreign Affairs commissioned several reports, enabling me to spend time in Afghanistan and donor countries' capitals to collect data. The Ford Foundation awarded a grant that made it possible to take time out and start on the book in earnest. The Carnegie Endowment for International Peace, where I was a non-resident fellow for a time, helped provide access in Washington. The Research Council of Norway funded a project on post-conflict violence that included Afghanistan as a case. The Norwegian Center for Peacebuilding (NOREF) supported recent research in a joint project with the Peace Research Institute, Oslo (PRIO), to which the German Marshall Fund of the United States also contributed. The Norwegian Ministry of Foreign Affairs funded an annual series of seminars on Afghanistan organized jointly by PRIO and the Chr. Michelsen Institute, which enabled us to bring in external analysts and other speakers to maintain a continuous dialogue about Afghan affairs.

Participation in other conferences and seminars over the years has contributed in numerous ways. I wish in particular to thank (in alphabetical order) Mariano Aguirre for inviting me to several seminars at FRIDE in Madrid, Roland Paris and Tim Sisk for including me in the Research Partnership on Statebuilding that was a multi-year event, Whit Mason and Martin Krygier for the conference on rule of law in Afghanistan held at the University of New South Wales, Roland Paris, Ted Newman and Oliver Richmond for the Sarajevo workshop on liberal peacebuilding, William Maley for hosting me at the Asia-Pacific College of Diplomacy at the Australian National University, Michael

Pugh for the conference on transforming war economies in Plymouth, Amin Saikal for seminars at the Australian National University, Conrad Schetter for the conference in Bonn on Afghan local politics, Susanne Schmeidl for the workshop on peacebuilding in Amersfoort, Shahrbanou Tadjbakhsh for the seminar on liberal peacebuilding at the Sciences Po in Paris, the Canadian Armed Forces for a very different kind of conference in Ottawa—a biannual NATO meeting on PSYOPS in counterinsurgency and stabilization operations—Andrew Wilder for the conference on 'Winning Hearts and Minds' at Wilton Park, and Susan Woodward for the workshop on aid and statebuilding at the Graduate Center, CUNY, as well as for constructive comments and warm support throughout. In Norway, conferences on Afghanistan at the Nansenskolen and Krigsskolen (the Norwegian Army Academy) provided contrasting but equally interesting perspectives. The invitation from Jonathan Goodhand last year to give the Eighth Anthony Hyman Memorial lecture at SOAS was the final straw that made me reassemble the pieces I had collected over the years into a sharpened thesis.

I have had the good fortune to work with colleagues on research projects that have contributed directly or indirectly to this book. Joint publications are duly credited in the footnotes; I also wish to acknowledge co-authors or co-researchers: Orzala Ashraf, Kaja Borchgrevink, Torunn Wimpelmann Chaudhary, Aziz Hakimi, Kristian Berg Harpviken, Jolyon Leslie, Arve Ofstad, Abdul Najimi, Akbar Sarwari and Arne Strand.

Friends and colleagues have read and commented on earlier versions of parts of this book: Martine van Bijlert, Torunn Wimpelmann Chaudhary, Aziz Hakimi, Michael Hartmann, Amin Saikal and Arne Strand. Special thanks to William Maley who read the entire manuscript, pointed out mistakes and challenged my analysis on critical points. Special thanks also to Howard Adelman—friend, colleague and mentor—who read, commented on, and critiqued all the chapters and has been a source of continuous inspiration and encouragement. All have saved me from factual mistakes and questionable interpretations; whatever remains of both kinds are exclusively mine.

Over the years, many other friends and colleagues have helped me think through the enormously complicated issues of international intervention in Afghanistan, but I wish to single out three Afghan friends: Mohammedi, my government 'minder' during my first visits to the country who, despite his formal position, was extraordinarily informative, friendly and helpful and, despite or because of his young age, had a deep commitment to a progressive and peaceful Afghanistan; Hedayat, who patiently entertained my questions about Afghan affairs in conversations that started in Washington and continued in Delhi, Peshawar and Kabul; and Najimi, my wise and favourite travel companion in Afghanistan.

Finally, I wish to acknowledge a deep debt of gratitude to my husband, Garry, and to our children, Arne, Finn and Toril, for their patience, support and understanding throughout the journey. I promise them—the next one will be shorter.

1

INTRODUCTION

THE LIBERAL PROJECT

A decade after the US-led invasion of Afghanistan in October 2001 felled the Taliban regime and triggered a massive international effort to create a new social order, there were about 150,000 NATO and other allied forces in Afghanistan—more than the Soviet Union had at the height of its engagement. Aid commitments had been in the magnitude of US$5–8 billion a year; the Afghan National Development Strategy (2008–2013) was estimated to require US$10 billion a year. Around sixty governmental donors and forty-seven troop contributing countries were operating in the country. There were parallel structures of administration on virtually all levels of government. International advisers, contractors and NGOs were ubiquitous. About two-thirds of all aid was channelled through an 'external budget' administered directly by foreign donors.

What were the results of this huge presence and infusion of capital? There were some positive indicators, particularly in the health and educational sector. A few ministries functioned reasonably well (notably the Ministry of Finance, the Ministry of Public Health and the Ministry of Reconstruction and Rural Development). In the rural development sector, the National Solidarity Programme was a showcase of success. On the other side of the ledger were massive corruption, poor governance, the uncertainty of economic growth in the aid bubble, a steadily expanding insurgency and mounting violence that affected combatants and civilians alike. The UN reported that 7,120 civilians were killed and injured in 2010 as a result of the war, an increase of 19 per cent over the same period the previous year.[1] Comparisons with the ill-fated interventions of the US in Vietnam and the Soviets in Afghanistan had become common. The US commander of the combined forces in Afghanistan had warned in late 2009 that NATO was on the point of losing the war. The surge announced by President Barack Obama in December of the same year was widely understood as part of an exit strategy. It seemed that the Western coalition had arrived at a point where, in effect, it had to fight its way out.

How did it come to this? That is the principal question of this book. It subdivides into two themes. The first deals with the dynamic of the intervention and the related peacebuilding mission. What were the forces shaping this grand international project? What explains the apparent systemic bias towards a deeper and broader involvement? It occurred despite an initial celebration in the UN of 'a light footprint' and a conservative political doctrine in Washington that eschewed 'nation-building' as a task suitable for US foreign policy. Nevertheless, a transformational, multinational project to secure, reconstruct, modernize and democratize Afghanistan took form and grew steadily despite—or because of—increasing evidence that earlier aid efforts had not produced the expected results. As difficulties appeared, goals slipped and conflict intensified, the international reaction was to get more deeply involved. The response was sometimes more of the same (more troops, more money, more technical assistance), and sometimes 'this' rather than 'that' (bottom-up rather than top-down statebuilding, supporting informal mechanisms of justice rather than formal institutions of justice). How do we explain this process? Was it the result of a deliberate strategy, or did the international community stray onto a path not originally intended but from which it could not extricate itself—a quagmire of sorts?

A second set of questions explores the reasons for the very modest results of the international engagement. Conventional explanations have focused on the difficult context—the negative reverberations from the war in Iraq and the sanctuary enjoyed by the Afghan insurgents in Pakistan—as well as the initially limited resources committed by the United States in the first post-Taliban years. This book explores a different trajectory. It asks to what extent the international project itself was part of the problem rather than a solution. If so, what were the reasons? Did the enterprise itself contain tensions and contradictions that contributed to the lack of progress?

The book is constructed as a narrative. After describing the starting point—the vision of a 'light footprint'—the narrative is organized thematically according to the principal tasks undertaken by the UN and the US-led coalition. The dual military function of defeating terrorists and insurgents while providing 'security assistance' to the Afghan government is examined in chapters 3 and 4; the principal civilian aid activities are discussed in chapters 5–7 (statebuilding, democracy assistance and legal reform). Yet a narrative is never just a plain description; like all narratives, this one also has themes and perspectives that frame the story. To make them explicit, the remainder of this chapter will outline the interpretative framework that guides the narrative, and, where appropriate, provide contextual information that is useful for understanding the forces of involvement and explaining their consequences.

But first, a few clarifications. The term 'project' is used throughout this book as short-hand for the international engagement that took form soon after 2001 to establish a stable, internationally 'responsible' and internally liberal, political order in Afghanistan. It did not always seem to be 'a project'—it was not entirely clear who the participants were, and who worked for, or against, whom. The term nevertheless seems appropriate. It conveys the overarching sense of purpose and the common structures that developed. On the military side, a more unified command structure emerged, anchored in NATO but led by the United States. On the civilian side, successive structures to coordinate the aid agencies culminated in the Joint Coordination and Management Board, composed of the Afghan government and its main international supporters. The UN spread—or tried to spread—an umbrella of authority over the peacebuilding enterprise and established an assistance mission, UNAMA, for this purpose. The Afghans were part of the project as well, mostly in roles defined as local/national 'partner' or 'beneficiary'. Other Afghans had declared *jihad* against the project from the beginning, and their numbers were growing throughout the first post-2001 decade.

It might be objected that the narrative focuses overwhelmingly on the problems of the enterprise, ignoring its achievements and the improvement in the lives of many Afghans after 2001. Yes, there were islands of progress. Nevertheless, the focus is on the overarching problems because they seem greater and, certainly by early 2011, more consequential in terms of the cost and suffering of all parties concerned, and also because they form a striking contrast to the ambitious aims of the project and the high hopes it generated.

3

Forces of Involvement

As the difficulties of the US-led forces in Afghanistan mounted despite progressively greater commitment of resources and troops, the analogy of the Vietnam War and the dreaded quagmire-word started to appear. But 'quagmire' suggests an agency that is innocent of purpose and weak in action; in the physical world, a quagmire drags down a victim who has strayed into a dangerous area and only sinks in deeper while struggling to get out. This hardly describes US policy even in Vietnam, and some critics at the time offered a contrary analysis. The now classic 1971 article by Leslie Gelb entitled, 'Vietnam: The System Worked' offers an intriguing parallel with the present international engagement in Afghanistan. Gelb's main argument can be summarized as follows:

- 'The deepening involvement was not inadvertent. It flowed with sureness from the perceived stakes and attendant high objectives'. US leaders considered it 'vital not to lose Vietnam by force to Communism' (pp. 140–41). The loss would affect the US's position as a global power and have very adverse domestic repercussions by 'opening floodgates to domestic criticism and attack for being "soft" on Communism' (p. 143).
- Once the US had established itself in Vietnam, bureaucratic judgements and stakes played a part. 'The Foreign Service had to prove that it could bring about political stability in Saigon and "build a nation". The CIA had to prove that pacification would work. AID had to prove that millions of dollars in assistance and advice could bring political returns' (p. 144).
- Each administration had to confront only the costs relevant at the time of their holding office, and each 'was prepared to pay the costs it could foresee for itself.... Each could at least pass the baton on to the next' (p. 145).
- The leaders were aware that the war was going badly and after a certain point did not expect to win militarily. Nevertheless, 'they allowed the impression of "winnability" to grow in order to justify their already heavy investment and domestic support for the war. The strategy was to persevere' (p. 152).[2]

Arguably, the analysis captures the key factors that worked to deepen the international project in Afghanistan as well. It was not simply a quagmire dynamic. Substituting 'international terrorism' for 'Communism' and 'liberal peace' for 'the free world' gives us the strategic doctrines and ideological elements that framed the launching of the project and thereafter helped sustain it. Bureaucratic momentum, organizational interests, aid lobbies and a cascading of objectives further deepened the commitment, making it progressively harder to turn around and change course.

Strategic Engagement

The international involvement in Afghanistan in late 2001 rested on two separate but interrelated foundations. The US military intervention—Operation Enduring Freedom, launched soon after the attacks on New York and Washington—was designed to eliminate an international terrorist network and its Taliban host. The Bush Administration's explicit policy of regime change triggered a much broader response in the international community, designed to create a new social order in Afghanistan. Both the military intervention and the peacebuilding mission reflected strategic decisions to engage.

The Military Intervention

In a sense, the US invasion of Afghanistan was a curious accident of history. Enraged by the attacks on New York and Washington, the Bush Administration invaded a country where the US previously had demonstrated only limited and vicarious interests. While the invasion of Iraq in 2003 was part of a broader imperial design for the Middle East, Central Asia was of peripheral concern to the neo-conservatives who at the time dominated the strategic thinking of the Bush Administration. Yet strategic considerations in a broader sense determined the invasion of Afghanistan. Responding to the 9/11 attacks by going to war in Afghanistan was perfectly in line with the Administration's national security doctrine that celebrated *Realpolitik* and the importance of military power in the conduct of US foreign policy.

The Administration's decision to remove the Taliban regime, rather than take focused, punitive measures against Al-Qaeda alone, proved to be a critical juncture. The stage was now set for a wider war, which quickly developed from the step-wise interaction between hostile forces. US troops raided Afghan villages to hunt for both Taliban and

Al-Qaeda (or the AQT, as the US military referred to the enemy at the time), and empowered Afghan militias to go after their local Taliban rivals. Negotiations and amnesty were mostly ruled out. New acts of international terrorism steadied the resolve of the US and its allies to defeat the problem at its presumed roots in Afghanistan and, increasingly, in Pakistan as well. Pakistan provided sanctuary to the Taliban and associated foreign fighters—as Pakistan always has done for Afghan rebels. The widening war itself generated new objectives. Having invested a great deal of efforts to defeat the insurgents, the intervening powers needed to end the conflict on terms that did not reflect unfavourably on their international prestige and power. At this point, the US-led engagement touched fundamental national security interests that went far beyond the significance of Afghanistan itself.

The Peacebuilding Mission

Efforts by the UN and many of its members to create a new and better post-Taliban order in Afghanistan formed the second pillar of the enterprise. This pillar was embedded in a much larger construct—the international peacebuilding regime that had developed after the end of the Cold War to stabilize 'failed states' and consolidate post-war settlements.

The peacebuilding regime had grown steadily in the UN system after the concept was launched in the Secretary-General's 'Agenda for Peace' report in 1992. A rapid expansion in peace operations was accompanied by efforts to strengthen the role of the UN, particularly after the disastrous missions in Rwanda and Bosnia. The year 2000 was a watershed in the reform process. The so-called Brahimi report on UN peace operations was issued, prepared by a high-level panel established by UN Secretary-General Kofi Annan and led by Lakhdar Brahimi, a former Foreign Minister of Algeria and UN special envoy to Afghanistan.[3] Referencing past problems, the report emphasized the need for proactive responses, integrated missions and broad, although realistic, mandates. It was a widely cited call to energize the UN to better keep and build the peace in the world's trouble spots. The message was shortly afterwards underlined by the High-level Panel on International Threats, Challenges and Change, also established by Kofi Annan. Its 2004 report stressed the world's growing interdependence and the consequent globalization of threats and security concerns.[4] Failed states and terrorism recognized no borders, the report warned. Civil wars had negative externalities that extended far beyond the area of the immediate fighting. Countries that had once experienced civil war were likely to relapse into renewed war. The conclusions hastened efforts to form a UN peacebuilding commission. Established in December 2005, the Commission was mandated to 'bring together all relevant actors to marshal resources and to advise on the proposed integrated strategies for post-conflict peacebuilding and recovery'.[5]

The UN peacebuilding regime and the international project in Afghanistan developed in tandem and were mutually supportive. UN principles formed the normative foundation for international peace-building, originally expressed in the UN Charter and related standards of human rights and norms to protect vulnerable populations. But the ideals were also underpinned by a solid dose of *Realpolitik*, as the con-clusions of the High-level Panel on International Threats, Challenges and Change showed. If peace and security in the modern, globalized world were more than ever indivisible, rich and powerful states clearly had a self-interest in assisting crisis-ridden societies. Afghanistan in 2001 appeared as exhibit A in the case for normatively founded peace-building as well as the right of established powers to deal with failed states for reasons of national security. As a result, it attracted enor-mous international attention.

Afghanistan also represented a huge growth sector for the many actors engaged in peacebuilding on a global scale. Even before the US invasions of Afghanistan and Iraq, a multinational entity involved in post-conflict assistance had developed, consisting of public and private aid agencies, financial institutions, economic development actors, and organizations specializing in providing assistance in matters of justice, good governance, rights issues, and so on. The entire apparatus was harnessed to a strong belief in social engineering. A nomenclature was developing as well: 'peacebuilding' usually included all the civilian activities plus the non-lethal parts of the military engagement (security sector reform, for example), while 'statebuilding' referred to public sec-tor reforms in law, administration and finance as well as the underly-ing assumption that an effective central state is essential to sustain peace.[6] Accumulated knowledge of 'best practices' that drew on peace operations in the 1990s—Cambodia, Bosnia, Kosovo, Mozambique, El Salvador, Guatemala and East Timor—was being codified by experts and international aid agencies. The academic world and policy-oriented think tanks followed apace. So did the literature; in 2009 it had become so vast that the Oxford University Press published a lexicon of post-conflict peacebuilding.

These diverse and formidable forces converged on Afghanistan to create, and later to maintain and sustain, the second pillar of the international project. Donors embraced the standard items in the peacebuilding package, commonly known as 'the liberal peace'—democratization, good governance according to principles of accountability and transparency, human rights, the rule of law, security sector reform and a market-based economy.[7] To reformers inside and outside Afghanistan, the genuinely liberal and enlightened ideals of 'the liberal peace' seemed self-evident signposts of progress. They formed a stark contrast to the record of the Taliban regime, as well as the violence of warlord rule and the civil war that preceded it. Perhaps the most convincing rationale for the massive assistance project was the destruction wrought by almost a quarter century of revolutionary violence, military invasion, civil wars and repressive rulers.

To radical critics, the project looked quite different. The radical critique of the international peacebuilding regime—and by inference the version that took form in Afghanistan—argues that peacebuilding is a tool in the general strategy of domination pursued by the powerful states in the world system.[8] Peacebuilding is designed to restore order in failed states and crisis situations that otherwise would threaten the international hierarchy of power. In this view, the forces of involvement in failed states such as Afghanistan are grounded in strategic thinking about the power of states, not altruistic norms and good intentions. The language of peacebuilding itself is viewed as a form of ideology; by masking deep inequalities of power, terms such as sovereignty, partnership and local ownership constitute a subtle and indirect form of control. Whichever the case, one need not accept the full conclusions of the radical critics in order to recognize that the peacebuilding project in Afghanistan was part of a much larger and powerful international phenomenon, 'an enormous international experiment' as Paris and Sisk call it,[9] which drove the early involvement and sustained its continuation.

Muddling Through? Vested Interests, Expanding Lobbies, and Cascading Policy Objectives

In conventional policy analysis, particular outcomes are explained not primarily by the existence of a grand strategy or the force of 'an enormous international experiment', and certainly not by this alone. Rather, policy is seen as the outcome of a fragmented decision-making structure and muddled process.[10] To understand better the evolution of the international project and the form it took in Afghanistan, we must shift the focus to structures and processes closer to the ground.

Micro-level policy analysis is based on the premise of limited or 'bounded rationality'. The pursuit of rational action by and in organizations, as James March writes, is 'frustrated by irremediable limitations of individuals and organizations, by intrinsic properties of the worlds in which organizations operate, and by unintended raps of adaptive action'.[11] In addition, the decision-making process is typically diverse and internally competitive, with each unit pursuing its own organizational interest. These features are certainly familiar from the international efforts to establish the post-Taliban order in Afghanistan. The very large number of international actors involved, each with a subset of national organizational actors, magnified the disjointed effect. Yet in a generic sense these features are present in all organizational behaviour and policy-making processes. The puzzle in the Afghan case is not the incoherence in the international engagement, but an apparently systemic bias towards deeper and broader involvement in response to the emerging signs of problems, rather than drawing back, taking stock, and exploring radically different alternatives.

Vested Interests and Expanding Lobbies

The first crisis of confidence in the peacebuilding project in Afghanistan appeared as the mid-decade was approaching. The initial optimism and expectations of peace and prosperity that had been noticeable among both Afghans and international actors were starting to dissipate in the face of escalating violence and a slow pace of economic reconstruction. Among the first to respond with alarm and call for more resources were the aid agencies in the UN system and the private aid organizations. The UN humanitarian agencies had a formal mandate to assist—including providing food aid and helping refugees return—and the UNDP had established major programmes to assist the transitional administration soon after the invasion. International and Afghan aid organizations constituted a powerful lobby as well. The Tokyo conference of donors in January 2002, where over $5 billion was pledged for relief and reconstruction, had opened up a bonanza for the aid organizations.[12] Over 1,600 NGOs were already registered with the Afghan Ministry of Planning in 2003.[13] Although not working under formal mandates like the UN agencies, the NGOs had a professional interest in securing a steady flow of resources that would enable them to pursue their institutional mission. They also had an organizational interest in maintaining or, better, expanding their share of the aid market. As further discussed in chapter 5, the aid lobby constituted a powerful voice for more. They were joined by Afghan government officials. Recognizing the usual short attention span of international donors, they called for a massive lift to create 'a virtuous cycle' of economic growth and peace, as the then Minister of Finance, Ashraf Ghani, forcefully argued.

By mid-decade, NATO gave the aid lobby powerful new momentum. The alliance had in 2003 taken command of the international security assistance force (ISAF) and was increasingly frustrated over the inability of the civilian aid apparatus to deliver results that could win popular support for the Afghan government. As discussed in chapter 4, the emerging doctrine in NATO held that defeating the Taliban required more effective delivery of public goods. In 2006 the alliance adopted the so-called Comprehensive Approach, which called for closer integration between development, governance and military strategy. The doctrinal shift meant strong and steady international resource commitments in existing fields, as well as an expanded agenda. On the military side, the US responded to the mid-decade signs of an increasing insurgency by pressuring its allies to provide more troops, thereby widening the circle of vested military interests in the venture. Washington subsequently added more forces of its own and switched to a new, counterinsurgency strategy, infusing new hopes that steadied the coalition on its course, as discussed in chapter 3.

Cascading Objectives

The Comprehensive Approach pursued by NATO and many donors set off a veritable cascading of policy objectives that led to expanded and interlinked activities.

Aid agencies provided more resources to provinces where their soldiers were operating, and the military could not be withdrawn without endangering the aid projects. Coalition militaries increasingly went into the aid business as well, and more sectors were targeted for assistance. As Paddy Ashdown told the then Prime Minister Gordon Brown, to fight the war against the Taliban the international project took on several wars on many fronts—against poverty, narcotics, abuse of power, and corruption.[14]

The expanded agenda required more international resources and involvement. At the same time, the engagement was yielding added value that sustained the commitment. Growing involvement in combat operations in Afghanistan gave NATO operational experience in dealing with unconventional threats. This was valuable to an organization that towards the end of the decade was developing a new strategic concept to guide it through the next ten years. Afghanistan-like challenges might well appear in the future, requiring 'a fit and flexible' response, NATO Secretary-General Anders Fogh-Rasumussen told member states.[15] Other NATO officials spoke approvingly of a 'transformational' experience.[16]

The US military, for its part, had constructed bases and other forms of support structure that had potential future use. Even if not maintained by the US as permanent bases, the huge infrastructure built at the air bases in Bagram north of Kabul and in Kandahar in the south could serve as access points in line with the Pentagon's post-Cold War concept of flexible, forward operational facilities.[17] Arguably the US military did not enter Afghanistan in search of new overseas bases, and NATO did not take command over ISAF to gain counterinsurgency experience. Rather, these can be understood as externalities of sorts, strategic benefits that arose *post hoc* from the engagement and represented assets in a new international environment. Once established in Afghanistan, the US and its allies had a valuable strategic foothold in relation to regional international relations, particularly vis-à-vis Iran and the rising power of China and India.

Over time, two well-known mechanisms reinforced the deepening and broadening engagement. Additional commitments were justified with reference to previous investments ('the investment trap'). When the insurgency gained force around mid-decade, US and NATO officials sought to mobilize more support by claiming that the future of the alliance was at stake in Afghanistan. The claim reflected an element of truth—an outcome that looked like a defeat would clearly harm the prestige and hence the power of the alliance—but the inflation in rhetoric magnified the effect. NATO was in effect caught in a 'rhetoric trap' of its own making.

11

The Peacebuilding Claim for More

The deepening involvement reflected not only the broad range of interests that had been vested in achieving the original objectives, but also new ones that had developed along the way. The process drew support from emerging doctrines of peacebuilding, which held that strong commitments of international troops and finance were necessary to stabilize the peace in post-conflict situations and lay the foundation for democratic development.[18] The claim appeared in theoretically-oriented academic literature as well as policy-oriented studies. In this perspective, the initial 'light footprint' in Afghanistan appeared as a serious mistake, driven by the overpowering US interest in Iraq rather than realities on the ground in Afghanistan. The point was cited by proponents of a stronger commitment as a major reason for the limited results to date; to turn the situation around, more aid commitments and military forces were needed. The view was articulated by a disparate but powerful lobby of analysts, diplomats, aid agencies and Afghan reformers. On the eve of the 2006 London aid conference, for instance, over twenty US Afghan specialists and former diplomats circulated an open letter calling for more aid to reconstruction and statebuilding.[19] The low utilization rate of funds (at the time around 40 per cent) was overlooked as the London conference pledged another $US10 billion in aid.

Some analysts took the argument further, arguing that an early window of opportunity had been lost. The thesis was presented in influential publications. The American expert on Afghanistan, Barnett Rubin, wrote in *Foreign Affairs* in early 2007:

In the immediate aftermath of the Taliban's overthrow, the presence of coalition troops….created an opportunity to build a functioning state…. Such a project would have meant additional troop deployments by the United States and its partners, especially in the border region, and rapid investment in reconstruction. It also would have required political reform and economic development in the tribal areas of Pakistan. Too little of this happened, and both Afghanistan and its international partners are paying the consequences.[20]

A leading Canadian scholar of post-conflict peacebuilding had come to the same conclusion. 'The United States and its allies should have made a serious commitment to Afghan security and reconstruction in late 2001 and early 2002, when the Taliban and Al-Qaeda were on the run. But they did not, and we are dealing with the consequences today', Roland Paris wrote in an Ottawa-based public policy publication in late 2006.[21] At the RAND Corporation in California, Seth Jones argued in a 2005 article published in *Survival*, the journal of the International Institute for Strategic Studies in London, that the US and its allies had failed to meet the 'benchmarks' in troops and finance required to stabilize Afghanistan in the early post-intervention years.[22] More of both was now necessary to avert failure. The prominent journalist Ahmed Rashid made the same point, categorically phrased in his later book:

In those critical days in the autumn of 2003, a few thousand more U.S. troops on the ground, more money for reconstruction, and a speedier rebuilding of the Afghan army and police could easily have turned the tide against the Taliban and enhanced the support of the population for the government. It was a moment when even a little could have gone a long way...[23]

The windows-thesis underpinned the claim for greater commitments on two accounts. Given past under-resourcing, greater commitments would mean a genuinely new departure rather than simply more of the same, and since greater investment would have worked in the past, it would probably work now. The argument had staying power, reappearing towards the end of the decade when events in Afghanistan were nearing another major fork in the road.[24]

But the claim rests on a counter-factual, and counter-factual history is hazardous, as Niall Ferguson reminds us.[25] The academic literature that finds a correlation between strong peace operations and a durable peace is based on statistical trends and relatively few cases. Exceptions occur, and case studies that would compare with Afghanistan have not been examined. Indeed, another counter-factual is *a priori* equally plausible: a stronger international presence in the early post-invasion phase might simply have introduced at an earlier point the negative reactions, problems and strains that appeared in the second half of the decade. Making this argument, however, would shift the analysis to an examination of the shortcomings of the international project itself. At the time, that was not the focus of the dominant thinking in either academic or policy circles.

Only a few analysts identified early on what they saw as inherently problematic features of the international project. In Washington, two scholars at the Carnegie Endowment for International Peace argued in early 2002 that the transformational statebuilding project being unveiled for Afghanistan was over-ambitious—a total 'fantasy'.[26] A more realistic approach, Marina Ottaway and Anatol Lieven wrote,

13

would be to work with existing power holders at the provincial and local levels on a more modest relief and reconstruction agenda, even if the local partners were unsavoury warlords. In peacebuilding circles the suggestion was dismissed with a certain moral indignation; the Afghan people deserved better than that.[27] Other observers pointed to the supply-side dynamic of aid projects as well as the intrusive and directive nature of the international presence. The Afghans were not treated as equal partners in the project despite the politically correct and ideologically attractive language of 'local ownership'. The agenda of liberal modernization created resistance in a society with strong conservative and traditional forces. The Bonn Agreement charting the post-2001 transition period was deeply flawed because it excluded the Taliban from the political arena (or only included them on the victors' terms), thus forcing the activists into military opposition. These views appeared in scattered articles and reports (to which the present author contributed).[28] A comprehensive analysis was already laid out in book form in 2004, written by Chris Johnson and Jolyon Leslie, two aid workers with long experience in Afghanistan. The book had a prescient sub-title: *The Mirage of Peace.*[29] At the time, however, their voices were barely heard or were shunted aside, and the book was savagely reviewed in the *Washington Post* by the anti-terrorist expert Peter Bergen.[30]

Explaining the Lack of Progress

Apart from resources, contextual limitations figure prominently in most explanations for the slow progress of the international project. The regional context was difficult (a 'bad neighbourhood'), Pakistan gave sanctuary and indirect support to the insurgents, and the war in Iraq had a polarizing effect. Inside Afghanistan, the huge poppy sector created a parallel illegal economy and power structure that fed crime, violence and the insurgency.[31] These are all pertinent factors. But there is more to the story, as conventional analysts also recognize.

Much of the mainstream criticism of the project has singled out particular policies pursued by the US-led coalition as misguided and flawed. That includes above all empowering the militias to help defeat Al-Qaeda and the Taliban, failing to hold the warlords accountable for past atrocities, and accepting abusive and corrupt power holders on the national and local level.[32] These decisions undermined the legitimacy of the Afghan government, and made it difficult to move forward on both the military and the peacebuilding side of the project. Although superficially correct, this analysis is insufficient. It was not simply a matter of choosing wrong, uninformed or misguided policies. The decisions reflected the very limited choice at hand given the fundamentally contradictory nature of the project. Empowering the militias, for instance, was the logical consequence of American policy to go after both the Taliban and Al-Qaeda. This necessarily meant working with Afghan counterparts, and the Afghan armed forces at the time were a collection of militias associated with local or regional strongmen. In this as in other respects, the peacebuilding agenda for reform and human rights clashed head on with the military agenda. Since US national security concerns were the origin of the entire project, short-term military imperatives won out. The result was a variation of what Michael Mann has called 'incoherent empire'. Reflecting on the American invasions of Afghanistan and Iraq, Mann, like Andrew Bacevich, sees an 'overconfident, hyperactive militarism' in American foreign policy.[33] Washington's ambitions may be to create 'order and benevolence' in the world, but the reliance on military responses instead 'creates more disorder and violence'. In Afghanistan, the tensions of building peace while waging war were persistent and palpable, contributing to an incoherent and ineffective project.

Similar tensions were evident within the peacebuilding sector. In part, the problem was the rush of donors and international advisers to build institutions, thereby replicating 'the errors of liberal imperialism in the nineteenth century' and producing 'empty institutions', as critics on the left maintain.[34] More fundamentally, the main reasons for the slow progress of liberal reforms were anchored in the internal tensions of the project itself.

A Contradictory Project

The peacebuilding agenda embedded a general contradiction between ends and means: the goal was to build an Afghan 'owned', liberal new order, but the means were heavy and intrusive external assistance. From this constellation flowed a number of tensions.

External assistance turned Afghanistan into a classic rentier state, which had several distinct features. With incentives stacked in favour of easy money, the steady inflow of aid discouraged the state from generating domestic revenue and building local administrative capacity.[35]

Because aid commitments far exceeded the country's absorptive capacity for project and fiscal management, international consultants and contractors were brought in. Over time, more skilled Afghans were employed as high-level advisers, but they were largely funded by foreign donors as well. Heavy dependence on external assistance in this way perpetuated itself, making an Afghan 'owned' order less likely.

The development of the rentier state collided with aspirations for a democratic polity. Since political accountability tends to follow the direction of resource flows, rentier status inhibits democratization.[36] With the Afghan national budget mostly financed by foreign governments and international financial institutions, the government's responsibility to account for the use of the funds was directed towards the donors rather than its own people. The Karzai government was in this respect no different from previous Afghan governments that also had presided over rentier states; they all failed the democratization test.

The heavy and intrusive nature of the foreign presence weakened the legitimacy of the government and hence the foundation for both state- and peacebuilding. It is worth recalling that two of the most remarkable cases of statebuilding in modern history have been the work of leaders who sought to strengthen the state *against* foreign threats, in Japan (the Meiji restoration) and Turkey (under Kemal Ataturk). Nationalism and anti-foreign sentiments provided the principal glue and justification for reforms; the foreign threat also gave the aspiring reformers strong incentives to embark upon change despite the risks and costs involved. While many reforms were Western-inspired, they were carried out by national leaders. In post-2001 Afghanistan, by contrast, foreigners have been the principal funders and drivers of the statebuilding project. The main patron, the United States, is also the leader of an international coalition that has declared war on militant Islam. This has enabled Afghan militants to appropriate the traditional sources of legitimacy in Afghanistan—Islam and nationalism.

On a different level, an international mission that is formally designed as a partnership, but is in practice dominated by external financial, military and technocratic power, produces tension between what we can call 'ownership' and 'control'. International actors want a measure of control over their programmes and the reform agenda; national actors press for the same in the name of 'local ownership' and the internationally sanctioned language of self-determination and sovereignty. Inherent in most aid projects, the tension was magnified in the Afghan case owing to the large and intrusive international presence and the high stakes involved. The tension worked like sand in the machinery of reconstruction and statebuilding. It drove the continuous tug of war over the modalities of aid, civil service reform and individual appointments, how to deal with corruption, how to fight the insurgency, the role of private security companies and the government's foreign policy orientation. By the end of the decade, the Karzai-led government and its international supporters were quarrelling in public.

The second major category of tension stemmed from the conflicting imperatives of waging war while simultaneously building peace. Most important, as noted above, local militias were armed and local alliances were made that conflicted with the principles of good governance (important for peacebuilding) as well as the establishment of a monopoly of force (central to statebuilding). When the international coalition later emphasized the need to build up the national security forces, this was done at a rate that was fiscally quite unsustainable, leaving the Afghan state with the prospect of even greater dependence on foreign aid or bankruptcy.

The military campaign waged by the US-led coalition forces generated its own tensions. A larger and more visible foreign military presence enabled the militants to depict the foreign soldiers as an occupation force. Civilian casualties caused by the coalition forces, and the night raids and detention they undertook, tended to alienate rather than win local 'hearts and minds'. Although many more civilians were killed by anti-government elements, to the population in contested areas the distinction was not so clear-cut. Foreign soldiers were targeted by the insurgents who used indiscriminate weaponry that often killed large numbers of civilians. In this and other ways, the coalition forces came to represent a source of insecurity rather than security.

Finally, the war seemed to have a multiplier effect on the internal tensions of the international project as a whole. The economic and political costs of the war to NATO and the allies led them to demand more and faster results across the board. Short-term objectives were privileged over long-term interests. Good local governance, for example, would in the long run serve military objectives by generating greater support for the Afghan government, but a local strongman who could deliver armed men, intelligence and protection of convoys had even greater short-term value for the coalition forces. The pressure for results to permit the US to wind down the war led to more external control and greater presence, as exemplified by Obama's military and civilian 'surge' in 2010. On the Afghan side, these pressures in turn created counter-pressures. In the office of the president, it led to a search for new friends and allies in the region that could lessen the government's dependence on the US-led coalition altogether.

* * *

A project torn by internal contradictions of this kind does not easily lend itself to repair by adding more foreign troops, funds and consultants. On the contrary, to the extent that these tensions are structurally embedded in the enterprise, investing more is likely to yield less. How this dynamic has worked in practice—and why the international community has nevertheless deepened its engagement in Afghanistan over the past decade—is narrated in in the chapters that follow.

2

THE POINT OF ENTRY

A LIGHT FOOTPRINT

The US invasion of Afghanistan in October 2001—Operation Enduring Freedom—was accompanied by strong words of support from
many UN members and several allies had offered to join the operation.
Yet there was a marked reluctance in Washington to take charge of the
aftermath of regime change. The UN also favoured a light mission.

Apart from removing the Taliban and ending Al-Qaeda's sanctuary
in Afghanistan, the Bush Administration made clear it had no interest
in Afghanistan and no taste for 'nation-building'. In the UN, there
were strong reservations against taking on major responsibilities in
what looked like an extraordinarily difficult post-conflict situation.
There was near consternation in the Secretariat when US Secretary of
State, Colin Powell, in mid-November asked the UN to form an
interim administration of international civil servants for Afghanistan
and to do so with 'speed, speed, speed'.[1] But while wary of the challenges a UN mission would face, UN member states repeatedly
affirmed that the international community had an obligation to promote stability, order and a representative government in Afghanistan.
To square these conflicting concerns required some nimble thinking.
The concept of a light international footprint proposed by Lakhdar
Brahimi seemed to fit the bill and was warmly embraced by the Security Council as the framework for international assistance.

The Dominant Narrative

The sense of an international obligation to assist Afghanistan rested on the dominant Western narrative of recent Afghan history. Its main theme was that in the early 1990s, the United States—the world's sole remaining superpower—had abandoned Afghanistan after the Soviet Union withdrew its troops as stipulated by the 1988 Geneva Accords. The troop withdrawal produced a political vacuum, and the failure of the US to step in opened the way for disaster. Abandoned by the West, Afghanistan slid into civil war, the Taliban took over and the country turned into a 'failed state' that produced massive human suffering at home and became a haven for terrorism abroad. The policy implication was that greater US-led involvement at the time would have prevented this course of events, and the lesson was widely cited in the UN system in late 2001: the international community must not walk away from Afghanistan again.

In the UN system, the abandonment thesis achieved the status of authoritative policy doctrine almost on par with the dominant historical verdict on the consequences of appeasement in Europe in the 1930s. It framed the deliberations on the international response in 2001and gave powerful external legitimacy to the subsequent presence. Towards the end of the decade, the narrative figured prominently in warnings against a hasty withdrawal of the US-led coalition forces: doing so would invite a repeat of history and a return to civil war in Afghanistan.

The historical events on which the thesis is based are uncontroversial. It starts with a success story: the UN succeeded in brokering the Geneva Accords of April 1988 that facilitated the withdrawal of Soviet forces. For almost a decade, the Soviet military intervention in Afghanistan had been one of the most intractable conflicts in the international system. The patient work of the UN diplomat Diego Cordovez to negotiate a Soviet exit was a high point for the UN at a time when the organization remained hamstrung by superpower rivalry. Nevertheless, the hoped-for peace did not materialize. The Geneva Accords failed to include a mechanism for an internal settlement among the Afghan parties. Both the United States and the Soviet Union were permitted to continue arming their respect clients under a 'negative symmetry' clause that was not abrogated until August 1991 (the abrogation taking effect on 31 December 1991). Shortly thereafter, in April 1992, President Najibullah fled the presidential office to seek asylum in the UN compound in Kabul.[2] To fill the gaping hole in the Geneva Accords, the UN had assigned a special envy, Benon Sevan, to promote negotiations between the Najibullah government and the anti-Communist Afghan *mujahedin* factions. Several proposals were aired with the backing of Najibullah and his Soviet supporters, most prominently a government of national unity and a demilitarization of the capital to be overseen by an international force. The *mujahedin* had their sights on total victory, however, and rejected the proposals, as did the United States and Pakistan, their principal remaining patrons.[3] Their competitive race to take Kabul started a four-year civil war (1992–96) and, for the first time since the cycle of organized violence started with the April Revolution in 1978, wrought large-scale destruction on the capital itself. In the countryside, anarchic conditions led to the rise of the Taliban, assisted by Pakistan. The Taliban seized the capital in 1996 and soon controlled nearly 90 per cent of the country.

That continued US engagement in Afghanistan would have led to a better outcome is probable but not certain. For a start, the outcome would have depended on the quality of that involvement. As it was, Washington's role during a critical period after the Soviet withdrawal (1989–92) was distinctly unhelpful to peace. The United States continued to arm the most militant *mujahedin* factions and opposed negotiations on compromise settlements.

The UN stayed engaged, and the General Assembly authorized the establishment of a Special Mission (UNSMA) in December 1993 to promote negotiations among the rival Afghan factions. Working without much support from the major powers, the UN failed to halt the unfolding civil wars, first among the *mujahedin* and subsequently between the factions that formed the Northern Alliance and those who joined the Taliban. The regional powers—Russia, Pakistan, Iran and, from further afield, Saudi Arabia—engaged in low-level competitive intervention that fuelled the conflict. In 1997, the UN Secretary-General appointed Lakhdar Brahimi as head of UNSMA to break the deadlock. Brahimi worked on two parallel tracks. To improve the regional dynamic, he established a contact group of neighbouring states as well as the major powers, the so-called 6+2 group.[4] He also tried to promote talks between the Taliban and the Northern Alliance. It was all in vain and in late 1999 the UN suspended ('froze') the mission's mandate in an overt admission of failure.

International aid organizations continued to provide assistance and some operated inside the country throughout the 1990s. Towards the end of the decade, attempts were made to coordinate the aid operations into a more coherent response. No more successful than Brahimi's diplomacy, the so-called Strategic Framework came up against opposing interests, in this case among donors who were divided in their views of the Taliban and whether and to what extent it was possible to work with the regime.[5]

By this time, Afghanistan had figured repeatedly on the agenda of the Security Council. Several resolutions towards the end of the 1990s condemned the Taliban for supporting international terrorism, engaging in narcotics production and violating women's rights. After the bombing of the US embassies in Nairobi and Dar es Salaam in the autumn of 1998, the Security Council imposed economic sanctions on the Taliban regime (Res. 1267), and demanded that Osama bin Laden be turned over to the United States or other appropriate authorities to be tried for international terrorism. A subsequent resolution in December 2000 (Res. 1333) reiterated these demands and tightened the sanctions. The resolution called for an embargo on arms and other forms of military assistance to all the Afghan factions, but singled out the Taliban in a separate passage. By the time the Taliban demolished the ancient, giant Buddha statutes in Bamyian in the summer of 2001, the regime was firmly established as an international criminal outcast. The attacks on New York and Washington in September powerfully confirmed that status and reinforced the message of the dominant narrative. In the Security Council, the international mission to reconstruct Afghanistan was formulated in the spirit of 'never again'. '[Our common efforts remain the same:.... to ensure that Afghanistan never again is used as a breeding and staging ground for terrorism or for traffic in drugs', Brahimi told the Security Council when presenting the plan for a post-Taliban transitional administration in November 2001.[6]

But while the dominant narrative ended with a call for action, the difficult questions remained to be defined. What was to be done, and who should lead? Here conflicting interests and sober assessments of the situation in Afghanistan converged to recommend a limited international involvement.

Washington: A Narrow Focus

The huge US presence in Afghanistan in early 2011 presents a striking contrast to the narrow and specific aims of the Bush Administration when it invaded the country in late 2001. The vast distance that US policy has travelled during this decade tends to overshadow its quite modest starting point, which was a limited exercise of military power to exact revenge for the attacks on the United States and promote US national security interests.

In developing its initial response to the attacks, the Administration of George W. Bush took note of the abandonment thesis. The overriding lesson from the 1990s, cited in a high-level meeting with the President in October, was 'don't leave a vacuum'.[7] But a US lead role did not follow. The Bush Administration had limited interests in Afghanistan itself and looked to other countries and organizations to take major responsibility for constructing the post-Taliban order. In this regard, the Administration carried forward earlier themes in US policy. During the Cold War, Afghanistan—like many other countries in the developing world—became an arena for superpower rivalry, but in itself lacked economic, political or strategic value to warrant long-term engagement. The Soviet withdrawal in 1989 occasioned only limited debate in Washington. The debate divided into three main groups: the 'bleeders' who wanted to continue an uncompromising anti-Communist policy towards Kabul to punish the Soviet Union; the 'dealers' who wanted the United States to use its influence to support an inclusive settlement among Afghan factions that included moderate Communists; and 'the disengagers' who advocated 'systematic disengagement from wars that were seen as unattractive, unpopular, unsellable, expensive, messy and entangling', as a later report noted.[8] When the Soviet Union finally collapsed at the end of 1991, the disengagers won out and cited with approval an editorial in *The Times* of London: 'The world has no business in that country's tribal disputes and blood feuds'.[9]

When the Bush Administration took office in 2001, the theme of the disengagers again moved to the forefront of policy. The new team presented a view of US national interests that celebrated the logic of power politics, laid out by the President's National Security Adviser Condoleezza Rice in a much-cited article in *Foreign Affairs*.[10] In this calculus of conventional *Realpolitik*, husbanding and projecting power

23

on prioritized goals is a principle of first order. Relations with other large powers are most important. Next comes supporting allies, while 'rogue regimes' and hostile powers must be dealt with 'decisively' at all times, Rice wrote. Hitting hard to eliminate the Taliban and Al-Qaeda after the attacks on the United States flowed logically from this view; staying on in Afghanistan to reconstruct a new order made little sense. Even in late September 2001, when the US Air Force was preparing to pulverize the Taliban, Bush held to a minimalist objective: 'We are not into nation-building. We are focussed on justice', that is, killing or capturing Al-Qaeda and Taliban members, above all Osama bin Laden.[11] In internal White House discussions, considerations of what would happen after the Taliban regime was removed had appeared as an afterthought. On 4 October, just after the US had started bombing Afghanistan, Bush had famously asked: 'Who will run the country?'[12] None of his advisers appeared to have any answer, except that it would have to be other countries and the UN.

The assumption that the US military would create regime change while leaving allies and international organizations with the task of picking up the pieces was not unique to the Bush Administration. The Clinton Administration had promoted a similar division of labour between the US and the European Union in Kosovo. Yet the point was expressed with unusual candour by the Bush Administration. Responding to British Prime Minister Tony Blair's call for the international community not to walk away from Afghanistan again, Bush said:

[W]e've got to work for a stable Afghanistan so that her neighbors don't fear terrorist activity again coming out of that country. ...[I]t would be helpful, of course, to eradicate narco-trafficking out of Afghanistan, as well. I believe that the United Nations would—could provide the framework necessary to help meet those conditions. It would be a useful function for the United Nations to take over the so-called 'nation-building'—I would call it the stabilization of a future government—after our military mission is complete. We'll participate; other countries will participate.[13]

The Administration's rapid shift in attention to Iraq was another, and at the time unstated, reason for letting the UN take responsibility for 'nation-building' in Afghanistan. In the foreign policy universe of the neoconservatives who surrounded the President, the UN and Afghanistan alike occupied a peripheral place.

Nevertheless, it was realized that the United States could not simply walk away. US aid agencies had been developing a capacity for post-conflict assistance during the 1990s, and started to plan in early October for ways to aid the reconstruction of post-Taliban Afghanistan. Expecting that there would be 'nation building on a huge scale', a cabinet meeting at the level of deputies began discussing aid programmes in food production, health, education for women and small-scale infrastructure projects. They also planned to ask other major donors and the international financial institutions to make 'multi-billion dollar' commitments.[14]

The State Department established a high-level inter-agency team to deal with transitional issues.[15] An immediate issue of concern was the ethnic composition of the Afghan government that would take power after the Taliban. As the main ally of the United States during the invasion, the Northern Alliance had risen to a position of unprecedented power. But as a coalition of Afghanistan's main minorities—Tajiks, Uzbeks and Hazaras, with a core Tajiks from the Panjshir valley—the Northern Alliance could not alone lead the transitional administration. American officials, particularly in the CIA, stressed early on that the transitional administration had to be headed by a Pashtun. While the precise proportion of Pashtuns is uncertain, they constitute the single largest ethnic group (around 40 per cent) and have traditionally ruled at the central state level. Although the Pashtuns had been the backbone of the Taliban, not all Pashtuns had supported the regime, and there were powerful Pashtun factions among the Afghan diaspora. American officials wanted Pashtun leadership of the transitional administration for foreign policy reasons as well. During the wars of the 1990s, the Northern Alliance had developed links with Iran, Russia and Turkey, but had much less contact with the United States. The CIA's somewhat limited involvement with anti-Taliban forces in this period had mainly been with Pashtuns in the southeast. Washington consequently looked in this direction for a candidate to head an interim government, and found him in Hamid Karzai. It fell to the State Department's newly appointed 'ambassador to the Afghan opposition', James Dobbins, to promote Karzai's candidacy in the UN and to the Northern Alliance.[16]

The second major issue of concern to Washington was the impact of security arrangements during the transitional period on US military operations against Taliban and Al-Qaeda. It had been clear from the outset that US forces would not contribute to an international peace-keeping force in Afghanistan. The function of US military forces, according to the Bush Administration, was not peacekeeping or nation-building, but combat and deterrence in defence of US vital national interests. In the words of Condoleezza Rice: 'The military is a special instrument. It is lethal, and it is meant to be. It is not a civilian police force. It is not a political referee. And it is most certainly not designed to build a civilian society'.[17] An international peacekeeping force formed by other nations was a different matter, and found particular support in the State Department. The Department's special coordinator for Afghanistan, Richard Haass, was actively promoting the idea of an international peacekeeping force among allies.[18] Colin Powell likewise thought a peacekeeping force was necessary,[19] and in mid-November, when the Northern Alliance forces were on the outskirts of Kabul, called for the formation of a 'coalition of the willing'. The US military had objections, however, and their concerns significantly influenced the formation and deployment of the force that eventually was established.

The UN Steps Up

Washington's limited interests in Afghanistan enabled the United Nations to step up to the invitation to lead on the civilian side. The ability of the often slow-moving and unwieldy organization to rapidly chart a consensus-based transitional mechanism was in no small measure due to Brahimi, who had been reappointed as UN special envoy. A seasoned diplomat with previous experience in Afghanistan, and leader of the recent report on UN peace operations that carried his name,[20] Brahimi was in a position to play a critical role. He used to the full an authority that was both formal and authentically steeped in deep knowledge. His first task was to orchestrate a complicated and multi-layered diplomacy in support of a transitional plan. The strategy was threefold: develop a consensus among the victorious Afghan factions on a transitional mechanism; obtain agreement among Afghanistan's neighbours and the major powers, above all the 6+2, on the principles of the transition; and prevent the political transition from being over-taken by developments on the ground.[21] Time was short. Brahimi had been appointed Special Representative of the Secretary-General (SRSG) on 3 October, just before the US started the bombing campaign that decimated the ranks of the Taliban. Across the border, international relief agencies were assembling, ready to move in and establish operations with or without a transitional authority in place.

Brahimi's solution was a vision of a light international footprint. Some in the UN system disagreed, including his predecessor as UN special envoy to Afghanistan, and later Special Representative of the European Union to Afghanistan, Francesc Vendrell, who favoured a more robust intervention. Yet Brahimi's views resonated more strongly in October-November 2001. The risks and dangers of getting too deeply involved in Afghanistan were widely cited, as were the enormity of the challenges ahead and the institutional risks of failure for the agency that took them on. The idea of establishing a UN administration in Afghanistan along the lines of the international administration of East Timor and Kosovo barely got off the ground before it was shelved. The initial discussion is nevertheless of interest as it reveals concerns that later emerged with full force.

The idea of a UN administration in Afghanistan had appeared fleetingly in the public discussion before being dramatically resurrected by Colin Powell in the Security Council on 12 November. The suggestions arose mainly because of the precedents in East Timor and Kosovo less than two years previously, which had generated interest as innovative instruments of peacebuilding. The analogy halted on several accounts, however. East Timor and Kosovo had both emerged as separate political entities after seceding from an internationally recognized state. In Kosovo's case, international administration helped mask the uncertain legal status of the breakaway state; in East Timor, the legal basis for independence was clear, but limited local capacity led to UN administration in an interim period before independence. Afghanistan, by contrast, was a sovereign country and a member of the UN. The UN debate on the evolving conflict in Afghanistan and on international assistance had always been conducted in the language of sovereignty and self-determination. A UN transitional administration in Afghanistan would have to be requested by some relevant Afghan entity in a process lacking precedents. Brahimi himself was acutely sensitive to issues of self-determination. As a former Foreign Minister of Algeria, a country that had fought a long and costly war for independence, he would not countenance neo-trusteeship even as a transitional device.

Other concerns applied to both a UN administration and a heavy assistance mission. In the critical months of late 2001 when the international response took shape, Afghanistan was portrayed in public discussion and the international media as a vast and complicated country, posing what in the UN discourse were called challenging issues of conflict management. The UN had tried its hand there for more than a decade, with little result. Even if the Taliban seemed on the way to rapid defeat, peace was not assured and the problems were legion. Conflict among the heavily armed *mujahedin* groups could erupt. There were deep-seated political antagonisms. Millions of internally displaced persons and refugees were waiting to return. The infrastructure was poor. The neighbours had a track record of supporting competing armed factions. Senior and experienced diplomats in the UN system who had worked in Afghanistan painted a dark picture. Sergio Vieira de Mello, the distinguished UN diplomat, who had worked for the UN in many of the world's conflict areas as well as Afghanistan, had found Afghanistan 'the most difficult place to work on earth'.[22] From his subsequent position as head of the UN transitional administration in East Timor, Vieira de Mello warned that the East Timor model was not appropriate to Afghanistan.[23]

Security concerns were fundamental, as Simon Chesterman has pointed out.[24] A hands-on mission with a broad mandate, let alone a fully fledged transitional administration patterned after Kosovo and East Timor, would mean posting international civil servants to remote areas on the provincial and district level. There was no ready international force to provide security for such a structure, and no obvious other policing agents in a country divided into competing fiefdoms of local militias, a history of a flourishing narcotics industry, active networks of smugglers, and 'a pervasive presence of non-Afghan armed and terrorist groups', as Brahimi told the Security Council on 13 November.[25]

There were underlying questions of authority and legitimacy. Posed explicitly in a formal trusteeship arrangement, serious internal legitimacy issues had arisen even in the UN administrations of East Timor and Kosovo where the organization had been welcomed as an important agency of national liberation.[26] In East Timor, for instance, Sergio Vieira de Mello had faced angry demonstrators assembling in the courtyard of his gubernatorial palace to demand greater Timorese participation. That was barely three months after he had arrived to head the UN transitional administration.

Institutional concerns suggested caution as well. Many UN member states, and above all the UN Secretariat, wished to protect the organization from a difficult mission that carried risk of failure and could damage its credibility. Caution had dictated UN response in earlier crises, and the scars from Rwanda and Bosnia were still painful.[27] In 2001, the UN was relishing the success of its administration in East Timor. A less than prudent involvement in Afghanistan could spoil this promising record. Discussing the prospects in the autumn of 2001, UN officials emphasized the enormity of the task ahead and tried to dampen expectations. Some pointedly referred to Somalia and Bosnia as examples of what could go wrong. Brahimi weighed in with his own experience from Afghanistan. In his first major press conference in mid-October, he recalled the frustrations and difficulties that earlier had made him resign as special envoy to the country. The international community had to proceed with caution. 'The UN is not seeking a transitional administration or peacekeeping or anything like that', he said; the UN was in Afghanistan only to help the Afghans form a government and to recover and reconstruct.[28]

The need to bring the discussion to a conclusion became painfully clear during the second week of November. While the UN debated, the Northern Alliance militias were advancing to the outskirts of Kabul. The political framework for the transition now had to be authoritatively defined so as to prevent the militias of one faction from taking control of the capital. Factional control would complicate the transitional gambit. There were also fears that the Northern Alliance militias would turn on the ethnically mixed population of Kabul and target Pashtuns (as they were doing then and later in the north). To gain more time, Brahimi and the State Department team working on the political transition had asked the US military to slow the offensive. The US military had agreed to delay the bombing of Taliban defences on the Shomali plains north of Kabul as well as some of their positions in the north, but not to stop the Northern Alliance's rapid advance towards Kabul. The advance occurred well before a political deal had been concluded, and prompted Colin Powell's call for the UN to act with 'speed, speed, speed' in putting together a transitional administration.

The 6+2 group, meanwhile, was laying down the ground rules for a future government. Meeting on 12 November, the foreign ministers declared that a 'broad-based multi-ethnic, politically balanced, freely chosen Afghan administration' should be established.[29] The declaration echoed earlier Security Council resolutions that had called for the establishment of a 'broad-based, multi-ethnic, and fully representative' government in Afghanistan,[30] but did not address the question of what should be done in the interim. The next day, Brahimi moved the process one step further.

The big challenge, he told the Security Council, was to create good governance. To be sustainable, governing institutions must be Afghan; a transitional administration run by Afghans will be 'far more credible, acceptable and legitimate' than one run by the UN or another constellation of foreigners. Plans were under way to establish a transitional administration of Afghans, he said, but this administration had to be shielded against a premature and overwhelming onrush from the international aid regime. 'Parachuting a large number of international experts into Afghanistan could overwhelm the nascent transitional administration and interfere with the building of local capacity'. Nor was a large number of experts required, Brahimi said. A considerable number of Afghans among the exile population had skills and training that could be utilized in the planned transitional administration and reduce the demand for international staff.[31]

The speech had been in preparation since early October and was the product of intensive consultations and careful diplomatic footwork at the UN and in the region. Hence it reflected the political consensus at the time. But it clearly carried Brahimi's imprint and was promoted under his preferred designation of a 'light footprint'. The catchy term took hold. While Brahimi did not define its meaning precisely, the main message was clear: the Afghans should run the show.

The UN's previous involvement in Afghanistan had left some ideas for a suitable process to establish an Afghan-run transitional authority. The mechanism proposed by Benon Sevan in the dying days of the Najibullah government was clearly relevant, although as a failed initiative it was given little credit. Sevan's plan called for assembling a large group of Afghans in a neutral place outside the region—Vienna was proposed. The gathering would select a smaller group which would call a traditional Afghan grand assembly, a *loya jirga*, which in turn would appoint an interim government. Brahimi's team now developed a similar mechanism, starting with an interim authority to be elected by Afghan representatives in Bonn, a transitional administration to be selected later in Kabul by a traditional Afghan assembly (*loya jirga*), and then direct, popular election of a president and members of parliament according to a new constitution (to be promulgated in the meantime). Shortly afterwards, the mechanism was duly approved in Bonn in early December by the Northern Alliance and Afghan factions in exile.

A Multinational Force?

Getting agreement on security arrangements for the transitional period was more difficult. The American forces were on a mission to hunt down Al-Qaeda and the Taliban—not to provide public security or maintain peace. There was no coherent Afghan army, only potentially conflicting armed factions and sundry militias. That left an international peacekeeping force as the default option.

One of the main Afghan exile factions had already called for a UN peacekeeping force in early October. Zahir Shah, the former King of Afghanistan and the titular head of the Rome-based faction, had made the request in a letter the UN Secretary-General soon after a visit from Richard Haass in the State Department, a timing that suggested parallel interests. The letter had an unsettling effect in the Secretariat. Appearing before the Security Council in mid-October, Brahimi underlined that UN priorities in Afghanistan were to assist with humanitarian relief, the political transition, and longer-term reconstruction. He urged the Security Council not to rush into accepting a peacekeeping operation in Afghanistan.[32] The main reasons had been elaborated in the so-called Brahimi report issued just the previous year, and soon established as the authoritative framework for UN discussion on peace operations. The report stressed that effective operations required clear and realistic mandates. Resolutions of good will had to be matched by capacity and willingness to implement the mission. Previous peace operations had demonstrated a problematic gap between Security Council resolutions in this regard. The consequences had been demonstrated in different ways in both Rwanda and Bosnia, where the UN hoisted the flag to maintain the peace or establish 'safe havens', but genocide and mass murder followed. In an organization still grappling with the aftermath of these disasters, Brahimi's call for caution was welcomed. As Brahimi later noted at a press conference, there had been no rush of countries offering to send troops to Afghanistan.

The historic opposition of Afghans to foreign military forces greatly added to the reluctance. The British and the Soviet experiences were told and retold. Afghanistan was the graveyard of empires and of expeditionary forces. Journalists dug out the story of the lone British survivor from the withdrawal of the British Army of the Indus in 1842 after the first Anglo-Afghan war. The survivor, Dr William Bryden, had apparently been spared to tell the horrors of the withdrawals when the

31

column was set upon by Afghan tribes and demolished. Wounded and dazed, Dr Bryden was hanging on to his horse as it stumbled across the Khyber Pass to what is now Pakistan.[33] Brahimi added his view in words that made the media round. 'Afghanistan is a very difficult country. They are a very proud people. They don't like to be ordered around by foreigners...[especially] those in military uniforms'.[34]

Other leaders called for a multinational force operating under a UN mandate but organized as a 'coalition of the willing'. The British Foreign Secretary, Jack Straw, canvassed Muslim countries for support to establish an international Muslim force. The British government thought Turkey was an obvious candidate; apart from having a Muslim population, Turkey was also a NATO member.[35] Morocco, Bangladesh and Jordan were mentioned as likely contributors. The US bombing of Afghanistan, however, made governments of Muslim populations reluctant to sign up for a coalition force associated with the US invasion. President Bush's characterization of the military campaign as 'a crusade' did not make their task easier. Even a staunch ally like the King of Jordan withdrew a previous offer to provide troops in support of Operation Enduring Freedom.

Brahimi's own stated preference was for an Afghan police or security force. He was holding to this option as late as mid-October, but a month later had relented.[36] The Northern Alliance forces were now on the outskirts of Kabul, a political transition mechanism had not been established, and the security element in the transitional equation was missing. On 13 November, he again took centre stage in the Security Council. Recognizing that 'without a credible security arrangement.... [n]o political settlement can be implemented', he proceeded to outline the options.[37] An all-Afghan security force could not be constituted in time. A UN force was not advisable. It would take time to put together; and, more important, 'any security force established in the absence of a credible cease-fire agreement or political settlement... could quickly find itself in the role of combatant. This is not a role for "Blue Helmets".' That left a multinational force formed by a 'coalition of the willing' as the default option.

The idea of a multinational force moved forward, but its status was still unclear when the victorious Afghan factions and international representatives assembled in Bonn two weeks later, at the end of November. No country had offered to lead such a force and only one had made a non-binding offer to contribute. That was Germany, whose government was eager to project its image as international peacemaker and hosted the conference.

The parties assembled in Bonn nevertheless agreed to invite the international community to 'assist in the maintenance of security for Kabul and its surrounding areas'.[38] Like the rest of the Bonn Agreement, the clause governing the international force was made in haste. The entire Agreement was concluded in just over a week and was a framework rather than a detailed settlement. The provision for a multinational security force was the handiwork of the chief American and British representatives at the Bonn conference, US Ambassador James Dobbins and Robert Cooper, a close foreign policy adviser to Prime Minister Tony Blair.[39] Both men were overtly interventionist. 'The idea that Afghans could adequately secure their country after a twenty-three year civil war struck me as naïve and irresponsible', Dobbins later wrote to explain why he had lobbied hard for a large international force.[40] Cooper's interventionism was more extreme and ideologically articulate. His advocacy of 'a new imperialism' in April 2002 made quite a stir even at a time when several public intellectuals in the Anglo-American world were exploring the values of liberal imperialism.[41] In the post-9/11 international system, Cooper argued, intervention was necessary to deal with 'failed states', terrorism and similar threats facing the established powers; interventions that promoted human rights, cosmopolitan values, and free markets were beneficial for the target population as well.

Their home capitals were divided. In Washington, the State Department strongly supported the idea, although Secretary of Defense Donald Rumsfeld opposed it with equal force. British military leaders were deeply sceptical as well, but Tony Blair firmly believed in military intervention as a tool of liberal internationalism. Indeed, the Prime Minister had been so eager to send British forces to stabilize Afghanistan that he had already dispatched a contingent of what was planned as 'thousands of British forces'. Landing at Bagram air base just north of Kabul in mid-November, the British troops were met by Northern Alliance leaders who told them they were not welcome, and that ended the operation.[42] A multinational force that was formally requested by the Afghans in the Bonn Agreement and endorsed by Washington found ready support from Blair. A British contingent was rapidly dispatched to Kabul to form the core of the British-led International Security Assistance Force (ISAF).

As Dobbins and Cooper had anticipated, the proposal had met with stiff resistance from the British military. 'Rumours had it that chief of the UK Defence Staff had been strongly opposed to Britain taking on the ISAF mission....Blair had only dissuaded him from resigning in protest after promising that the United Kingdom's commitment there would be short lived', Dobbins later wrote.[43] Nearly institutionalized memories of the defeats suffered by British imperial armies in Afghanistan during the nineteenth century were a cloud in the horizon, but there were more immediate concerns. The mandate was unclear and elastic. In the words of the Security Council resolution that authorized the mission, it would 'assist the Afghan Interim Authority in the maintenance of security in Kabul and its surrounding areas, so that the Afghan Interim Authority as well as the personnel of the United Nations can operate in a secure environment'.[44] More important for the British military was the unwillingness of US military officials to participate or even support the force in any form. The US forces in Afghanistan were focused on defeating the Taliban and Al-Qaeda; they refused to commit to assist the multinational force with logistical or other assistance, including extracting the contingent if needed. The general message communicated by the US military was that the multinational force was as an 'ineffectual or amateurish operation' which they were 'leery about being drawn into supporting".[45]

The operational area of the proposed multinational force was controversial from the start. Kabul was an obvious priority area. The importance of securing the capital as a neutral political space was a major lesson from the civil war in the 1990s when rival factions had fought over the city. A secure environment in the capital would permit the interim administration to function and the transition to proceed on schedule. Proponents of the force wished to see it deployed to Afghanistan's other main cities as well, in order to provide a more general stabilization function, as Dobbins and Cooper argued. The acting Defence Minister of the Northern Alliance, General Muhammad Qassem Fahim, agreed, although for other reasons. Since his forces currently in Kabul would be required by the Bonn Agreement to withdraw from the city, this would give an advantage to armed factions that controlled the other main cities. Some were associated with the Northern Alliance but had an independent power base, notably Ismail Khan in Herat and Abdul Rashid Dostum and Muhammad Atta in the north. Others were independent Pashtun commanders in the east (Jalalabad) and the south

(Kandahar). Placing international contingents in these cities would neutralize that advantage. As a result, an additional sentence was inserted in the Accords that permitted an international security force 'as appropriate, [to be] progressively expanded to other urban centres and other areas'. The clause opened the door to a subsequent expansion of ISAF in what became a major and controversial escalation of the international military presence.

* * *

In the early days after 9/11, when the Afghan situation appeared particularly chaotic and unpredictable, Brahimi had recounted the story of a man who climbed a palm tree in the desert and brought his shoes along. Asked why he did not leave his shoes on the ground, he answered that if he found a way out on the top he need not return to pick them up. After the Bonn conference, it seemed to many that perhaps there was a way out on the top after all.

The Bonn Agreement itself contributed to a new-found optimism and belief in the future. The Agreement was widely considered a great success. Almost miraculously, the Afghan factions had come together. Even the nominal President, Burhanuddin Rabbani, whose United Front/Northern Alliance government had represented Afghanistan in the UN and in whose name the Northern Alliance had seized Kabul, agreed to step aside in favour of a new leader anointed by the United States, with only a gracious acknowledgement in the Agreement of the contributions he and the other *mujahedin* had made to the country by defeating the Communists. With the partial exception of Pakistan, which had recognized and supported the Islamic Emirate of the Taliban, the 6+2 as well as the large number of other countries represented in Bonn supported the transitional scheme. The UN system had mobilized international cooperation to ensure that Afghanistan would not again become a 'failed state' that threatened the stability of the region and the world beyond. Even Iran and the United States had a moment where their interests converged, as their representatives in Bonn acknowledged.

At the Tokyo pledging conference in January the following year the tone was upbeat. The Taliban were defeated or kept on the run by US forces. Kabul basked in a newfound sense of freedom and hope, and the population welcomed the British ISAF forces. There were dangers ahead and the task was enormous, but the emphasis now was on tackling the challenges ahead. The caution that Brahimi had counselled in October 2001 was fading.

3

AMERICAN BOOTS ON THE GROUND

In retrospect, the discussion among US military planners as they prepared to invade Afghanistan in October 2001 seems oddly prescient. Operation Enduring Freedom (OEF) was designed to have a very light footprint, based on a combination of US airpower and Afghan militias with a small contingent of US ground forces. In late 2001, the advance party consisted of Special Operations Forces and around a thousand Marines. More US forces were added in early 2002 to mop up remnants of Al-Qaeda and the Taliban. The option of a large, conventional invasion force was never seriously discussed. There were time constraints—the US military had no plans for an invasion force of this kind. Further, President George W. Bush was in a hurry to 'get some scalps', as he told his advisers.[1] Given that the wounds of Vietnam had never really healed—the pains, though no longer acute, were still felt— the US military did not want another land war in Asia. Equally if not more important, the lessons from the Soviet experience figured centrally in the planning of the US military. General Tommy Franks, head of the Central Command, was very clear: 'We don't want to repeat the Soviets' mistakes.... There's nothing to be gained by blundering around those mountains and gorges with armored battalions chasing a lightly armed enemy...'[2] That meant a small invasion force. Even for the subsequent mopping-up operations, Franks envisioned no more than a total of 'about 10 000 American soldiers, airmen, special operators, and helicopter air assault crews, along with robust in-country close air support'. A force much larger than that, it was feared, would appear as an invading force and mobilize resistance far beyond the militants.

Simple arithmetic reinforced the point: 'Analysis of the Soviet experience indicated that the larger a foreign force... the more target it produces, which in turn increases the size and intensity of any insurgent effort directed against it', an analyst writing in the journal of the US Army concluded.[3]

The alternative approach based on a combination of US airpower, Special Forces and Afghan militias—soon dubbed the 'Afghan model' of intervention—proved a 'powerful and robust' instrument for defeating the Taliban regime, as its proponents argued.[4] It was much less effective in hunting down Al-Qaeda and Taliban members who had escaped towards the mountainous region on the border with Pakistan. One reason was poor organization among the Afghans, reflecting lack of voice and preparatory time. For security reasons, American advisers did not inform the Afghans in advance of the operation, and so they had little time to prepare. One local commander said he was given notice only a few hours before the offensive started: 'My father told me, "just go", so I ... took 700 soldiers. We got there, but I don't know for what. We had no food or anything'. More important were motivational factors. Having routed the Taliban from Kabul and provincial strongholds, Afghan commanders were inclined to consider the war over. They had little interest in pursuing Taliban leaders on the run, and even less in pursuing 'the Arabs', as foreign fighters were called. In the eastern Nangarhar province, local commanders were reluctant to leave their home territories, preferring 'to stake out their own turf', as one American military adviser reported. In the local calculus of power, this was more important than joining the Americans on the chase. Another American adviser recalled that he had to 'sit down and negotiate with General Hazrat Ali [leader of a local Afghan militia] and convince him to stay in the fight'. Clearly, the willingness of the Afghans to pursue Al-Qaeda was 'built on U.S. diplomacy and cash, not internal motivation'.[5] Despite heavy cash handouts, however, Afghans fought poorly and some even took money from the militants to help them escape to Pakistan.

The mistaken assumption of common interest between the Afghan militias and the coalition forces cooled the enthusiasm in American military circles for the Afghan model. While the militias were still needed for their local knowledge and manpower, they could not substitute for the coalition forces, which were introduced in growing numbers to deal with the remaining challenges. In the first major mopping-up operation after the invasion, Operation Anaconda in March 2002, around 1,700 US infantry troops as well as Special Operations Forces from some allies were airlifted into the eastern border area. Afghan militias were used in subsequent operations, but their loyalty was a continuing and growing concern. During a major operation in early 2004 (Mountain Storm), US forces experienced incidents where militias had fired on the Americans, because—it was reported—of infiltration of Taliban elements.[6] By this time, the US and its allies were making increasing use of the Afghan army—which they had started reconstituting and training—as well as the national police. Even by the end of the decade, however, regular Afghan units were only assigned a supplementary and subordinate role. If the growing insurgency were to be fought militarily, US and allied forces had to be deployed in increasing numbers.

Escalation: The First Round

It soon became evident that the early mopping-up operations in important respects had failed. Even the large Operation Anaconda in March 2002, which had cleared the designated area and killed hundreds of militants (an estimated 500–800, as against eight coalition casualties), did not prevent militants from escaping further into the mountainous border area or, more commonly, into Pakistan. As reports of renewed militant activity in the east and southeast came in, the coalition forces launched successive sweeps to net and eliminate the militants. Operations were conducted in Paktia and Zabul in August 2003, and the much larger Operation Avalanche along much of the eastern border area in December which involved around two thousand US and other coalition forces as well as some Afghan militias. Operation Avalanche did not engage major concentrations of militants, but, in what was to become a disturbingly familiar pattern, fifteen children were accidentally killed and a large number of villagers suspected of working with the militants were taken away.

The militants started to regroup in Pakistan in 2002 and soon thereafter flexed their muscles in Afghanistan.[7] Incidents that had the character of anti-government or anti-foreign political violence increased markedly towards the end of 2003. The UN Mission in Afghanistan (UNAMA) reported that attacks against civilians associated with the foreign presence during the last three months of 2003 had exceeded the total number of similar attacks during the entire previous two year-period after the signing of the Bonn agreement. The attacks were clustered in the east and south of the country and mainly directed against visible but 'soft targets'. At one point there was an attack every second day—against UN offices and personnel in white vehicles, and NGO offices and personnel, including Afghans working for foreign NGOs. There were also kidnappings of foreign engineers working on the Kabul-Kandahar road.[8] An ICRC official was murdered in Uruzugan in March. Several incidents took place in Kandahar and the troubled province of Ghazni, halfway between Kabul and Kandahar. In Kabul, a bomb went off that blew out half the windows in the Intercontinental Hotel. The UN started marking most of the southeast as a no-go zone for its personnel. Lakhdar Brahimi, who had served as Special Representative of the Secretary-General and head of UNAMA and was due to leave his position at the end of 2003, said in a parting message that unless the security situation improved, the UN might have to abandon its efforts to stabilize the country. A group of UN Security Council ambassadors on a mission to Afghanistan in November came away expressing deep concern over the worsening situation.

Not all the violence was the work of the militants. Afghanistan's tortured history had left a large potential for revengeful acts and vigilante justice, in addition to common disputes over land, water, and smuggling routes, and plain banditry. All flourished in the unsettled aftermath of regime change and the invasion. The Taliban nevertheless took responsibility for many of the attacks, thereby presenting themselves as a coherent movement that had returned and retained the capacity to strike at will. Taliban-signed leaflets were distributed to the foreign press calling for a boycott of the presidential elections scheduled for 2004. Other leaflets announced a *jihad* against US troops and warned Afghans not to work with foreigners or the government. Taliban spokesmen claimed their forces controlled large parts of the southern province of Zabul.[9]

The US military reported Taliban incursions in the southern Helmand province already in mid-2002, and a year later the American commanding general in Afghanistan told American journalists that the Taliban had come back.[10] US intelligence agencies were starting to revise their earlier estimates that the Taliban had been decimated. They now concluded that the militants had regrouped in a major way, infiltrating the southern provinces and showing a boldness not seen since they were driven from power in November-December 2001.[11] Looking at the policy implications for the United States, Secretary of Defense Rumsfeld concluded in his end-of-the year assessment in 2003 that the future would be 'a long hard slog' in both Afghanistan and Iraq.[12]

The deteriorating situation in Afghanistan created contradictory pressures on the Bush Administration. The war in Iraq had absolute priority. In this light, Afghanistan appeared as a diversion and nuisance, and Rumsfeld—perhaps in a moment of wishful thinking—had declared in May 2003 that major combat operations in Afghanistan were over. Yet Afghanistan kept intruding. Osama bin Laden had not been captured, and the question haunted Bush at every press conference. A Taliban-led insurgency in league with Al-Qaeda would pose a major problem for the Administration in domestic politics as well as foreign policy. The next year, 2004, was a presidential election year in both the US and Afghanistan—Bush was running for re-election and Karzai, who was leading the transitional administration, was up for popular election. In the meantime, Washington needed to demonstrate some progress in the two wars in which it was engaged. Developments in Iraq were not encouraging, despite the President's declaration of 'mission accomplished' a couple of months after the invasion. By comparison, Afghanistan seemed a relatively easier place to produce a visible measure of success. The Taliban had raised their heads, but not much more. The political transition agreed to in Bonn had so far proceeded largely on schedule. The US intervention continued to command broad international as well as domestic support—Afghanistan was still 'the good war'. The upcoming presidential election in Afghanistan was an opportunity to validate both the intervention and its aftermath.

A team of Administration officials started in August 2003 to develop a strategy that could produced the desired indicators of progress ahead of the elections. The President's principal adviser on Afghan affairs, Zalmay Khalilzad, was dispatched as Ambassador to Afghanistan with an additional $1.2 billion in aid and a free hand to ensure that free and fair elections would result in victory for Karzai. A large number of senior American advisers—news reports spoke of one hundred—were sent to work with Afghan ministers to strengthen 'statebuilding' at the central level. In Washington, the responsibility for managing reconstruction aid was moved from the State Department to the White House. On the military side, the Administration wanted to send more troops, but, as American troops were tied up in Iraq, shifted the pressure on to its allies to contribute. The result was a reversal of US policy on the question of ISAF's expansion. With Washington's approval of ISAF expansion beyond Kabul, the UN Security Council passed a resolution to this effect in October 2003, opening the way for both a fresh deployment of allied troops and an enlarged operational area (see chapter 4).

US forces in Afghanistan nevertheless did increase in this period, at first gradually, and then quite markedly. Small but steady increases in 2002–03 had brought US force levels to the maximum envisaged by General Franks for the post-invasion phase, about 10,000. In late 2003 and 2004 that number almost doubled again to just under 20,000.[13] The latest increase reflected the growing power of the insurgency and the wish to keep up the pressure on the militants, particularly during the pre-election period. 'We want to make sure that that [election] event goes well', the Chairman of the Joint Chiefs of Staff, General Richard B. Myers, said in March 2004 as he announced that an additional 2000 marines would be sent to Afghanistan.[14] New military operations were launched. In the five-month 'Mountain Storm', which started in March 2004, US commando teams went on search-and-destroy missions in seven provinces, stretching from Kunar in the northeast to Kandahar in the south. Often inserted by helicopter in remote areas, the teams raided villages and engaged suspected militants with the help of close air support. But the operations also continued after the elections. No sooner was 'Mountain Storm' over than another started, this one called 'Lightning Freedom', which lasted from December 2004 until February 2005. Back-to-back operations seemed to have become an established pattern. Special resources were also introduced, including a team of US specialists that had been involved in the search for Saddam Hussein and was transferred to Afghanistan with the aim of capturing top-level Al-Qaeda operatives.

A doubling of force levels to nearly 20,000 over a couple of years would under most circumstances have aroused some attention in Washington and been formalized in a statement of policy. Instead, the increase was accompanied by near-total silence, a symptom of the unawareness in political circles and the media of what was happening. There was no statement of policy from the Administration and no reaction in Congress. Members of the House Armed Services Committee were surprised when told by Defense Department officials in mid-

2004 that the US had 17,900 troops in Afghanistan—they had thought it rather lower, around 12,000.[15] There was confusion in the media and even at higher levels of government about the figures. The Deputy Solicitor General used the figure of 11,000 in April 2004, while a small news item in the *New York Times* the following month reported that US troop numbers had swollen to 20,000 as a result of rotations. It seemed a textbook case of the kind of disjointed incrementalism that transforms a series of small steps into *de facto* policy. Heavily focused on the larger war in Iraq, the Bush administration had committed a substantial number of combat troops in Afghanistan, a step that raised the stakes and amounted to a significant policy commitment, without having made a deliberate decision to do so. NATO, which had taken over operational responsibility for ISAF in 2003, was going down the same road.

Mid-Decade: Second Round of Escalation

A new spiral of violence started to uncoil around mid-decade. Demands from the Iraq theatre had made Washington turn to its allies

Fig. 1. US troops in Afghanistan (in '000)

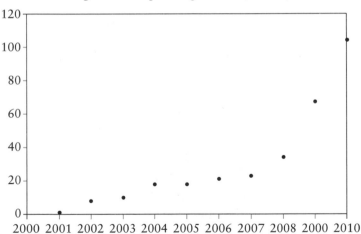

Sources: Author's compilation from The Afghanistan Conflict Monitor (http://www.afghanconflictmonitor.org/hsrp/), US Congressional Research Service reports and news reports.

43

to boost troop levels in Afghanistan, particularly in the southeast where the resistance was gathering strength. The Canadians, the British and the Dutch complied, joining the US in a major military offensive launched in preparation for the deployment of fresh—but, the US military expected, inexperienced—allied troops. To prepare the ground and soften the resistance, a major operation was launched. Operation Mountain Thrust was the largest and the longest offensive undertaken by the coalition forces since the invasion. Starting with air strikes in March 2006, the operation peaked in June-July as some 10,000 troops from the US and its NATO allies and a contingent from the newly formed Afghan National Army mounted a sustained campaign with close air support over a wide swathe of territory in the southern provinces, including Kandahar, Helmand, Uruzgan and Zabul. The offensive involved protracted and intense fighting that caused huge casualties among the militants—coalition spokesmen cited 5–600 after only the first two weeks of fighting—an unknown number of deaths among civilians, and new flows of displaced persons estimated in the tens of thousands.[16]

Yet the results were inconclusive. The operation was designed to break the back of the militants in the south by inflicting heavy casualties, but the militants were able to absorb large casualties. The new ISAF commander, who arrived in July just as the operation was being completed, made a sombre assessment. 'We need to realize that we could actually fail here', the British General David Richards said in what became a widely cited statement.[17] The head of the UN mission (UNAMA), Tom Koenigs, concluded that the Taliban simply could not be defeated by repeated military offensives. The Taliban were a 'grassroots movement' whose reservoir of fighters was 'practically limitless', he said. 'The movement will not be overcome by high casualty figures'.[18] There were reports of amazing bravery—or foolhardiness—as lightly armed militants stormed the positions of the coalition forces in flip-flops.[19] There were also reports of increasing professionalism in organization, tactics and weaponry that reflected external training and other assistance. Assessing the capabilities of the militants in June 2006, at the height of the operation, a US general gave them high marks. The coalition forces now faced 'thousands of heavily armed Taliban ...aggressive and smart in their tactics'. They operated in battalion sized units, and—he added in a not so subtle reference to Pakistan's role—had 'excellent weapons, new IED technology, commercial communications gear and new field equipment'. They appeared to have received 'excellent tactical, camouflage and marksmanship training'.[20]

The insurgents demonstrated their growing strength and diversity of tactics in other ways as well. Suicide attacks—previously unknown in Afghanistan—had first occurred in 2004 (three attacks) but then increased sharply: 17 incidents in 2005 and 123 in 2006.[21] It produced the expected shock effects. Incidents involving improvised explosive devices (IEDs) increased 142 per cent from 2004 to 2005. By 2005, the militants were no longer primarily hitting 'soft targets' but inflicting significant losses on the foreign forces as well. OEF and ISAF casualties more than doubled from 2004 to 2005 (from 58 to 130).[22] The overall strength of the insurgency was indicated by the sharp rise in what coalition forces called 'AGE-initiated security incidents' (that is, those initiated by anti-government elements). In 2006, when the militants were being hammered for several months by Operation Mountain Thrust, the number of violent incidents attributed to them nevertheless more than doubled and kept rising (see Fig. 2).

Among the international supporters of the government, the mid-decade evidence of a deteriorating security environment was interpreted as a wake-up call for more assistance and a stronger commitment. The under-investment thesis discussed above (chapter 1) appeared in full force. A range of individuals, organizations and agencies already involved in Afghanistan argued that Iraq had overshadowed Afghanistan, allowing things to slip. Unless greater commitments were made, Afghanistan would be lost. An editorial in the *New York Times* on the eve of the NATO summit meeting in November 2006 captured the dominant mood.

NATO is failing its most significant post-Soviet test: stabilizing Afghanistan. Violence is spiraling as the Taliban and Al-Qaeda reassert their power. The economy is addicted to opium production. The pro-Western government in Kabul looks increasingly powerless and irrelevant. Unless NATO's members commit to sending in more troops and more resources, Afghanistan could go the way of Iraq. There may not be many more chances after this week's meeting.[23]

The summit meeting in Riga dramatized the deteriorating situation and was an opportunity for the governments that already had troops in Afghanistan to appeal to other members to join in. Yet the alliance was at a juncture where several difficult questions intersected to complicate efforts to generate stronger commitments.

45

Fig 2. Security incidents initiated by anti-government elements (AGE)

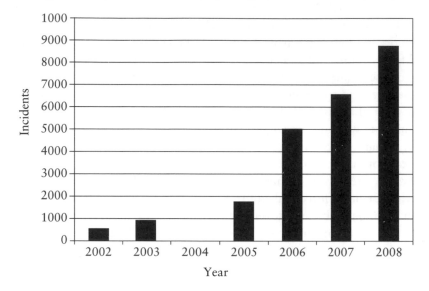

Sources: Author's compilation based on CentCom public figures and Anthony H. Cordesman and Nicholas B. Greenough, *The Afghan War. A Survey of 'Metrics'*. Washington, DC: CSIS, 2009). http://csis.org/publication/afghan-warUS.

Within the alliance, NATO's approach to the conflict was being reassessed by European allies that had been asked to provide troops. A year before the Riga summit, the Danish and the British government had started to develop concepts and plans for an 'integrated approach'— or a 'comprehensive approach' in alliance language. The aim was to bring civilian and military assets closer together in NATO stabilization missions in general and in Afghanistan in particular. The central theme of an 'integrated approach' seemed uncontroversial: that the 'creation of sustainable peace in societies ravaged by war hinges on providing security, humanitarian assistance, reconstruction and development, governance and the rule of law in a concerted and coordinated manner', as a Danish report later put it.[24] In a NATO context, however, these notions were linked to a number of critical questions facing the alliance as it was adjusting to the post-Cold War and post-9/11 international environment. Did a 'comprehensive approach' suggest that

NATO should take on a global role and consistently operate out-of-area and outside Europe? Should the military establishments of the alliance develop new capabilities to fill gaps in stabilization and peace operations left by civilian actors? Should civilian activities be coordinated with the military or vice versa?

In relation to Afghanistan, the most divisive question was whether a comprehensive approach meant a classic counterinsurgency strategy of clear-hold-and build that started with intensive combat operations, such as the newly completed Mountain Thrust in the south, or whether doctrine should privilege reconstruction and Afghan capacity building in a mission cast as stabilization rather than combat, of the kind that Germany and other European allies were developing in the north and west of the country.[25] By the time the heads of state and governments met in Riga in November 2006, there was no agreement on these issues, either in their general form or in relation to Afghanistan. US pressure on its allies to send more troops to the southern provinces in Afghanistan forced the issue.

In an ironic twist, the dialectics of intra-alliance disagreement over substantive policy generated a declaratory policy of strong and enduring support for Afghanistan, as well as inflated rhetoric about the stakes involved. As if to paper over the substantive divisions over policy, the joint declaration of the Riga meeting described NATO's commitment in ambitious, unambiguous and wide-ranging terms. NATO was standing with the government and people of Afghanistan 'to build a stable, democratic and prosperous society.... We are committed to an enduring role....Contributing to peace and stability in Afghanistan is NATO's key priority...[We] pledge to ensure that ISAF has the forces, resources and flexibility needed to ensure the mission's continued success'. The principle of an integrated approach was also acknowledged: 'There can be no security in Afghanistan without development, and no development without security....[ISAF] Provincial Reconstruction Teams are increasingly at the leading edge of NATO's effort supported by military forces capable of providing the security and stability needed to foster civilian activity'.[26] In terms of declared policy, at least, the Riga meeting deepened NATO's commitment to a multi-purpose mission of peace, democracy and stability in Afghanistan.

Other factors worked in the same direction. Afghanistan was NATO's first 'out-of-area' mission, and the first in the post-9/11 international security environment. Having taken operational responsibility for ISAF in August 2003 and subsequently expanded its command to cover the entire country, NATO had invested significant status in the project. The Afghanistan mission, moreover, evolved in a context of efforts by the alliance to redefine its functions and thereby remain relevant in a rapidly changing international strategic environment. A creature of the Cold War, NATO had initially adapted to the dissolution of the Soviet Union by adding stabilization and peacekeeping operations to its original mandate.[27] The 9/11 events had brought other threats to the fore, and the Riga meeting emphasized the importance of non-conventional threat scenarios. The General Political Guidance adopted by the Riga meeting to guide development of strategic doctrine recognized that 'for the foreseeable future, the principal threats to the Alliance are international terrorism and the proliferation of weapons of mass destruction and their delivery systems, as well as instability caused by failed or failing states...' As a source of international terrorism and a case of a failed state as commonly defined, Afghanistan was putting NATO to a double test. At stake was not only the past investment in securing the country as a stable and friendly state, but NATOs capacity to meet unconventional security threats and thereby position itself as a powerful actor on the global scene.

A stream of rhetoric from alliance leaders to the effect that NATO's credibility was at stake sharpened the point and raised the stakes. The policy rhetoric was in part designed to extract additional resources from European allies to the Afghan mission. The Secretary-General, Jaap de Hoop Scheffer—whose own (Dutch) government had committed troops to a controversial deployment in the south—warned that the outcome in Afghanistan would affect the credibility and possibly the very survival of the alliance. So did the Bush Administration. In a particularly hard-hitting speech, Secretary of Defense Robert Gates took reluctant allies to task at a meeting organized by NATO's military leadership in October 2007. Afghanistan, he said, was a test of the alliance's capacity to respond proactively to the unconventional military challenges of the twenty-first century—that is, to help 'quell ethnic conflicts, fight terrorists, and rebuild communities......The failure to meet commitments puts the Afghan mission—and with it, the credibility of NATO—at real risk'.[28] This definition of risk permitted no failure and drove the alliance to invest even more of its military resources and prestige in Afghanistan.

A similar perverse effect operated in countries where governments sent troops to Afghanistan in order to meet obligations to NATO or the US, but faced domestic critics of the war. Grand objectives of peace, security and democracy in Afghanistan were cited to justify deployment. Some invoked a 'domino' version of international terrorism. The British seemed particularly inclined to grand rhetoric. Visiting British troops in southern Afghanistan on the eve of the Riga meeting, Prime Minister Tony Blair made a speech that turned the sands of Helmand into a decisive battlefront in matters of global war and peace: 'Here, in this extraordinary piece of desert, is where the future of world security in the early twenty-first century is going to be played out'.[29] Similar claims were also made by British military leaders. General David Richards, who took over as ISAF commander in mid-2006 and warned that NATO could fail in Afghanistan, also warned that this must not be allowed to happen: 'I think of my own daughters in London and the risk they would be in'.[30] Rhetoric of this kind served as glue to fasten policy to a path of deepening involvement. Any compromise or withdrawal from these lofty objectives or dangerous scenarios would require a steep climb-down in rhetoric and invite criticism from political opponents of hypocrisy, defeat or sell-out.

At one point the war in Iraq likewise stacked the political incentives in favour of increasing NATO commitments to Afghanistan. With requests from the US to contribute to both wars, some European allies found it much easier for domestic political reasons to deploy to Afghanistan—particularly to the relatively quiet northern and central areas, and for purposes that could be described as stabilization and reconstruction (see chapter 4). By mid-decade, a similar dynamic was evident within the United States as well. As the violence in Iraq seemed to spiral out of control, critics in the US fastened onto Afghanistan as the more critical place to fight the 'War on Terror' and where more support should be given. Quite apart from the merits of the argument, it served to demonstrate that critics of the Iraq war were still firm on national security issues. The argument had already surfaced during the 2004 elections and continued to reappear, both in the context of the under-investment thesis in Afghanistan and the growing concern in Washington to find an exit from the Iraq war. The report of a major bipartisan Iraq Study Group presented in December 2006, for instance, suggested that the US should re-evaluate its policy towards Iraq but maintain a strong military and economic presence in Afghanistan.[31]

The group did not elaborate on its reasoning—it seemed to be a matter of maintaining an overall balance so as not to give opponents at home and adversaries as well as friends abroad the impression of a major power in retreat.

By the second half of the decade, then, the US and NATO had significantly increased their military presence in Afghanistan. In part it was the result of a growing momentum generated by domestic and foreign policy concerns unrelated to Afghanistan *per se*, inflated rhetoric, and the prestige of the alliance and its leading member. It was also, of course, a response to the growing insurgency.

The Taliban—The Growth of a Movement

The return and revival of what is commonly called the Taliban movement is a complex phenomenon, not fully understood and poorly documented. While it is not the main focus of this book, a brief review of the movement's growth is necessary to better understand the role of the international military presence as a precipitating factor in the rise of the insurgency.

The principal dynamic in the return of the Taliban is reasonably well established. Driven from power, excluded politically from the transitional process established in Bonn, denied amnesty by the new US-supported government, but not totally defeated, the Taliban retreated to Pakistan. There they nursed their wounds and prepared a return to drive out the foreign forces and re-establish the Islamic Emirate. The senior commanders coalesced around Mullah Omar in Quetta. The semi-autonomous network of Jalaluddin Haqqani, a veteran *mujahed* from the anti-Soviet resistance, regrouped in Pakistan's North Waziristan, and Gulbuddin Hekmatyar, who had led Hezb-e-Islami since the mid-1970s and had most recently been in exile in Iran, also returned to Pakistan. ISI and the Pakistan government provided critical protection and support, enabling the insurgency to gather force.[32]

In this sequence of events, the exclusionary element looms large in a recent study of the Taliban in Kandahar by Anand Gopal, an Indian journalist based in Afghanistan who conducted extensive interviews with parties to the conflict. In a 'window-of-opportunity' thesis, Gopal argues that there was an opening soon after the invasion for making peace with senior Taliban leaders. Several Taliban leaders approached

Karzai, offering to lay down their arms in return for amnesty. Rebuffed, they had no option but to seek safety in Pakistan, where they joined the struggle led by Mullah Omar. Lesser Taliban commanders in Kandahar were prepared to accept the new government and tried to quietly melt away in their villages, but they were attacked, harassed, tortured and jailed by the new power holders. Those who survived fled to Pakistan with family and friends to join the resistance. As a result, Gopal concludes

[t]he resurgence of the Taliban in Kandahar was not....merely a result of a lack of [coalition] troop presence in the early years. Rather, it was due to specific policies pursued by the Kandahar government and its American backers. A significant part of the senior Taliban leadership in Kandahar had surrendered or attempted to surrender to the Afghan government. But intense harassment left many of them with the feeling that there was no option but to flee to Pakistan and reorganize their movement...[T]he problem was political—the lack of a reconciliation process...[33]

Gopal maintains further that US authorities were instrumental in discouraging Karzai from discussing surrender and amnesty guarantees with the Taliban leaders who approached him, while the US military in the Kandahar area empowered new leaders and let them freely go after their Taliban rivals.[34] His thesis is indirectly supported by two independent Western analysts who have closely studied the movement, Antonio Giustozzi and Thomas Ruttig. 'Relatively few' of the old Taliban initially responded positively to Mullah Omar's call to a new *jihad* in 2002–3; '[b]ut later their number rose, as a result of threats (by Afghan intelligence, Westerns troops in Afghanistan and their minders in Pakistan) to be arrested and deported to the Guantanamo system', Ruttig writes.[35] The argument dovetails with the overall thrust of US policy in Afghanistan, that is, to bring about regime change, defeat the Taliban and Al-Qaeda—which in US military jargon were joined in the acronym AQT—and generally to refuse to talk with 'terrorists'.

A more reconciliatory attitude towards members of the former regime would possibly have been more effective than military force in nipping the insurgency in the bud. However, as noted in the discussion of the other windows-thesis in chapter 1, the 'what ifs' of history are tricky. What we do know is that the US military pressure generated counter-pressure, and the step-by-step interaction of hostile forces produced a steadily escalating violence for the next decade.

Other factors contributed as well. The sanctuary in Pakistan was a critical enabling condition for the insurgency—and quite predictably so. The sanctuary function was a long-established tradition in the border area, in modern times dating back to the 1920s when Nadir Shah mobilized support in the northwest of what was then British India for his march on Kabul. In the 1980s, when the *mujahedin* fought the Afghan Communist government and its Soviet supporters, the sanctuary became highly developed and institutionalized. An arena for channelling aid, training fighters, and running the political activities of the *mujahedin*, the sanctuary operated with the official blessing of the Pakistan government, the US and its major allies. After 2001, the Taliban and other Afghan militants received permission to stay and organize the struggle, as well as *de facto* protection and covert support from Pakistani agents, although the extent and nature of the links remain unclear. Given the altered international context, the Pakistan government now tried to establish conditions of plausible deniability. A tripartite commission consisting of the Pakistani and Afghan government and ISAF's leadership provided an institutional forum for discussing cross-border cooperation. Towards the end of the decade US pressure on the sanctuary increased markedly. Drone attacks multiplied. Taliban leaders were harassed and occasionally arrested by the Pakistan government, and Pakistan military forces launched repeated offensives in the semi-autonomous tribal areas where both Afghan and Pakistan militants were located.

The Taliban also received support from further afield. The American invasion of Iraq in March 2003 dramatically sharpened the conflict between the US-led 'War on Terror' and militant Islam, enabling the Taliban to draw on a larger international network of support, particularly in the Middle East. The Taliban started to incorporate new techniques of struggle, organization and propagandizing. By the second half of the decade, analysts were using the term 'Neo-Taliban', although to what extent new forces and techniques prevailed is disputed.[36] In important respects, however, the link to the wider *jihad* was a 'poisoned chalice', as Alia Brahimi writes. The link 'provides the legitimising rhetoric of self-defence against the global Crusader and an arsenal of technological innovation, yet it brings with it a fanatical foreign presence and tactics like suicide bombing and beheading which alienate the populace and sow division within the ranks'.[37]

The Taliban movement experienced problems of this kind.[38] In addition, to the enemies of the Taliban, the ties with international *jihadi*s served to validate the US invasion and continued war, although the point was strenuously countered by the Taliban's nationalist orientation in word and action. In fact, no Talib was ever involved in an attack outside Afghanistan and the movement's focus was entirely on change within the country.

While external support helped empower and sustain the insurgents, the driving forces were local and national. US military analysts estimated that three-quarters of the insurgents were fighting within five kilometres of their homes, a telling indicator of the local nature of the movement.[39] The militants were able to exploit a wide range of conditions: the failure of the post-2001 order to deliver a 'peace dividend' in the form of economic and physical security, the rule of incompetent, abusive and corrupt strongmen and government authorities, and increasingly negative reactions to the international military forces. Turned into political outsiders in 2001, many withdrew before they were militarily defeated and were biding their time, waiting for an opportunity to regain power and recruit supporters by tapping into local conflicts and grievances. Gradually, the ranks of the militants swelled; the 'caravan effect', as Bernt Glatzer called it, set in.[40] During the 1990s, people had attached themselves to the Taliban for a variety of different reasons, and they were increasingly doing the same again.

For some, the pursuit of local conflicts over water, land and power, and tribal and family feuds were reasons for joining the movement, as described in revealing detail in a volume by independent analysts and published in 2009.[41] Some grievances seemed relatively small. Pashtun villagers in Wardak, for instance, feared being harassed and accused of being Taliban if they travelled to Kabul wearing their turbans.[42] Others were major. Sarah Chayes recounts the systematic harassment and violence meted out by Gul Aga Sherzai, the militia leader whom the Americans helped install as Governor in Kandahar, where he ruled for about three years before being transferred as Governor to the eastern province of Nangarhar.[43] When such rulers were demoted by coalition forces, as happened to Governor Sher Mohammad Akhundzada of Helmand, their networks became potential allies of the militants. In Ghazni, commanders associated with the old Taliban regime capitalized on local resentment against Tajik policemen who were sent into the Pashtun heartland where they harassed local shopkeepers and other villagers.[44] In Zabul, the majority tribes and landed elite (Hotak/Tokhi) had been ousted after 2001 and members of a local minority tribe had been appointed to government positions. The change was part of a divide-and-rule strategy in Kabul, but was justified by the fact that some Tokhi had been prominent Taliban leaders.[45] Deprived of power and demoted, the new 'outsiders' were potential Taliban allies.

In this context of shifting and conflictual local politics, movements with external networks exchanged money and weapons in return for allegiance and willingness to fight. This was the way the *mujahedin* had operated during the resistance against the Communists in the 1980s, and this was the way the insurgent networks operated after 2001. American and NATO intelligence had arrived at a similar conclusion. The Taliban are 'localized, regionalized, syndicated', the American head of ISAF, General David McKiernan, told a public audience in Washington in 2008.[46]

The Impact of the International Military Presence

Reasons for joining an insurgent movement are obviously diverse, and often complex and composite in nature. Researching the return of the Taliban in Uruzgan, Martine van Bijlert found that locals used a nuanced vocabulary to describe different types of fighters and reasons for joining.[47] Yet for all its diversity, the Taliban caravan that moved forward at the end of the decade had a distinct shape and direction, defined by the overarching aim of repelling the foreign invaders and restoring an Islamist state in Afghanistan. Both the old and the new Taliban were essentially religious movements focused on capturing state power. Mullahs of varying stature and formal education formed the core of both.[48] But even more ordinary fighters expressed their reasons for joining in nationalist and religious terms when talking to outsiders, as an enterprising Canadian journalist based in Kandahar found when he succeeded in making contact with a fairly large sample of ordinary fighters.[49] This is hardly surprising. Islam has for centuries dominated the political discourse in Afghanistan, and moves even more to the forefront in times of crisis. As Olivier Roy wrote of the resistance to the Soviet and Afghan Communists during the 1980s, 'it is the external threat which gives Islam its energising power'.[50]

In this perspective, the steady increase in US and allied troops who often behaved like an occupation force generated considerable 'energising power'. Their presence gave the militants more targets to attack and more grievances to exploit in a resistance validated by Islam. The logic was tellingly recognized by the British Secretary for Defence, Des Browne, who noted that the British contingent deployed to Helmand in April 2006 was attacked as soon as it arrived. The presence of British troops seemed to 'energise' the Taliban, as he put it.[51] The more numerous US forces who had spread out in a larger area since the invasion appeared to have a similar effect.

In the rural Pashtun heartland, the string of operations carried out by US forces up and down the eastern border areas since 2002 had created fear and antagonism that resonated beyond the circle of militants. The Americans were infidels in a society that was tribal in social structure, culturally conservative and closed to outsiders who had not been invited. They behaved like an occupation force, moving at will anywhere their operational plans required, searching villages without asking permission or informing local authorities, and violating fundamental cultural codes of propriety by bursting into private family quarters. Property was destroyed and villagers killed, whether they were technically speaking civilians, Taliban or both. Night raids carried out by Special Operations Forces caused particular resentment. Suspects disappeared into American-run detention centres in Afghanistan that seemed to be black holes, for years inaccessible even to the ICRC and the Afghan Independent Human Rights Commission.[52] Tribal elders in vain sent delegations to Kabul to protest that the foreign troops did not consult them before entering their villages, and killed or took away their relatives. The word got around. '[T]he Americans bomb the wrong kind of people and imprison innocent people', the elders in a village in Logar told a team of foreigner researchers who surveyed local attitudes in late 2004—their area had not even been directly affected by the violence.[53]

A more specific and highly emotive cause for complaint was civilian casualties caused by US and NATO airpower. The problem had been a national political issue since the invasion, when it was dramatized by the attack of US planes on a wedding party in Uruzgan in 2002. Mistaking celebratory gunshots as hostile fire from an area that had been a Taliban stronghold, the pilot repeatedly strafed the area, killing up to fifty villagers from two prominent clans.[54] Similar incidents of mistaken identity or 'collateral damage' among civilians followed. While the aggregate number was low during the first half of the decade, individual cases were highly publicized and publicly condemned by President Karzai. Thus, in December 2003, Karzai expressed his 'profound shock' over the collateral damage of nine children in Ghazni. In February 2004 he ordered a government inquiry into the 'unfortunate' casualties of a similar incident in Uruzgan. After repeated cases of civilian deaths caused by American air power in early 2005, he demanded that US forces exercise 'extreme caution' and consult with the Afghan government on operational plans.[55] A year later, Karzai brought himself and his audience to tears when recounting a similar incident, denounced 'the cruelty imposed on his people' and expressed despair over his inability to stop 'the coalition [forces] from killing our children'.[56]

Whether Karzai himself was genuinely moved or wished to distance himself from the actions of his allies is not the issue; the more significant aspect is that he felt compelled to invoke the 'us/them' language of nationalism, in which the international forces were cast as the offender and the Afghans as the victims. The choice of words was a recognition of the power of nationalism in Afghan reactions to the international presence, particularly when faced with the most controversial consequences of that deployment. The nationalist appeal was even more explicit in the President's reaction to the general casualty rates caused by the large operation 'Mountain Thrust' launched by the coalition forces in the south in mid-2006. Although the manifest purpose was to eliminate Taliban fighters, Karzai publicly protested: 'It is not acceptable that in all this fighting, Afghans are dying. In the past three to four weeks, 500 to 600 Afghans were killed. Even if they are Taliban, they are sons of this land'.[57]

Karzai had good reasons to stress his nationalist creditentials to compensate in some measure for his extreme dependence on foreign powers. But nationalism also gave a measure of coherence and popular legitimacy to an insurgency that otherwise was localized and syndicated in nature, and so did Islam. History alone suggested as much. The *jihad* against the Soviet invasion in 1979 had been powerfully charged by the forces of Islam and nationalism; on this point all analysts agree. Nevertheless, the lessons seemed lost. Western analysts who had written authoritatively on the *jihad* against the Soviets examined the US-led invasion and the subsequent international project in a quite different framework.[58] This time around there was little recognition of the role of Islam and nationalism as powerful forces of the resistance. The parallel with the Soviet invasion—and the related conclusion that more forces would generate more resistance—was rarely drawn. Perhaps the analysts assigned too much weight to the differences. Admittedly, the coalition forces did not reach the Soviet level until the end of the decade. The 2004 Constitution recognized Islam, while the early communist governments in Kabul explicitly denied Islam as a source of law and government authority. The Western-led intervention was initially welcomed by large segments of the population, while the Soviet invasion was deemed illegitimate by many Afghans from the very outset. Perhaps, also, the analysts were blinded by the good intentions of the project.

Eschewing the Soviet parallel, the conventional, Western strategic narrative had to look elsewhere to explain the growth of the insurgency and found it in factors external to the intervention itself. Three main factors were emphasized: the weaknesses of the Afghan government, Pakistan's support for the insurgents, and widespread poverty that enabled the Taliban to enlist large numbers of local Afghans who made up the rank and file of the movement. In this schema, only the hard-core militants were ideologically driven by their publicly stated aim to drive out the foreign infidels and restore the Islamic Emirate. For most, the action of becoming an insurgent was 'accidental', in the catchy phrase of David Kilcullen, a military officer, anthropologist and adviser to the Pentagon.[59]

This narrative provided foundational authority for the more-is-more policy that dominated the international response for almost a decade after the US-led invasion, powerfully underpinning the build-up of international troops and infusion of capital and advisers. Rather than being part of the problem, a greater international presence was seen as the solution; it would create more security, better governance, and less poverty. The first reconciliation scheme launched by the government with British and American support in 2005 was premised on the same narrative. The scheme sought in effect to buy back Taliban soldiers.[60] The counterinsurgency doctrine similarly presumed that development would stabilize restive areas and legitimized the entry of the military as an aid actor. In fact, the considerable sums of money used by the military to 'win hearts and minds' on the ground seemed not to have the intended effect, according to field studies conducted by a team of scholars led by Andrew Wilder, a long-time analyst of Afghan affairs.[61] Nevertheless, the strategic narrative stubbornly remained, filtering down to coalition soldiers in the field who tried to understand why villagers turned hostile. In a telling scene from the documentary film *Restrepo*, a stern-faced US army colonel tells the village elders in Koregal Valley in Kunar not to let their sons join the Taliban. 'The Taliban will pay your sons just 5 dollars to go and shoot at my men', he says, and offers a better deal: 'We'll give you progress—a road'.[62]

Challenges to the conventional strategic narrative had started to appear around mid-decade, pointing to the importance of the foreign military presence itself as a cause of the insurgency and suggesting parallels with the Soviet period.[63] By the end of the decade, this view had become more commonplace, with nationalism and religion appearing as principal drivers of the insurgency beyond its Pashtun core. As Thomas Ruttig wrote in 2009:

While the Taleban (sic) are still a predominantly Pashtun movement, their appeal amongst non-Pashtun groups is increasing. The deepening sense of occupation, undercurrents of anti-Westernism based on perceptions of an 'anti-Muslim' Western world and Islamic moral superiority, a surge of international Muslim solidarity (linked to developments in the Middle East) and the joint mujahedin history establish common ideological denominators between the Taleban and a wider range of former mujahedin.... Enormous growing anger about the behaviour of foreign forces has already brought groups closer to the insurgency that earlier had supported the international engagement in Afghanistan.[64]

A Way Out on Top of the Palm Tree?

In 2007 the US Secretary of Defense, Robert Gates, had been working on a strategy to maximize allied input and get the most out of the total resources committed to Afghanistan in line with the principles and intentions of the Riga summit meeting. It was by now clear that simply asking for more soldiers would not convince NATO allies and their increasingly sceptical public opinion, or even the military establishments in member countries. A change in strategy as signalled at Riga seemed necessary. Gates started working on what was billed as an integrated approach that would bring the various elements of the allied presence in Afghanistan together in a coherent counterinsurgency strategy. Reconstruction, development and counter-narcotics activities would now be coordinated with security aspects in a common framework with clear objectives, timelines and benchmarks. Parallel work on an integrated approach was under way in the British government. By the time the next NATO summit was held in Bucharest in April 2008, the new Comprehensive Strategic, Political, Military Plan for Afghanistan was ready for approval.

Armed with new plans and approaches, the US government pressed its allies for more troops. At the time of the Bucharest meeting, the US/ISAF force commander in Afghanistan, General Dan K. McNeill, was calling for three more combat brigades to address the growing insurgency. With the US still heavily involved in Iraq, Gates was leaning on the allies. The latter had by then already contributed almost as many troops as the US had in Afghanistan, and were reluctant to add more (see chapter 4). When the new US/ISAF force commander, General David McKiernan, took over from McNeill in mid-2008 and also requested more troops, the Bush Administration relented. As McKiernan described it, the situation had deteriorated to the point where additional forces were necessary to protect the southern approaches to the capital itself. He needed an additional brigade combat team for deployment to the nearby provinces of Wardak and Logar, where insurgents had become increasingly active. The prospect of a Taliban stranglehold on Kabul was real. In December 2008, Gates announced that the US would send another 20,000 troops to fill the gap in combat forces as well as meeting the new priority need for trainers and mentors for the Afghan security forces.[65]

When the new Obama Administration took office in January 2009, US troop presence had increased to around 34,000 and more were in the pipeline. US allies had contributed around 30,000. The total number was now approaching the Soviet level in the early 1980s, not including civilian contractors. The insurgency, however, was also growing. The insurgents had spread geographically towards the north, the west and the central region, had changed tactics, and used a range of techniques, especially refined IED methods apparently imported from Iraq. They continued to receive international support. Although not as nationally diverse as the forces under NATO command, the Taliban were attracting a number of Chechen, Uzbek, Saudi and European fighters. The violence followed apace. Statistics collected by the US military showed a sharp leap in security incidents initiated by 'anti-government elements' (see Fig. 2 above). The end-of-year report to Congress for 2008 by the US Department of Defense was bleak: the insurgency was 'complex and adaptive', 'constantly evolving', and had 'increased its influence and access to the population'.[66]

The Surge

In office, President Barack Obama did what candidate Obama had said he would do on the campaign trail—his administration would progressively withdraw from Iraq and focus on Afghanistan, which was deemed the important war from the viewpoint of US national security interests. Already in February the Administration had conducted its first strategy review, resulting in the decision to send 21,000 troops, including 4,000 instructors to accelerate the Afghanization of the war. Military analysts in Washington warned that the additional deployment would be insufficient to contain what was now described as 'a raging insurgency', and predicted the mini-surge would be followed by more.[67] And so it was. The Administration's second review, which started in September 2009 and lasted until December, found that an additional 30,000 troops were needed. The number of civilian advisers and consultants would increase from 300 to 1,000 in line with the requirements of the integrated approach.

The combined new commitments of 51,000 troops in the first year of the Obama Administration were the greatest single increase in deployment since the invasion. Like the similar surge just launched in Iraq, the additional troops were presented as the critical mass of force required to turn the situation around. Yet the decision appeared to rest more on a political than a military calculus. For the Democrats, a strengthened military engagement in Afghanistan helped to compensate politically for the commitment to withdraw from Iraq and thereby protect them from criticism on the right of being weak on national security. At the same time, growing resistance among Democrats to the war, the lack of strong indicators of progress, and the increasingly frequent comparisons with Vietnam and the Soviet experience made Obama promise that withdrawals would start in mid-2011. It was an attempt to placate all sides and, as Leslie Gelb had written of the Vietnam War, reflected fears that withdrawal in the face of adversity would weaken American power and prestige and encourage a dangerous enemy—now in the form of international terrorism. Moreover, as in President Kennedy's case, election concerns appeared to weigh heavily. Kennedy had famously said in early 1963 that he wanted to withdraw from Vietnam but 'I can't do it until 1965—until after I'm re-elected'.[68] If Obama were to be a second-term president, he had to steer a middle course and try to please all sides, critical observers concluded.[69]

Pressures from the US military strongly weighted the decision in favour of a surge. The account by Bob Woodward shows the pressure from the military, supported by Hillary Clinton in the State Department, was relentless.[70] An important new player in this respect was General Stanley McChrystal, who in mid-2009 had been appointed to lead the US and allied forces in Afghanistan. Like all ISAF commanders before him, McChrystal asked for more troops, but unlike his predecessors, he lobbied publicly to influence the strategy review, calling for an increase of 30–40,000 troops. The general's readiness to go public—culminating in a clumsy interview that cost him his job—contributed to an open discussion in the United States over the troop reinforcements. The size of the projected increase, the apparent futility of earlier investments, and the diminishing shadow of the Iraq war ensured that this time an increase in force levels would not go unnoticed. The Soviet experience in Afghanistan was brought into the discussion as well. An article on the op-ed page of the *New York Times* made the rounds on the internet and the blogger sites. It was the story of a much-decorated general who asked his government for more troops to Afghanistan; his soldiers controlled the town, but could not hold the territory it had seized from the insurgents; without extra troops and equipment, 'without a lot more men, this war will continue for a very, very long time', he concluded. The general in question was not McChrystal, but Sergei Ahkromeyev, the commander of the Soviet armed forces, who made the case to the Soviet Union's Politburo on 13 November 1986.[71]

McChrystal was one step ahead of Ahkromeyev, however. Like Secretary of Defense Gates, McChrystal and his advisers recognized that simply focusing on more troops would not do. There had to be a sense of refined or revised strategy to ensure that 'more' would indeed be 'more'. He put the case bluntly in his report to the Secretary of Defense in August 2009, which was leaked to the public in September, just as the Obama review of strategy commenced:

Success is achievable, but it will not be attained simply by trying harder or 'doubling down' on the previous strategy. Additional resources are required, but focusing on force or resource requirements misses the point entirely. The key take away from this assessment is the urgent need for a significant change to our strategy and the way that we think and operate'.[72]

The message was delivered against a backdrop of a grave situation and short timelines. The report warned that:

[a]lthough considerable effort and sacrifice have resulted in some progress, many indicators suggest the overall situation is deteriorating. We face not only a resilient and growing insurgency; there is also a crisis of confidence among Afghans...that undermines our credibility and emboldens the insurgents...[A] perception that our resolve is uncertain makes Afghans reluctant to align with us against the insurgents... Failure to gain the initiative and reverse insurgent momentum in the near-term (12 months) ... risks an outcome where defeating the insurgency is no longer possible.[73]

McChrystal probably oversold the novelty of the new strategy, which he described as classic counterinsurgency (COIN). As noted above, NATO had been moving in this direction for the past three years. The US Army and Marine Corps had already issued the new doctrine for counterinsurgency in June 2006 (FM 3–24). ISAF military spokesmen had discussed the massive Operation 'Mountain Thrust' in mid-2006 in a language that was almost identical with the McChrystal report: 'One component is the insurgency, and that is mostly confined to the south and east of the country.... But hunting down and killing insurgents won't lead to an end of violence... Leaders need to provide an environment in which people aren't attracted to extremist viewpoints'. That meant improving the economy, the infrastructure, rule of law, and dealing with corruption.[74] At NATO meetings in early 2007, high-level Pentagon officials had referred to US military operations in Afghanistan as counterinsurgency.[75]

The Pentagon's annual review of the progress of the war likewise showed that the change in strategy preceded McChrystal. At the end of 2008, that is, a year before McChrystal announced a 'significant change of strategy', the review described the operations in Afghanistan as a 'comprehensive counterinsurgency strategy' based on concepts of clear, hold and build, with a military component focused on 'degrading insurgent capacity, developing the Afghan security forces, border management and counterterrorism'.[76] '[B]uilding an effective Afghan government', in turn, was seen as an integral part of this strategy.[77] McChrystal's call for a 'population-centric' strategy aimed at protecting populations paraphrased the recommendations of the US force commander who had served in Afghanistan in 2003–05. Reflecting on the lessons from that period, General David Barno had concluded that a 'people-centric' counterinsurgency based on respect and tolerance was necessary.[78] Nevertheless, the inability of NATO to break the back of the insurgency made it imperative to present initiatives that at least appeared as new and promising.

McChrystal did offer some change. Resources would be focused on select key districts that were most vulnerable or contested. The 'clear-hold-and-build' doctrine was revised to 'shape-clear-hold-and-build', and the Operational Plan was modified accordingly. The change of leadership also seemed to offer fresh hope. McChrystal's reputation as an unconventional general with a background in Special Operations created expectations of a new turn and a new chance. A meeting of NATO defence ministers in Istanbul in February 2010 captured the atmosphere.

The defence ministers had been briefed on the Pentagon review for the preceding year. It made for depressing reading. The insurgents had 'robust means of sustaining its operation' in the form of external as well as internal funding, and '[a] ready supply of recruits .... drawn from the frustrated population, where insurgents exploit poverty, tribal friction and lack of governance to grow their ranks'. The major strengths of the insurgency were 'speed and decisiveness' of information, organizational capability and operational reach, power to intimidate, increasing ability to provide shadow governance and growing 'sophistication in conducting complex attacks'.[79] To deal with this, the NATO defence ministers looked both to more forces and to strategic innovation. When McChrystal arrived in Istanbul and presented his counterinsurgency plan, he was greeted with relief and enthusiasm. His presentation got almost 'a hallelujah' response', a participant later recalled.[80] Perhaps there was a way out of the top of the palm tree after all, as Brahimi had mused almost nine years earlier.

Marjah: How 'More' Became 'Less'

The first major application of McChrystal's 'new' strategy was a large offensive in Marjah, a cluster of villages in Helmand where the Taliban had entrenched themselves. It was launched with much fanfare, but soon revealed fundamental weaknesses.

For a start, the Taliban chose to fall back rather than confront the massive, high-tech NATO force of some 15,000 soldiers led by the US and with participation from the UK, other allies and the Afghan National Army. Once the coalition forces were in town, the Taliban slowly crept back in. In June, more than three months after the invading force had taken Marjah, fighting was occurring almost daily. The coalition forces were taking casualties that were higher than during the initial offensive. Reconstruction stalled, paralyzed by fear among the villagers of Taliban retaliation. Anyone found having installed water pumps distributed by USAID, or being in the possession of dollars, was vulnerable to retaliation. USAID's employment-creating projects had funding to hire 10,000 residents, but only 1,200 villagers had signed up, and only a quarter of the 4,000 water pumps had been distributed.[81] Afghan government officials who had been flown in from Kabul were fearful as well. Most chose to stay in the provincial capital rather than move to Marjah. Four months after the offensive, only one of fifteen line ministries was in place in Marjah.

If some 15 000 troops could not provide security to a community of 60,000 persons—an astounding ratio of 1:4, and much higher than standard COIN density recommendations—[82] then clearly the problem was complex. For a start, the invasion had created a lot of local enemies. In addition to the Taliban, potential adversaries included local elders who had chosen or been forced to co-operate with the Taliban. Villagers who had lost relatives or property during the invasion, or whose families had been forced to flee, were hardly positively inclined. Then there were the drug smugglers. A survey conducted in Marjah soon after the offensive by an international NGO found that two-thirds of the villagers were more negative towards the NATO-ISAF forces after the offensive than before and did not want a strong international force presence in their area. Nor did they want the Taliban back. It was a means-ends problem, the analysts concluded; the coalition campaign was poorly conducted and badly communicated.[83]

Part of the 'means' problem was the difficulty of establishing a system of public order after the Taliban were chased out. The local police had been dismissed en masse on suspicion of involvement in the drug trade and/or collaboration with the Taliban. A new contingent from the national police force (ANP) was flown in. The new policemen were from non-Pashtun minorities, mostly Tajik. They did not speak the local language (Pashto), and their presence touched a raw nerve. Ethnic tensions had divided the country during the civil war in the 1990s and deepened with the victory of the Tajik-led Northern Alliance over the Pashtun-based Taliban in 2001. Having captured control of the Ministry of Interior and its police department, Tajiks were strongly represented in the ANP both at the departmental level and among the rank and file. An ANP contingent from the outside would thus most likely be a non-Pashtun force. The introduction of a Tajik police force in the Pashtun heartland, however, provoked such protests from the elders in Marjah that it had to be withdrawn. As a back-up solution, new policemen were recruited locally, armed by the coalition forces and, as they initially lacked uniforms, given a yellow belt to signify their position and power. Apart from the yellow belt, it was not clear that the new police force was qualitatively different from the old one, or—as a yellow belt could easily be traded—who were wearing them.

A critical part of McChrystal's plan had been to fly in what he famously described as 'government in a box'. The box was duly flown in containing officials from the principal central government ministries as well as numerous British and American technical experts and 'stabilization advisers'. Most of them stayed in the provincial capital, however, afraid to venture into the more remote and insecure Marjah. Someone in the vast American civilian-military complex in Afghanistan had found a candidate for the position of district governor among the Afghan diaspora in Germany, and he was flown in as well. Haji Zahir had been outside Afghanistan for about thirty years and as an outsider knew little of the local patterns of amity and enmity. While this placed him above the fray, it also meant he could not navigate in the sensitive and—given the war—high-stake local politics, nor mobilize support. He did not even have the advantage of having a strong reformist profile; rather, he had spent four years in a German jail for having stabbed his stepson (who had admonished him for beating his wife). Haji Zahir did not last long in the job. Already in mid-July, four months after the invasion, he was replaced by a man sent down from Kabul and described by coalition spokesmen as having more managerial capabilities.

Altogether, the operation revealed fundamental weaknesses of knowledge and legitimacy. The attacking force did not know who or where the Taliban were, and the villagers had no incentives to provide information, knowing that the foreign troops would leave in due course. The Afghan police, as noted above, were foreign in a different way. The composition of the Afghan army units in the area is not known. In general, the Pashtuns have since 2001 lost their traditional dominant position in the army, especially in the officer corps. Recruitment from Pashtun areas has been slow and close to nil in the south.[84] In the Marjah campaign, the very name of the operation—*Moshtarak*—had conflictual ethnic associations. A Dari word meaning 'together', it had been much used by the Northern Alliance during the second half of the 1990s when its militias were locked in a bitter fight with the Taliban that included horrific massacres on all sides. Finally, the operation pointed to the central paradox of a counterinsurgency strategy. Credible and trusted local partners are critical to success, but the absence of such partners is a main reason for the insurgency in the first place. Flying in a 'government in a box' to an area where previous representatives of the central government had enjoyed little legitimacy or support—and where local autonomy was highly valued—was unlikely to fix the problem.

Whatever it would take to improve the situation, time was of the essence. Obama had announced he wanted a policy review at the end of the year to assess the results of 'the surge'. The outcome would heavily influence decisions pegged to the July 2011 date identified as the beginning of the US troop withdrawals. The ISAF command adjusted strategy to emphasize 'kinetic' operations to kill and capture insurgents rather than classic COIN operations to win over the population, as in Marjah. The short-term result was in these terms successful. In May-July 2010 alone, ISAF press releases claimed to have killed over one thousand insurgents and captured nearly two thousand. Night raids were stepped up as well, to average three operations per night.[85] This approach framed the large ISAF offensives in Kandahar later in the year as well, but whether it gained the United States and its allies more than a short-term tactical advantage was uncertain. The insurgents had fallen back, many probably to Pakistan, but the Taliban's fighting rhythm was seasonal. The British general in command of the southern region, Nick Carter, cautioned that the full impact of the offensives would not be evident until the next spring when the snow on the mountain passes had melted.[86]

Contradictions Between Waging War and Building Peace

The Marjah operation captured in concentrated form the tensions between waging war and simultaneously building peace that tore at the fabric of the international project in Afghanistan. NATO's counterinsurgency or integrated approach assumed that the costs to the local population of establishing security—including civilian loss of life, displacement and destruction to property—were outweighed by the benefits of reconstruction, good governance and development that followed. Much of the growing popular reaction to the foreign presence in Afghanistan, however, arose precisely from such costs. What to the coalition forces and counterinsurgency experts was 'establishing security' could in the perspective of the intended beneficiaries seem unacceptable costs even if at the outset they were not hostile to the foreign forces or might glad to be rid of the Taliban. The juxtaposition of two different reports of a June 2007 offensive on Sangin—a disputed area in northern Helmand where control had gone back and forth—graphically illustrates the point. The first is a description by a US army public relations officer:

Nicknamed the 'Red Devils', [the US paratroopers] played a key role in...the largest air assault mission ... in [the] region since the Soviet Union's occupation in the 1980s.... In the Sangin district, paratroopers began their assault by clearing buildings and ridding the area of Taliban.... In the next couple of days, the regiment swept through the countryside with little resistance in search of weapons caches and the Taliban.... Paratroopers [then] entered the second phase of the operation, focusing on winning hearts and minds.... 'In Sangin we were really successful', said [battalion commander] Mennes. 'We stood up the first couple of shuras and after that the Afghans started running their own'. The regiment hosted three shuras for the locals and a medical engagement to help Afghans who need treatment.[87]

An independent journalist who had been embedded with the troops gave this description of the same events:

More than 100 bearded elders [had] assembled in the portico of the Sangin district centre....British and U.S. officials, military and civilian, rose in turn with promises of schools, hospitals, roads and canals. There were polite speeches of gratitude from the elders, and carefully worded requests for faster aid. But then a U.S. Special Forces commander sprang to his feet, silencing the gathering. 'How are we going to [give you assistance] ... if you continue to let Taliban come into your villages?...' When the Special Forces commander fell silent, the elders erupted in murmurs and shouts... 'The troops have taken over my land...to make a checkpoint!' shouted one. 'I have just two acres of land and 20 people to feed. I have to grow poppy', yelled another.... Afterwards, one of the elders, Haji Mohammed Yaqub said he believed the valley was indeed now quiet enough for the road work to begin... But he added, it was probably too late for the NATO force to be welcomed by most residents. *'They have destroyed people's houses and their lives'*, he said. *'So, what do they expect?*[88]

Three years later, the scene was repeated numerous times during the intensified fighting in southern Afghanistan. One event that graphically exposed the dilemmas involved received international attention. Preparing for the US-led offensive in the Arghandab River Valley in Kandahar in July-October 2010, the Taliban had entered three villages in the path of the expected campaign and told the population to leave. The Taliban then wired the compounds with explosives and left. After initial slow efforts to clear the villages manually, US forces resorted to airpower. The villages and some of the surrounding orchards were completely flattened, as shown on before-and-after aerial photos posted on the internet.[89] There was now little left to 'hold', and no one left to 'build' since the population had dispersed. Those who returned were embittered over the losses and reluctant to cooperate with the coalition forces. 'The friendlies' were all gone, the US colonel in charge of the operation said.[90]

Perhaps the most damaging impact of the coalition offensives was from civilian casualties, a point fully recognized in principle by the US military. Successive commanders of US and ISAF forces had grappled with the problem. Already in 2004 the US force commander, General Barno, had disallowed air strikes based on technical intelligence and limited the use of airpower to situations of close combat and when called in by troops on the ground, even if this meant tactical sacrifice. A large margin for error nevertheless remained, and successive incidents occurred. Adoption of a counterinsurgency strategy that underlined the importance of winning 'hearts and minds' made General McChrystal issue a Tactical Directive in July 2009, urging his commanders to 'weigh the gain of using CAS [close air support] against the cost of civilian casualties'.[91] A year later, General David Petraeus did the same: '[U]se only the firepower needed to win a fight.... We cannot kill or capture our way to victory...if we kill civilians or damage their property in the course of our operations, we will create more enemies than our operations eliminate'.[92]

It had some effect. UNAMA concluded that civilian casualties caused by the international and Afghan government forces had decreased by 18 per cent in the first ten months of 2010 as compared to the same period the previous year. At the same time, the insurgents had dramatically increased their activity, claiming many more civilian lives—over three-quarters of the total. Still, that left the pro-government forces with responsibility for 742 civilian deaths, most of them caused by coalition aerial attacks, and individual incidents continued to cause outrage among Afghans.[93] The day before Petraeus issued his guidelines, for instance, national and international media reported that attacks by coalition forces on a village in northern Helmand had caused a large number of civilian casualties. Some reports said fifty, citing Afghan government officials. Local witnesses spoke of pulling bodies of women and children out of the rubble. President Karzai condemned the attack as 'morally and humanly unacceptable'; a statement that NATO officials said was 'not helpful'.[94]

The continuation of the problem, albeit at a lower level, suggested that the causes were structural. One factor was the nature of the war; the US and its allies were fighting an insurgency, making it difficult to distinguish between combatant and non-combatant. Civilian casualties were also a result of NATO's access to and reliance on close air support in order to protect its own forces. A consequence of the way modern democracies fight distant wars, the strategy meant in effect that the human cost was disproportionately shifted onto the local population. There was also an intelligence problem. Lack of verifiable intelligence and limited knowledge of the social environment in which the troops operated caused mistaken targeting and misguided approaches, and produced unintended consequences. NATO had by 2010 accumulated a significant apparatus for collecting intelligence, and more was on its way. General Petraeus said: 'Some of it's unmanned, some of it's manned, some of it is optics, optics on towers, some of it is optics on blimps, more blimps, more towers, more unmanned aircraft of various types, more manned aircraft of various types, more intelligence tools of various types, etc., etc'.[95]

But the challenge lay in understanding what this meant on the ground level. Interpretation of data required insight into Afghan society and politics as well as deep local knowledge.[96] Neither the US nor its allies had invested in institutions to develop such knowledge, having suddenly invaded a country in which they previously had shown little interest. Once in the country, the coalition forces focused their intelligence efforts on understanding the enemy rather than the environment in which they themselves operated, an assessment team led by a US general concluded in 2010. After almost a decade of operations in Afghanistan, the intelligence community 'still finds itself unable to answer fundamental questions about....the people we are trying to protect and persuade'.[97]

One obvious consequence was that the coalition forces were open to manipulation by competing Afghan factions. A continuous string of events throughout the decade can for illustrative purposes be summarized by two incidents. The first appears as a classic failure of intelligence. On 20 December 2001 a convoy of tribal elders was travelling from the eastern border area of Khost towards Kabul to attend the inauguration of Hamid Karzai as president of the Interim Administration. The elders were sent by a leading militant commander, Jalaluddin Haqqani, in an evident gesture of goodwill and to explore the possibilities for peace. The US military, however, were informed that these were Taliban on the way to Kabul, and dispatched planes to attack the convoy. About sixty persons were killed. Speculation was rife that the informant was Pacha Khan Zadran, an arch rival of both Karzai and Haqqani.[98] It is also possible that the US military were deliberately targeting Haqqani's people. In the following year, US Special Forces tried to kill Haqqani at least three times.[99] Either way, the attack squashed any consideration Haqqani might have had of reconciling with Kabul. His men soon became one of the leading and most feared militant groups working with the Taliban.

The second incident, eight years later, illustrates the propensity for unintended consequences when foreign forces tried to shape a complex tribal environment through what in NATO language would be 'a comprehensive approach'. In January 2010 US military commanders in Nangarhar signed an anti-Taliban pact with some of the leaders of one local Shinwari tribe, promising $1 million in return for a promise to keep out the Taliban, stop poppy production and refrain from corruption. Initially hailed as a successful local defence initiative (see chapter 5), the scheme soon went bad. Another sub-tribe that was not offered a deal became hostile, and the governor of Nangarhar accused the Americans of bypassing the central government structure. The sub-tribe empowered with a fresh inflow of dollars started to press old land claims against the sub-tribe that had been left out, leading to hostilities that left ten dead.[100]

* * *

By the end of the decade, the costs and unintended consequences of the foreign military presence contributed to the growing frustration, anger and anti-foreign sentiments among the Afghan people. These sentiments also stemmed from a growing despair over the costs of a war that seemed to have no end. Visiting Kandahar in mid-2010, a foreign analyst found people were weary of yet another NATO-ISAF campaign in the province. '[T]here are operations all the time, they don't change anything', but more importantly, she wrote, 'the whole subject seemed a distraction from the real issues: why is the situation getting worse all the time and why is there still no serious strategy, after more than eight years?'[101] Other analysts found the mood in Kandahar deeply negative towards the foreign military forces. A poll conducted in the city and several districts of the province in June 2010 found that large majorities of the respondents did not think the international forces protected the local population, believed they did not respect Islam or local tradition, and said working with them was wrong.[102] If this response was representative, it meant the internationals had lost the war according to the reasoning in the updated US Army/Marine Corps field manual on counterinsurgency. Here, the principle of 'lose moral legitimacy, lose the war' is prominently displayed in a caption.

Whether accidentally killed by international forces, intentionally targeted by militants in suicide bombings, or caught in the cross-fire between the two, ordinary civilians paid a heavy price. The violence generated a measure of alienation towards all the parties involved, yet it is a testimony to the strength of the militant movements, as well as the fear they inspired, that the insurgency continued to find ready recruits. The large, diverse and visible international presence, by contrast, was a ready target for popular anger, whether related to the issue at hand or generated by underlying grievances of other kinds. Perceived offences against Islam, for instance, were certain to trigger street riots and attacks on Western buildings and persons. Protests against the Danish cartoons of the Prophet led to attacks of this kind in Kabul, Herat and Balkh in February 2006. The following year, reports that guards at Guantánamo had desecrated the Qur'an unleashed violence in Jalalabad. A traffic accident involving American troops in Kabul in May 2006 caused widespread violence and buildings were torched. An incident during the riots recounted by an American journalist seems emblematic: when the street mob came upon a package of books with the address written in English, one of the rioters grabbed it and hacked away with a knife until all the books were destroyed. It was as if the English words represented an evil enemy, the journalist later wrote.[103] For a Western-inspired peacebuilding operation, it was an ominous sign.

4

PROVIDING SECURITY ASSISTANCE

The International Security Assistance Force (ISAF), as we have seen (chapter 2), was originally conceived as an entity quite separate from the US combat forces that were pursuing Taliban and Al-Qaeda. ISAF was designed to assist the transitional government in Kabul in establishing a secure environment for reconstruction. That much was agreed in Bonn, and the Security Council, acting with unusual speed, authorized the force on 20 December, a few days after the Bonn Agreement was signed. The British had agreed to lead, and a small contingent was on its way to Kabul in January 2002. No sooner had it landed than a veritable campaign to expand its mandate and mission started. It succeeded. ISAF gradually expanded in mandate, task and size. Moreover, NATO took operational responsibility for the force the following year, and a merger between ISAF and the American OEF was gradually effected. By the end of the decade, both forces were operating under the NATO/ISAF umbrella (although American Special Forces were not), and had become organizationally indistinguishable. Functionally, the joint force had also become more uniform. ISAF units that had originally been deployed to provide 'security assistance' were undertaking combat operations, while a range of civil activities were aligned with American and allied combat operations in the spirit of NATO's 'comprehensive approach' and counterinsurgency doctrine.

ISAF's expansion reflected some of the forces that drove the increasing US deployment, but the growth and partial transformation of the force also tell a different story. In part, the expansion was rooted in the success of the mission in executing its original mandate: to facilitate the political transition by ensuring that Kabul was a safe and politically neutral place.

Securing the Centre

ISAF's overarching purpose was to signal that the UN and its members were committed to a new, post-Taliban order in Afghanistan. Its more specific and immediate function was to prevent a recurrence of the fight over Kabul among Afghan factions that had happened after Soviet troops withdrew in 1989, with devastating consequences for the city and its population. This time, the Northern Alliance armies that had taken the city had agreed in principle to withdraw. ISAF's presence in Kabul was to make certain that they kept to their promise and, more generally, to ensure that the other parts of the transitional arrangement outlined in Bonn could proceed in a neutral, peaceful and secure environment. In effect, ISAF was to be a surrogate army of the Afghan transitional state and a police force in the capital as well. At the time, only the Kabul traffic police seemed to have survived institutionally as an effective and centrally organized force.

By and large, ISAF succeeded in securing the centre. Inevitably, there were setbacks. Not all arms and armies of the Northern Alliance were immediately moved out of the city. The Afghan secret police (the National Security Directorate)—an institution dating back to the 1970s that had become one of the most powerful agencies during the Communist period—was the only other police institution to quickly recover from the decades of upheaval. It was now controlled by the Northern Alliance faction under Defence Minister Fahim, and back in operation. Most demonstratively, its agents were visibly present to monitor the debates of the first *ad hoc* national assembly (the Emergency *Loya Jirga*), which met in Kabul in June 2002 to select the head of the transitional administration (Karzai had only been provisionally named so in Bonn).[1] Their presence inside the assembly hall put a damper on the proceedings. Some delegates felt harassed and threatened, and at least one political activist fled the country under UN protection. Yet the assembly proceedings went ahead, bestowing a broader Afghan legitimacy on the transitional government than had been possible in Bonn. It was the first important step in the post-war transition. The next important transitional event was a constitutional assembly, scheduled to be held in Kabul the following year. This event proceeded on schedule and within prescribed forms as around 500 delegates from all over the country assembled in the capital to debate and adopt a new constitution. ISAF again provided the necessary security.

The force also helped to avert a military coup in 2003 by the Northern Alliance leader Marshal Fahim, who was smarting from US and UN pressure to reduce his influence and demobilize his men. As rumours of a planned coup grew, ISAF 'rolled out tanks to protect the presidential palace', and the city remained quiet.[2] More generally, ISAF's presence helped create sufficient safety and order in Kabul to permit the newly established government and its international partners to start rebuilding the city, aid returning refugees, provide humanitarian assistance, and reopen schools and the university. There certainly was crime, abuse and insecurity, but a sense of normalcy prevailed that permitted commercial and political activities to resume. ISAF sought to compensate to some degree for the absence of an effective police force in the early days by occasionally taking on what the UN called 'lawless elements' in the city.[3] At one point, for instance, British soldiers cordoned off an area on the outskirts of Kabul to protect the inhabitants against raids by criminal gangs.

The contingent that carried out these diverse and demanding tasks, the Kabul Multinational Brigade, was less than 5,000 strong. The initial deployment consisted of 1,500 British troops, assisted by a newly formed battalion of the Afghan National Guard trained by the British. The small size was partly a concession to Northern Alliance concerns that a large force would constrain their freedom and undermine Afghan sovereignty; it was also all that the troop contributing countries would commit. As it turned out, size was not a decisive factor. The Kabul Multinational Brigade achieved a significant measure of success despite its small numbers, for three main reasons: adroit demonstration of presence, a credible link to US air power, and the willingness of the principal Afghan leaders with capacity to shape the security situation in Kabul at this time to buy into the Bonn Agreement.

Adroit demonstration of presence partly meant frequent patrolling. During the first few months, the British-led brigade mounted some thirty patrols a day in and around Kabul, many of them jointly with various elements of Afghan forces.[4] Strategic positioning of armoured vehicles to demonstrate power and draw a line in the sand was important to deflect possible preparations for a coup, as noted above. The British commander of the force, General John McColl, was prepared to stand firm and risk confrontations that played out in the political arena. His first clash with Marshal Fahim had occurred during the Emergency *Loya Jirga*, when Fahim positioned his intelligence agents inside the assembly hall. Quite apart from considerations of free speech, this violated an agreement on procedures negotiated by the government and the UN. McColl was prepared to send in ISAF forces to clear out the agents and was confident that Fahim would back down. Before going ahead, however, he checked with Lakhdar Brahimi, who had arrived in Kabul soon after the Bonn conference as the Special Representative of the UN Secretary-General and was heading the UN mission in Afghanistan (UNAMA). Brahimi asked McColl to stop, evidently not wanting to court trouble that could spoil the high-profile, prestigious event, which was indeed the first test of the Bonn Agreement in which the UN and Brahimi personally had invested so much.[5] In the end Fahim was allowed to proceed, in what was an early signal that the international sponsors of the new order prioritized stability over democratic reform.

The irony is that McColl's gamble would in all probability have succeeded. ISAF itself had only symbolic power to coerce; its punch lay in its association with the vast and recently demonstrated US military power, particularly in the air. In Kabul at the time, the Afghans were referring to the B-52s as 'the new Vice and Virtue' after the ministry charged with upholding public morality that had become notorious during the Taliban regime. The B-52s had demonstrated their awesome power during the invasion and patrolled the skies afterwards. They were seen as the ultimate force that could discipline the spoilers of the Bonn Agreement even by the very mention of its name. As one story has it, already during the negotiations among the Afghan factions in Bonn, Brahimi—who served as facilitator—had passed the drawing of an aeroplane down the table to a recalcitrant Afghan delegate. Apocryphal or not, the story circulated to carry the message of American air power.

The beguiling power of the new 'Vice and Virtue' also created expectations about what the international forces could achieve outside Kabul in terms of providing 'security assistance'. An influential article by Michael Ignatieff, the Canadian public intellectual (and later member of Parliament), published in the *New York Times Magazine*, captured the tone.[6] Ignatieff had in mid-2002 travelled to the Northern part of Afghanistan where he witnessed UN officials trying to mediate between two local strongmen, General Abdul Rashid Dostum and General Atta Mohammed Noor. Considered 'first-tier warlords' with large armies, the two were nominally part of the Northern Alliance but were locked in a conflict over revenge, honour and territory in the north, particularly control over the prosperous northern city of Mazar-e-Sharif. The UN mediators were trying to avert further bloodshed by getting Dostum and Atta to pull back their tanks from the city. Standing in Dostum's fortress-like compound, Ignatieff observed the demonstration of American airpower:

The bulky American in combat camouflage, sleeveless pocket vest, wraparound sunglasses and floppy fishing hat is not going to talk to me. He may be C.I.A. or Special Forces, but either way, I'm not going to find out. These people don't talk to reporters. But in Mazar-i-Sharif, second city of Afghanistan, in this warlord's compound, with a Lexus and an Audi purring in the driveway, armed mujahedeen milling by the gate and musclemen standing guard in tight black T-shirts and flak jackets and sporting the latest semiautomatic weapons, the heavyset American is the one who matters. He comes with a team that includes a forward air controller, who can call in airstrikes from the big planes doing Daytona 500 loops high in the sky.

The experience helped shape Ignatieff's support for international intervention in a form he called Empire Lite.[7] Yet even big American planes doing Daytona loops in the sky could not bring the warlords of northern Afghanistan to heel. Dostum and Atta continued to quarrel and fight for two more years until they agreed on a peace pact in 2004. The agreement was essentially a demarcation of territory and access to related resources in the north, and both continued to jealously guard their autonomy and power vis-à-vis each other as well as the central government

The northern episode points to the third and critically important factor that helped ISAF achieve its mission in Kabul: the main Northern Alliance leaders who had the capacity to resist or unleash the Alliance's armies on the population basically decided to cooperate. As the principal local ally of the United States during the invasion, the Northern Alliance was poised to gain significant political power. The Bonn Agreement gave the inner circle of the Northern Alliance (*shura-e-nazar*) more than one foot inside the central government, including the Ministries of Interior (with the police), Defence, and Foreign Affairs. This gave them positions of power and patronage on the central level, and strong incentives to work with the international actors whose principal concern was to rebuild the state. They were on the way to capturing state power in a manner that had previously denied the country's ethnic minorities, except for a brief period during the civil war in the 1990s and a similar interlude in 1929 when a Tajik for the first and last time occupied the throne in Kabul, otherwise held by Durrani Pashtuns.

A basic common interest did not guarantee agreement on all issues, as Barnett and Zürcher point out in their modelling of contracts between international peacebuilders and local elites.[8] In the Afghan case there was serious disagreement over access to, and use of, central state power. Nevertheless, the Northern Alliance leaders were part of the centre that ISAF was mandated to serve, and they placed the possibility of increasing their power in the centre ahead of opposing the state from their base in the provinces. That put them in a rather different position from that of leaders whose principal concern was to develop and consolidate their provincial or regional power, the 'subnational elites' who in the Barnett and Zürcher model fiercely protect their local autonomy and power vis-à-vis the central government, and who certainly did so in post-Taliban Afghanistan. As a result, if ISAF were to expand beyond the capital with a mandate to extend the grip of the central government, it would operate in a distinctly less friendly environment than Kabul, not even counting a resurgent Taliban.

The relative success of ISAF in Kabul, and the contrasting insecurity caused by sundry 'warlords', smugglers and bandits in much of the rest of the country, nevertheless became a main argument for expanding the force to the rest of the country. No sooner had the initial resolution authorizing ISAF passed than the discussion on its expansion reopened.

The Case for and Against Expansion

The debate over ISAF's role in 2002–03 was nestled in a larger international discussion about post-conflict reconstruction and peacebuilding. In this perspective, the regime change in 2001 was an opportunity to rebuild, develop and modernize Afghanistan along the lines of 'the liberal peace'. Given the violent and anarchic conditions in much of the country, restoration of security was a foundational requirement for a post-war agenda writ large—promoting economic growth and development based on a market economy and foreign investment, democratic political activity, respect for human rights, and promotion of women's rights—and establishing a monopoly on legitimate force was a central ingredient of statebuilding. It followed that ISAF must expand beyond Kabul to do essentially, throughout the country, what it had done for the capital, but also to do more: to extend the authority of the transitional government in a countryside dominated by diverse militias and 'warlords'. ISAF expansion would signal the international community's commitment to reconstruct Afghanistan as a unitary state, support the UN-led demobilization of armed groups, and stand by the Bonn process as the path to a peaceful new order.

The case for ISAF expansion drew strength from the international peacebuilding regime that had developed steadily since the 1990s, as noted in chapter 1, and from the heady international confidence in the Afghan project that marked its early years. The Bonn process was on track. ISAF had been welcomed in Kabul—there had been no fighting, only a few tense stand-offs and some disquieting discoveries of explosives-rigged cars aimed at the force.[9] The prominent journalist Ahmed Rashid wrote in March 2002 that British ISAF soldiers were so popular in Kabul that they caused an 'instant traffic jam. Hordes of well-wishers—including blue *burqa* clad women and laughing children—crowd around them'.[10] The report did not seem atypical. Kabul's urban and partly middle-class population had suffered heavily under the Taliban regime, which had originated in an entirely different environment steeped in literalist interpretations of Islam and shaped by rural, traditional Pashtun values. The city genuinely received ISAF as a liberation force, which probably did more than anything else to overshadow the international image of Afghanistan as hostile to foreigners and the graveyard of empires. As the forbidding image faded, a growing number of prominent individuals, agencies and interest groups working in Afghanistan called for an expansion of ISAF. So did leading government figures, above all Hamid Karzai.

Brahimi, as noted (chapter 2), had already started to modify his initial deep scepticism towards an international force in mid-November 2001. The wording of his speech to the Security Council on 13 November, acknowledging a possible expansion of an international force beyond Kabul, was incorporated almost verbatim in the Bonn Agreement. As ISAF deployed without meeting resistance from the Northern Alliance militias, and was warmly welcomed by Kabul's population, Brahimi's remaining apprehensions seemed to melt away. At the international conference of donors in Tokyo in late January 2002 he came out strongly in favour of expanding ISAF to meet popular demands for peace and stability: 'People up and down the country are calling for the force to be deployed in other regions of Afghanistan. I do hope that the Security Council will respond to these requests'.[11] It was a far cry from his warnings three months earlier that the Afghans were a proud people who did not like to be ordered around by foreigners in uniform. Now he made the case for ISAF's expansion in increasingly urgent tones. His first major report to the Security Council in March 2002, presented in the name of the Secretary-General, expressed 'the hope' that the Security Council would support force expansion.[12] By mid-year, he 'strongly' advocated expansion, although still of a 'limited' kind.[13] The reservation echoed earlier concerns over risks and the reluctance of UN member countries to contribute.

The main argument for force expansion in these early reports to the Security Council rested primarily on security concerns arising from the weakness of the Afghan state and its lack of a monopoly on force. In the north, armed factions were fighting among themselves and Pashtun minorities were subjected to systematic harassment and violence. In the east, some governors appointed by the central authority were violently rejected by the local communities. In the south, attacks by militants were reported. Throughout the country, violence by local strongmen and general insecurity was a problem for both the local population and international aid workers. The July 2002 report to the Security Council described the situation in some detail:

In addition to actions by ex-Taliban and Al-Qa'idah forces that explicitly oppose the Bonn process, the presence of armed factions that nominally support the process continues to pose a threat to the consolidation of peace and civil government in the country. This is particularly problematic in the north, where a long-standing rivalry between the Jumbesh [Dostum] and Jamiat [Atta] factions negatively affects the general security situation. This rivalry has prevented the establishment of effective security in Mazar city, despite the efforts of the Interim Administration and UNAMA to establish a separation of forces and a neutral, multi-ethnic police force. In this context of impunity and insecurity, a number of armed attacks and robberies have been carried out against international aid organizations in the last several weeks....... Absent truly national security forces and the expansion of the International Security Assistance Force (ISAF), Afghanistan remains hostage to this prevailing insecurity. Lack of tangible improvement in the security situation could seriously undermine the political and reconstruction efforts.[14]

By early 2002 a veritable campaign for an expanded ISAF was under way at the UN.[15] The UN High Commissioner for Human Rights,

Mary Robinson, returned from a trip to Afghanistan in early 2002 to call for deployment of ISAF outside Kabul, citing the impossibility of rebuilding society and securing human rights 'if you have violence, if you have killings, if you have robberies, if you have looting, if you have women terrified'.[16] Human rights organizations carried a similar message. Human Rights Watch cited widespread violence against Pashtun minorities in the north to recommend immediate ISAF deployment to that region.[17] Aid agencies and NGOs poised to address the enormous need for assistance and chafing under security restrictions wanted ISAF to protect movement of personnel and materiel throughout the country. Experts, crisis management groups and think tanks joined the lobby. The International Crisis Group advocated an increase from the initial deployment of 4,500 to 25,000. The Washington-based Stimson Center called for 18,000 troops. The American analyst Barnett Rubin wrote in an op-ed in the *New York Times* that US failure to support ISAF expansion would be read as a sign of US disengagement and a defeat in the front line of the 'War on Terror'. All were cited in a major hearing in the US Senate in June 2002 that addressed the situation in Afghanistan.[18] During the hearing, two prominent senators, including the later Vice-President Joe Biden, urged the Bush Administration to help ISAF expand beyond Kabul in order to combat 'warlordism' and improve security for ordinary Afghans, particularly women.

Within Afghanistan, the most visible and committed advocate of expansion was Hamid Karzai, leader of the transitional administration. Karzai had no organized armed following of his own, which was an important reason why he was selected to head the interim administration. ISAF was in a sense Karzai's army. It was mandated 'to assist the Afghan Interim Authority in the maintenance of security in Kabul' (Res. 1386). It was a tangible commitment of international support to the administration he led and, more directly, a check on the armies that Marshal Fahim still controlled (although confined to barracks, or outside Kabul). A similar check on regional 'warlords' and lesser strongmen in the provinces would significantly boost the coercive capacity of the central state and Karzai's administration. Not surprisingly, in his first appearance before the UN Security Council on 30 January 2002, Karzai asked for ISAF to be deployed in the other main cities of the country. That meant above all Mazar-e-Sharif, Herat, Kandahar and Jalalabad. Located astride Afghanistan's principal trading and smuggling routes, these were resource bases for established ex-*mujahedin* leaders or lesser commanders who benefited from the US military presence. As such, the cities represented both a potential threat to the authority of the central state and a major source of revenue for the national treasury.

Among US allies who might be asked to contribute to an expanded ISAF, the reactions varied. British military leaders, it will be recalled (chapter 2), had strongly resisted leading the first contingent. The army chief eventually relented, but only agreed to a British lead for an initial three months and on the express condition that US military forces provided 'essential enabling support'.[19] The British subsequently agreed to another three months, but Turkey, the only country willing to take over the command, was reluctant as well, requesting logistical support from the US, a NATO commitment, and bilateral financial assistance to take on the mission.[20] These conditions applied to deployment in Kabul alone; expansion to other cities entailed additional risks and costs. At bottom was the ambiguous but potentially ambitious mandate of providing 'security assistance' to a weak central government, which enabled the different advocates of expansion to make their case. Some analysts favoured expansion as a symbolic exercise of power to maintain the post-Bonn momentum; others wanted an enforcement mission to secure relief supplies and development projects, or to protect women and ordinary Afghans against abuse, or for standing down armed factions in the provinces, protecting minorities, and so on. Collectively, the list of security problems facing Afghanistan that human rights activists, aid organizations, UN officials, analysts and the Afghan head of state wanted ISAF to take on suggested a gigantic 'mission creep' even before the force was on the ground. As if to underscore that the problem lay with the nature of the mission rather than resource restraints, the British military had no evident difficulties with the government's decision to send a force of 1,700 to serve with the US-led OEF in anti-terrorist combat operations in the southeast.[21] The additional force was requested by US General Tommy Franks and went to Afghanistan in March 2002, just as the debate on ISAF expansion was heating up.

In Washington, the US military continued to oppose expansion to prevent diversion from Operation Enduring Freedom. To the civilian leaders in the Department of Defense it was a diversion from the forthcoming invasion of Iraq. Secretary Rumsfeld was adamantly opposed and blocked further inter-agency discussion of the idea.[22] His deputy,

Paul Wolfowitz, took the message to Congress. At a hearing in June 2002, Wolfowitz conjured up the image of Afghanistan as a forbidden country to foreign soldiers. Pressed by the then Democratic Senate leader, Joe Biden, to explain why the Bush administration did not support the expansion of ISAF, Wolfowitz rolled out a map of Afghanistan superimposed on a map of the United States. It covered a large chunk of mainland United States. Wolfowitz then displayed a topographical map, pointing out rugged mountains in the northeast, and a huge desert in the southeast called the 'Desert of Death', as he noted. The point was clear—sending more US troops into this area was a dangerous proposition, and the US mission should be confined to its current anti-terrorist operation; European countries were welcome to expand ISAF on their own.[23] That effectively vetoed expansion. Senator Biden put the logic of force differential in blunt terms: without US participation or support from a US extraction force, 'it is not at all surprising to me that the little dog said: 'Well, wait a minute. We're not interested in expanding'.[24]

The Dynamic of Expansion

Less than a year later, the violent aftermath of the US invasion of Iraq had effectively eliminated the American veto on ISAF expansion. Faced with demands of the Iraqi theatre on US troops, and a still unsettled Afghan conflict, the US government started to actively solicit allied contributions to Afghanistan. An expanded ISAF became the main vehicle for managing the enlarged force. The process was facilitated by the decision, which had been reached a little earlier, that NATO would take operational responsibility for the force. The practical problems of finding a country able and willing to command ISAF on a six-month basis had been taxing. Even when ISAF was limited to Kabul, the rapid turnover in command meant uncertainty and lack of institutional memory that reduced its effectiveness. If operating in the entire country, ISAF needed a command structure with a stronger institutional anchor. NATO formally took command of ISAF in March 2003 and in October 2003 the Security Council authorized force expansion to 'areas of Afghanistan outside of Kabul' (Res. 1510).

NATO's leadership under SACEUR, General James Jones, immediately put the alliance's formidable planning capacity to work and produced a four-phased scheme for geographical expansion with a regional command structure and a timetable. ISAF initially expanded to the north and the west, where leadership of the regional commands was given to the major troop contributing countries, respectively Germany (RC-N) and Italy (RC-W). The southern area followed in 2005, where ISAF forces were placed under a regional command that rotated between Britain, the Netherlands and Canada. The last area to be formally brought into the scheme was the eastern region, where some of the US troops that had operated there since the invasion were placed in the ISAF chain of command. By the end of 2006, NATO's command structure formally extended to the entire country, and ISAF's website started producing maps of Afghanistan bedecked with a bewildering variety of national flags. By the end of the decade forty-seven countries had troops serving under ISAF's flag (including the US).[25] A parallel phased plan for functions was also prepared, although without a timetable: assessment and preparation, expansion, stabilization, transition (of responsibility to Afghan forces) and redeployment (exit).[26]

Backed by NATO's equally formidable political power and capacity for resource mobilization, the process ensured that ISAF would formally cover all parts of Afghanistan, and as rapidly as possible. Strictly speaking, this went beyond the Security Council resolution (1510) of 23 October 2003 that had authorized expansion. The resolution did not explicitly make the entire country an area of operations, but used the indefinite form: expansion to 'areas of Afghanistan outside of Kabul and its environs'. The terminology corresponded to the reference in the Bonn Agreement 'other urban centres and other areas' (Annex, para. 3). On the other hand, the clause in the resolution that mandated ISAF to assist the government in extending its authority to 'all parts of Afghanistan' seemed to negate any restrictions. Whichever the case, the distinction was hardly noticed as NATO firmly set ISAF on a course of full expansion.

NATO's entry as an organization fundamentally changed the political dynamic of the engagement by placing the alliance's credibility on the line. As discussed in the previous chapter, it gave member governments incentives to increase their individual commitments so as to avoid the appearance of collective failure. In this perspective, NATO's assuming institutional responsibility for ISAF appears as a gigantic mission creep; immediate, practical problems on the ground arising from a rotational command structure led to institutional commitments and—not so far down the line—the related need to protect the institution itself.

The mission expanded qualitatively as well. Resolution 1510 added three broad enabling clauses to the original resolution (1386) that had authorized the force in December 2001. The first, as noted, expanded its area of operation to 'all parts of the country'. Secondly, and in response to the concerns of the aid agencies, ISAF was to help create a secure environment for the reconstruction and humanitarian efforts. Finally, the resolution had an omnibus clause. ISAF was to provide security assistance 'for the performance of other tasks in support of the Bonn Agreement'. A few items were specifically mentioned—UN programmes to disarm all Afghan armed factions, programmes to reconstitute the national armed forces and the police, and security sector reform broadly understood. The mandate was now sufficiently broad to include virtually any activity covered by the letter and, if need be, the spirit of the Bonn Agreement to end collective violence and lay the foundations for a peaceful new order. By the end of the decade, the official ISAF website listed stability and security operations, assistance to develop Afghan security forces, support for reconstruction needs, assistance to humanitarian and counter-narcotics operations, and assistance to disarm illegal armed groups.[27]

Stabilization and/or Combat?

The main vehicle for allied contributions to an expanded and diversified ISAF was the Provincial Reconstruction Team (PRT). Designed by the US military for a mission with mixed military and civilian functions in a post-combat phase, the concept had been applied in earlier US operations. In late 2002 it was plucked off the shelf by the US force commander in Afghanistan in the expectation that US troops would make an early exit and allied forces would enter to stabilize the situation.[28] The first American PRT was established in Gardez in the eastern province of Paktia in January 2003. It was soon followed by one in each of the main regions of Afghanistan—Bamiyan, Kunduz, Mazar, Kandahar and Herat. Their role, according to the US Embassy in Kabul, was to extend the authority of the Afghan central government, improve security and assist reconstruction.[29]

The PRTs were initially designed for a stabilization mission that did not involve combat operations. They did not seem to require the kind of US commitment for back-up support originally required by the British and the Turks.[30] The early areas of expansion—the northern and central regions—were calm and considered friendly towards the international forces. Populated mainly by non-Pashtun ethnic groups, these areas had proved most resistant to Taliban control in the 1990s. The main task of the PRTs was to extend the central government's reach through being an authoritative presence, collecting information, and assisting with reconstruction. The point was emphasized by the German government when it sent a contingent to Kunduz in the north.[31] The government wanted to contribute to a peaceful new order in Afghanistan, and in this spirit had hosted the Bonn conference that finalized the transitional framework; however, for reasons deeply embedded in modern German history, the government did not want an engagement that might involve German forces in another war. The initial separation of command between ISAF and the OEF reinforced the distinction. The PRTs, it seemed, were instruments of peacebuilding, while the US-led OEF forces were fighting a war.

Deployment to the volatile southern region in late 2005 and early 2006 muddled the distinction. Staunch allies of the US (Canada and the British) or NATO supporters (the Netherlands, home country of the current Secretary-General of the alliance) stepped in with major contributions to keep NATO's scheduled roll-out of the regional commands on track and meet US requests for additional troops. Yet the PRT concept and the language of stabilization were also applied to these deployments. The result was confusion and lack of clarity regarding the purpose and expectations of the mission. In Canada, the process of decision-making leading to the deployment in Kandahar was confounded by a lack of coherence and transparency. The consequence was an 'unexpected war', as the careful study by Stein and Lang concluded.[32] In Britain, the Defence Secretary sent off the first contingent of British forces for Helmand in April 2006 with the reassuring words that he hoped no shots would be fired.[33]

To the Afghans, the distinction was irrelevant or unimportant. In some areas, the local population did distinguish between types of missions and the nationality of the soldiers,[34] but in other cases this was clearly not so. In the northern province of Faryab, for instance, a civilian shot by Norwegian forces for failing to stop at a checkpoint had inscribed on the banner above his grave that he was 'martyred by American soldiers'.[35] Surveys in Faryab showed that most respondents incorrectly believed the foreign soldiers in the province were all American.[36] To the militants, of course, any foreign soldier was a legitimate target, and the steady spread of NATO's colourful quilt of national contingents in ISAF constituted an equal number of provocations. Every attack in turn widened the PRT's distance from the local population, reduced the mobility of civil affairs units assigned to reconstruction, and created an atmosphere of mutual suspicion that invited escalation of violence. This was the case even in the north, where the German contingent operated under strict national guidelines that limited their mobility and actions. As the insurgency started to spread northwards, and other ISAF forces launched offensive operations, the Germans in ISAF's regional command headquarters switched to an offensive mode as well. In one infamous case in September 2009, a German colonel in Kunduz called in US air strikes after receiving reports that people were scavenging fuel from two stranded oil tankers apparently hijacked by the Taliban but accidentally driven off the road; the assumption was that any person out at night must be a Talib. The air strikes killed an estimated 140 local villagers.

The logic of escalating violence that progressively reduced the difference between 'stabilization' and a combat mission also led to a merger of the two commands. On a practical level, the difficulties of running separate operations in the same country, and sometimes in the same region, also favoured a merger. As more allied contributions arrived in 2006, and the establishment of NATO's structure of four regional commands was completed, the regular American forces were transferred to the ISAF command as well. The common command structure imposed some order on the international military presence in Afghanistan, although not all forces and operations were placed under the ISAF/NATO umbrella. A US general who was sent to Afghanistan in the closing days of the Bush Administration to assess the situation reported back that he found about ten 'distinct but overlapping wars in progress'.[37] Even within the ISAF structure, the complex command structure, the diversity of contributions, and the operational restrictions that several governments had imposed on the operation of their troops (the infamous 'national caveats') reduced military effectiveness.

There were more fundamental limitations as well. Most governments that contributed to ISAF did so for strategic reasons related to support of NATO—to fulfil obligations of membership or in the hope of becoming a member—or their bilateral relationship with the United States. Some did so in order to deflect US pressure to contribute to the war in Iraq.[38] They had limited interest in and often no prior experience in Afghanistan. Most had little or no institutionalized knowledge to inform the deployment. The vicarious nature of the commitment was well illustrated by the case of Ghor, one of the most isolated, destitute and neglected provinces in all of Afghanistan. By mid-decade a four-nation Provincial Reconstruction Team from Lithuania, Denmark, Iceland and Croatia had hunkered down. Apart from Denmark, which for years had been active on the NGO front in Afghanistan, none of these countries had a history of previous engagement in Afghanistan. One of them—Iceland—does not even have an army. The ambiguous mandate of 'security assistance' did not make it easier for international forces dropped into a local Afghan environment, usually on a six-month rotation basis, to explain their presence and do some good.

These limitations were particularly significant because the international forces were inserted into complex and often conflict-ridden local environments where providing 'security assistance' placed great demands on social skills and local knowledge. The core mandate—'extending the central government's authority'—meant dealing with local strongmen who were nominally friends but had little interest in accepting Kabul's authority, had strong incentives to exploit the power represented by the international forces, and often abused their populations. The security environment was further complicated by bandits, drug-running operators and long-standing local conflicts over land and water that often meshed with the militants' *jihad* against the government and its international supporters. An ISAF force outside Kabul, in other words, faced environments qualitatively different from and much more demanding than what the British-led force faced when landing in the capital in January 2002.

To understand more fully the dynamic of expansion, and what providing 'security assistance' meant in practice, the rest of this chapter examines two cases in detail—the Norwegian PRT in Faryab and the British contingent in Helmand. The two cases represent two extreme points in the spectrum of allied contributions. The small Norwegian PRT deployed to the initially calm northwestern province of Faryab and was cast as a stabilization mission. The much larger British Task Force went into the erstwhile heartland of the Taliban in Helmand; it was prepared for combat but had a civil component as well, in line with NATO's comprehensive approach. Both contingents ended up fighting a much stronger enemy than expected.

The Norwegians in Faryab: Local Accommodation and Military Expansion[39]

Arriving in 2004, the Norwegian contingent spent the first couple of years on mostly uneventful patrols in Faryab's hilly countryside, and lying low vis-à-vis the local power holders dominated by the Uzbek leader, General Dostum. The calm was disturbed only by a mob attack on the camp in early 2006. A year later problems appeared from a different direction. Taliban rebels were reported to be moving into Faryab from neighbouring Badghis province, and the PRT participated in several ISAF offensives to clean out insurgent areas. In a related boundary adjustment, a district in Badghis suspected of harbouring rebels was shifted to Faryab province, and thus into the Norwegian area of responsibility. By 2010, Norwegian forces were deeply involved in combat operations on a regular basis. How did these changes come about? Was it a form of 'mission creep'—a concept suggesting an unwilled process, a chain of events that landed the Norwegians, like the Canadians in Kandahar, in a war-like situation they did not anticipate and did not seek?

Norway had earlier contributed to both OEF and the ISAF brigade in Kabul. While the OEF contribution was opposed by the political Left at home, the main political parties supported it as an expression of sympathy for the United States after 9/11 and an affirmation of NATO's importance to Norway's national security. When ISAF expanded beyond Kabul under NATO command, the Norwegian government was again asked to contribute. With a small conscript-based army befitting a social democracy of around four million people, the government decided initially on a symbolic presence. A few soldiers were sent to join the British PRT in Faryab in mid-2004 as part of a general increase in the international forces to provide security during the presidential elections. When the British moved south the following year, the Norwegians agreed to lead the multinational PRT in Faryab. It did not seem a difficult decision. Norway was already participating in ISAF in Kabul. The additional deployment was modest—just under fifty soldiers in the first year—but demonstrated Norway's role as a loyal member of NATO. The Minister for Development Cooperation strongly supported it for reasons of aid policy. To the government, Faryab had the added advantage of being a calm province, far from the emerging trouble in the southeast. To the public at large, it seemed an appropriate engagement. Norwegian NGOs had a long history of working in Afghanistan, and strong solidarity networks had formed during the resistance to the Soviet invasion.

The transfer took effect on 1 September 2005, a couple of weeks before the general elections in Norway. The new Labour-Left coalition government promised to increase the Norwegian contribution to ISAF, explicitly justifying its policy as a means to strengthen the transatlantic partnership and develop NATO's ability to meet unconventional security threats.[40] At the same time, it terminated the more controversial participation in OEF and withdrew the even more controversial 'humanitarian' contingent that the previous centre-right government had sent to Iraq in support of the US invasion. Later contributions to ISAF were modest by NATO standards, although less so on a Norwegian scale. The PRT received some additional military personnel (the aid component was mostly channelled outside the PRT, in order to maintain a military-civilian separation), and a larger contingent of around 230 soldiers was assigned to the Quick Reaction Force (QRF) based in Mazar-i-Sharif, whose task was to assist or extricate the forces serving under ISAF's Regional Command North (RC-N).

Settling into Faryab

Although the Taliban had been decisively defeated, the northern region had other security problems. Most obvious was the conflict between the two major victorious 'warlords' in the north, Dostum and Atta, as well as clashes among lower-level commanders and their abuse of the local population. By mid-decade the situation had stabilized somewhat, partly because of the peace pact concluded by Atta and Dostum in 2004. Dostum remained the informal 'overlord' over Faryab and an adjacent province in the northwest, but was relying less on military coercion and more on political institutions, above all the political party Junbesh-i Milli-yi Islami and its youth organization. By the time the Norwegians took command of the Faryab PRT, Dostum had participated in presidential elections (and made a nice showing by getting 10 per cent of the vote). He was cooperating with the UN-supervised process of disarmament and reining in some of his most violence-prone commanders.[41] His party did well in the parliamentary elections in 2005, securing 23 seats out of a total of 249 in the Lower House.

Dostum's reorientation towards the political arena and attempts to enhance his power by working with the central government made it easier for the Norwegian PRT to provide 'security assistance' and help extend the authority of Kabul to the province. Yet general national trends were one thing and local level politics another. Dostum had developed a fearsome reputation as a military commander. He was also a wily politician who made and unmade alliances with ease. His human rights record was dismal. Not surprisingly, the primary concerns of the PRT as it settled into Faryab were related to Dostum and his larger-than-life image.

There were several issues. His Junbesh party dominated politics in Faryab and often sub-provincial power structures as well. All major appointments were controlled by Junbesh, at least by requiring its approval. Many appointments were at variance with the criteria of good governance, security, development and the extension of the central government's authority, all of which related to ISAF's mandate. Another concern was the continuing power and often abusive behaviour of Junbesh commanders, or commanders who had split off and operated autonomously. Several times delegations of Faryab elders approached the Norwegians to ask for protection against the informal as well as formal structures of power on issues that ranged from violence by the police or local commanders to land grabbing, illegal tax collection, and detention in private prisons. 'Security and justice were always on top of their list', an embassy official later recalled.[42]

The legacy of past conflict that followed ethnic lines belonged to a different category. Faryab was predominantly Uzbek (around fifty-six per cent of the population), with Tajiks the second largest group (just over twenty per cent), and Pashtuns forming a distinct but important minority (fourteen per cent). The Pashtun communities had mostly originated as favoured settlers who, issued with land grants from Pashtun kings, had migrated to the northwest from the central or eastern regions. Many had come in the late nineteenth century, but others had settled in the mid twentieth century. During the 1990s, violence among the militias had followed ethnic lines, with predictably disastrous consequences for the civilians. On the main axis of conflict in Faryab—Pashtun versus Uzbek—the reference points were mutual massacres. Dostum's (Uzbek) commanders had massacred Pashtuns, and the Taliban's (Pashtun) commanders had massacred Uzbeks. After the fall of the Taliban, retaliation against the Pashtun minorities in the north had been swift, widespread and vicious. Found guilty by ethnic association of having been Taliban or Taliban-supporters, Pashtuns were systematically harassed. Some were killed and many more forced to flee from their land, seeking refuge in IDP camps in the south. Dostum and his militias had led the way by massacring Taliban prisoners of war in Shebergan, just east of Faryab in late 2001. But conflict along ethnic lines also mobilized Uzbek against Tajik, and Tajik against Pashtun—not to speak of divisions among smaller solidarity groups which clashed over land, allegiance, positions, honour, or control over the two main opium smuggling routes that ran west and north through Faryab.

Walking into this landscape, the Norwegians at first trod carefully. 'We took our cue from the British in Mazar who had stressed the need to blend in with the local structures', one official recalled.[43] The PRT team moved into the British 'base', in fact an old bank building located in the provincial centre, Maimana. The military went on patrols, sometimes with the local police, to 'show the flag', monitor, observe and drink tea with local leaders. In Kabul, the embassy adjusted its economic aid programme for 2006 to include sizeable projects for the province.

While concerned with local issues of security and justice, the Norwegians had few means to address the problems.[44] The PRT had neither the local knowledge nor the capacity to take on local commanders. The team was quite small—even by late 2007 it consisted of only 150 soldiers from Norway and other Nordic and Baltic countries. Random or regular abuse of the local population was considered a matter for the police, outside a realistic interpretation of ISAF's mandate. Interventions aimed at the formal power structure would have to go via Afghan central authorities. On this point the Norwegians were adamant. They occasionally intervened; a particularly notorious and corrupt police chief, for instance, was removed with the help of the embassy's appeal to the Ministry of Interior. But appointment matters touched on the delicate balance between the centre and the provinces and were difficult to influence. In some cases the person concerned secured immunity in other ways; for instance, a troublesome commander associated with Dostum, Fataullah Khan, got himself elected to Parliament in 2005.

Suspicions and mistrust of Dostum among the Norwegians increased dramatically in March 2006, when the PRT camp suddenly was attacked. A mob stormed the outer perimeter of the building, shots were fired, stones thrown, and hand grenades tossed as well. The small PRT in the camp was only saved by the Quick Reaction Force based in Mazar. Fighter planes buzzed low to disperse the crowd, and some 120

British soldiers were brought in to help fight it back. The immediate cause of the attack was the publication of the Danish cartoons of the Prophet Muhammad, which provoked demonstrations and violence elsewhere in Afghanistan and in other countries as well, but only in Maimana did the rioters succeed in storming a NATO base. Not unreasonably, the PRT suspected it was a show of force by Junbesh to demonstrate its power and ensure non-interference in sensitive local matters. A video taken by the PRT of the rioters contained some familiar faces, and Junbesh clearly had the power to orchestrate—or prevent—demonstrations of popular fury. At the time, frustration was increasing throughout Afghanistan over a foreign presence that had failed to meet expectations of creating peace and prosperity. The sentiment exploded a couple of months later in Kabul, which saw widespread and much worse rioting. But even in the north—the stronghold of the Northern Alliance that had partnered with the United States in the invasion—the foreign presence was becoming an inflamed element. In a move that further widened the distance from the local population, the PRT in Faryab started building a new, heavily fortified base outside town.

To address security issues in the province more generally, the Norwegian Ambassador advocated the establishment of a Policy Action Group (PAG) for the northern region, composed of high-level Afghan and international civilian and military officials. A similar group had been initiated by the British to address issues in four southern provinces where the Taliban were gaining strength. The northern PAG barely got off the ground, however. The United States and Britain were focused on the growing insurgency in the south and the east and were uninterested. The Germans, who headed Regional Command North that included Faryab and eight other provinces in the north, firmly opposed the idea. The reaction indicated the depth of German caution. The very formation of such a group might suggest that the insurgency was spreading northwards and drawing critical attention at home. The German federal parliament had formally restricted the role of German forces in Afghanistan to prevent their involvement in combat operations, and its members were closely monitoring the situation.

Expansion

In mid-2007 several violent incidents occurred in the northern region that had the trademark of insurgent attacks. ISAF forces started to take

93

casualties.[45] In Kunduz, a suicide bomber detonated his explosives next to German soldiers on foot patrol in May 2007, killing three and wounding two, as well as hitting Afghan civilians. Another suicide bomber in the same area took aim at a car carrying private American security guards. In Faryab a few days later, a bomb carried by a donkey exploded near a PRT foot patrol, killing one Finnish soldier and wounding two Norwegians. For the Faryab PRT it was a watershed and a wake-up call. Routines for patrolling were changed and movement in the provincial centre, Maimana, was restricted. Nevertheless, in June a patrol just outside Maimana came under fire and one Norwegian soldier was wounded. A few months later, the car carrying the head of the PRT hit an IED and was destroyed (although the officer survived).

The incidents led to new security assessments. The insurgency seemed to be spreading into the north, whether in the form of older Taliban commanders who had lingered or the arrival of new cadres from the south, where the Taliban were pressed by British and American forces. An assessment appeared in UNAMA reports that upgraded part of the north, including Faryab, to medium and high risk. The independent analyst Antonio Giustozzi, who relied heavily on UN sources, concluded that the Taliban were back in the northwest.[46] A report prepared by the long-time Afghan analyst Peter Marsden for the Asian Development Bank in early 2007 was less certain. The report found 'a manageable level of risk' for development projects, although not from rebels alone, and recommended additional security measures for the Bank's infrastructure projects on the Ring Road that went through Badghis and Faryab.[47] ISAF, it must be assumed, operated with similar or higher risk ratings. Already in 2005, when the Norwegians took over the PRT lead, Faryab was ranked as 'high' on the insecurity scale. This was the second-highest point on the scale, signifying that 'the enemy' had the intention and capacity to attack.[48]

The Pashtun communities received particular attention in these security assessments. Several of Faryab's districts had sizeable Pashtun communities, but the Ghomarch district in neighbouring Badghis province was of special interest to the Faryab PRT. The district was almost entirely Pashtun, while in the province as a whole the Pashtun population was estimated to number less than 30 per cent.[49] The Pashtuns in Badghis had been politically 'in' during the Taliban regime, but after 2001 had become outsiders in local politics and consistently disadvantaged in relation to the majority Tajik population, whose Jamiat party controlled local administration and associated benefits. Ghormach was extraordinarily poor and neglected, even by rural Afghan standards, for other reasons also. While administratively part of Badghis, the district was isolated from the provincial centre and the rest of the province by a mountain range and a wide river. The provincial authorities—not to speak of the central government—had thin, if any, presence and control in Ghormach. The district was thus *de facto* autonomous, a likely area of discontents, and a natural safe haven for insurgents and criminals alike.

By early 2007 the Norwegians in Faryab had concluded that the trouble in 'their' province had its roots in Ghormach.[50] Crossing into Faryab from Ghormach was easy—Ghormach was topographically as naturally part of Faryab as it was cut off from Badghis. The problem from the PRT perspective was that ISAF jurisdiction followed Afghan administrative divisions and not topography. This placed Faryab and the Norwegians under Regional Command North (RC-North), led by the Germans, while Ghormach was in Regional Command West (RC-West), which was led by the Italians headquartered in faraway Herat. Under the Italians in the chain of command was the Spanish PRT, which had operational responsibility for Ghormach. But the Spaniards were based in the provincial capital of Badghis and thus cut off from Ghormach by the same mountain range and river that divided the local population. The roads were in bad condition and it would at best take the Spaniards a long day to get there. The road traversed another Pashtun-dominated district (Bala-e-Murgabh) whose population after 2001 was just as disadvantaged as that in Ghormach and inclined to be unfriendly. Local strongmen fighting over the opium production and trade routes further discouraged entry by outsiders. As a result, the Spaniards had mostly stayed out of Ghormach.

Being under RC-North, the PRT based in Faryab could in principle not cross into Ghormach without prior clearance from RC-West, which discouraged incursions from another command into 'its' area. The Germans who led the northern command and had some 4,000 troops in nearby Kunduz province were restricted by their own parliament from operating outside their regional command area. The Norwegians, however, were raring to go. Small observation teams had entered Ghormach in early 2007 to assess the security situation and had prepared an internal memo discussing ideas for including the district in their operational area.[51] The team scored an initial success when ISAF authorized two operations into Ghormach from RC-North. Both involved Norwegian and German forces, but the German contingents had to stop at the provincial border and watch the Norwegians, accompanied by Afghan army units, penetrate deep into Ghormach.

The first operation in November 2007 was a relative success. The area was 'cleared' of rebels, the ISAF troops withdrew, and relief, reconstruction and political work could begin. The Norwegian aid agency provided US$4.5 million for quick impact projects and a French NGO (ACTED) with previous experience in the area started the work from an office in the district centre. UNAMA set up a local *shura*, whose leader also functioned as district governor. For a while things seemed to be going well. Soon, however, the insurgents were returning, and ISAF planned another offensive to clear the district. Both UNAMA and the aid workers opposed this, fearing that the delicate work to establish political and humanitarian inroads had just begun and could easily be wrecked. Their opposition was in vain. Operation *Karez* was launched in May 2008.

After the operation was completed, the Norwegian-led PRT forces were again withdrawn from the district in line with standard procedures for observing ISAF regional command jurisdictions, although they continued informally to make forays across the provincial border. A unit of Afghan soldiers was left to man the Forward Operating Base established in Ghormach during the offensive (built on the remnants of a Russian base left over from the 1980s), but did so unwillingly, if at all, after the international troops had left. Local strongmen, rebels and criminals again had a free run of Ghormach, only more agitated than before, it must be assumed, after two offensives by the foreign soldiers. The local population had twice been caught in the cross-fire. Politically, the situation deteriorated as well. The *shura* fell apart in factional disputes, possibly over distribution of new infusions of aid money. In addition to ACTED, which resumed its work some time after *Karez*, American Special Forces had started operating in the district with small winning-hearts-and-minds projects. Unlike ACTED, they distorted the local power structure by bringing in Uzbek and Tajik aid workers, and paid salaries that a traditional NGO like ACTED could not match. In Faryab, the security situation deteriorated, suggesting either that the insurgents had been hard pressed by the offensives in Ghormach and had moved into neighbouring Faryab, or that they had simply expanded.

At this point—some time in mid-2008—the Norwegian government and the military decided that new steps were needed to address the now combined Faryab-Ghormach problem by allowing the PRT in Faryab free and regular access into the troubled district.[52] One solution would be to simply include Ghormach in the RC-North jurisdiction. This, however, was opposed by the Germans with reference to the Bundestag restrictions designed to keep the German forces in Afghanistan out of combat operations. The issues had become even more sensitive than before because ISAF's Quick Reaction Force based in Mazar—

whose function was to assist smaller operations in the command area—had by this time been taken over by the Germans, having previously been manned by the Norwegians. Including Ghormach in the RC-N jurisdiction increased the probability that German QRF forces would be called on to help other ISAF units during offensives. The Norwegian government assiduously worked the Berlin track with high-level diplomacy and meetings with Bundestag members to see if adjustments could be made, but had little success. Another option was then tried, to circumvent the Germans and the rigidities of the regional ISAF command structure altogether by having the Afghan government change provincial boundaries and include Ghormach district in Faryab. In late 2008, Norwegian diplomats and military officials redoubled their efforts in this direction. Approaches were made on the ministerial level to the Afghan Minister of Defence, Abdul Rahim Wardak, as well as directly to President Karzai when the Norwegian Ministers of Defence and Foreign Affairs visited Kabul. In a parallel move, the case was put forward at the highest level of ISAF and through the UN mission, which was now headed by a Norwegian (Kai Eide). By December 2008 agreement was reached, and President Karzai signed a decree that enlarged Faryab to include Ghormach.

The change put Ghormach into the Norwegian area of operations, although it did not automatically ensure German support. In fact, the German government decided that the original coordinates for the RC-North command area were still valid and would guide German operations regardless of Afghan provincial demarcations. The Norwegians had covered for this eventuality as well, having extracted informal assurances from the German high command and Minister of Defence that, *in extremis*, German forces would assist Norwegians operating in Ghormach. This was in line with the slightly greater flexibility granted by the Bundestag in 2008, which allowed German forces to operate outside the northern command area 'occasionally', and for purposes of providing 'limited support' to other ISAF troops.[53]

The ability of a small NATO country to circumvent the political objections of a major ally as well as the rigidities of the ISAF structure was not only due to Norwegian persistence. Other allies, particularly the United States, were frustrated over national caveats that restricted operations and over ISAF's cumbersome command structure. The first American ISAF commander, General McNeill, had shared the concerns of the Norwegians over the awkward division between the operational areas of RC-North and RC-West.[54] A small but eager ISAF nation that volunteered a proactive approach towards the enemy was surely welcome at the highest levels in ISAF, where the Americans predominated. With the added weight of the Americans, the scales tipped in favour of change.

The Afghan government was divided about, or indifferent to, the boundary adjustment. The Governor of Faryab did not cherish the prospect of getting a notoriously troublesome district that would likely soak up large amounts of aid money. The identification of Ghormach as a joint UNAMA-ISAF 'pilot action district' in 2008 carried the promise of additional resources, but escalating violence in the district blocked the scheme. President Karzai was most concerned about the implications for the upcoming presidential and provincial council elections, and decided that for these purposes Ghormach would remain a part of Badghis. The district would be included in Faryab only for military purposes, in response to Norwegian demands, and only temporarily as the presidential decree stated.

A Strategy of 'Mission Creep'

The story of the Norwegian approach to Ghormach is in part a classic story of 'mission creep'. Immediate problems on the ground led to expanded operations in an enlarged area. Yet there was nothing automatic or inevitable about the process. As the contrasting German case shows, political constraints can prevent 'mission creep'. The Norwegian forces did not face similar political restrictions. But the puzzle still remains: why was it that a small country with a self-image as a nation of peace, and a PRT that had been unwilling to confront troublesome local commanders, later took on proactively an area widely considered a hornets' nest of rebels, criminals and opium smugglers?

The logic of military operations was compelling. Unlike Dostum's commanders who had given the PRT some headaches, the Taliban were clearly the enemy. They were entering the Norwegian area of responsibility, but were sitting on the other side of an administrative boundary that protected them from hot pursuit by international forces. There are indications that the German military contingent would have been quite happy to do the same and were chafing under the political restrictions. In January 2009, after all the commotion about the boundary change and after the Bundestag-approved mandate had become more flexible, German forces in RC-North were planning to accompany the Norwegian PRT on a forthcoming operation into Ghormach.[55] Over the next two years, German forces frequently conducted patrols aimed at Taliban strongholds in their area.[56] This suggests that military institutional factors were at work.

The character of the Norwegian military establishment had indeed changed in recent years. A long-time contributor to UN peace-keeping operations, the Norwegian military had become more professional in line with the new demands posed by peace operations that involved enforcement operations. In Afghanistan, the principal forces conducting offensive operations in the south—the Americans, the Canadians, and the British—were also the closest points of reference for the Norwegian military. Even the Danes, it was said with some feigned surprise, were in the south. Norwegian military opinion had favoured deployment to the south rather than the north when an expanded ISAF contribution had first been discussed. Instead, Norwegian troops were sent to what was presumed to be a calm region to work alongside countries that hedged their contribution with caveats, caution or passivity. In this environment, professional and institutional incentives favoured decisive military action over a more cautious strategy of circling the wagons and monitoring the activities of the enemy across an administrative boundary line.

The Norwegian aid and diplomatic community supported an expansion of the operational area, citing the 'comprehensive and integrated approach' and its emphasis on a civilian development component. The poverty and neglect of Ghormach were undisputed. By late 2007, no international NGOs were working there, or even in the entire province of Badghis. Previous aid workers had pulled out when security conditions deteriorated (including MSF after five of their doctors were killed in June 2004). The Spanish PRT based in the provincial capital had US$10 million a year for development projects or force protection, but most of it was spent close to the provincial capital and benefited Tajik communities. Afghan NGOs were uninterested in implementing projects in the outlying district of a remote and difficult province. Even the national flagship programme for local development, the National Solidarity Programme (NSP), had no takers in Ghormach in 2007.[57] The district was completely 'under-serviced', a Norwegian official later said.[58] It simply cried out for assistance. In the conventional thinking that prevailed, that meant prior military operations to clear out the Taliban.

A more aggressive line arguably suited the Norwegian government as well. Norway had been hard pressed by the Americans to contribute troops to the southern region, but the Labour-led government had declined, fearing that the domestic political climate and its left-wing coalition partner would not accept deployment of Norwegian forces to a known combat area. Taking a more pro-active line in the north would remove some of the sting from the refusal to go south. In terms of domestic politics, an incremental change in Faryab would be much less controversial than deployment to the south, if it were noticed at all— indeed, it was not. Military spokesmen consistently underplayed the combat aspect of the operations to the Norwegian media.[59] Only later, when Norwegian casualties started to rise, did public awareness become apparent. The new awareness generated a debate over whether or not Norway was at war in Afghanistan, but this was not until the second half of 2009, well after the boundary adjustment had taken place and Norwegian forces had launched several offensive operations.

The Consequences

The Faryab story also tells us something about the consequences of ISAF's byzantine command structure and the impact of the much-discussed national 'caveats' on operations. ISAF's multinational structure and associated caveats clearly impeded military effectiveness; the NATO force resembled the proverbial giant pinned down by a myriad of Lilliputian ropes. But the ropes also constrained the scope and nature of the violence. When the ropes were loosened—as in the steps the Norwegians took with the support of the United States to adjust the provincial boundary—more offensive operations took place and the conflict escalated.

From 2009 and onwards, the Norwegians operated more frequently and freely in Ghormach. The boundary change was one factor, the other was the increase in American forces in the north in 2009, and particularly during the surge in 2010. The entry of American forces into the Faryab-Badghis area lessened Norwegian reliance on the Germans and permitted more offensive operations. Yet the consequent increased pressure on the rebels only seemed to generate more resistance.

Security conditions had deteriorated already in the first half of 2009. Work on the parts of the national highway that runs through Ghormach and other districts of Faryab came to a standstill as workers were killed or kidnapped. It was not the first time that construction had been interrupted on the Ring Road, the single most important infrastructure project in the entire country. In 2009, however, the situation in the northwestern sections had become so bad that the Asian Development Bank, which financed the western segments, started hiring a private police force of 500 men to protect the road workers. That the workers were foreign rather than hired locally made little sense to villagers steeped in poverty and underemployment, and probably made the foreign workers a particularly inviting target. Most were Chinese, brought in by the Chinese construction company that had secured the road contract from the ADB.

Faryab as a whole became more insecure and the Taliban tightened their grip. When the Norwegian PRT had first started to focus on Ghormach, Norwegian military intelligence sources had disagreed in their assessment. Were the rebels local or Taliban from the outside? Or opium smugglers and other strongmen who resisted outside intervention? Were they tightly or loosely organized? The Faryab-based PRT had been more inclined to see an organized Taliban-movement at work than Norwegian intelligence officers based further away in RC-North or in Norway. The spokesperson for the military headquarters in Norway said it would be 'quite wrong' to see the Afghans whom the Norwegians were fighting in Ghomrach in late 2007 as 'an advancing Taliban force'.[60] Less than three years later, however, the Taliban in the area had acquired the contours of a formidable and organized force. The Ghormach district *shura* of elders decided in May 2010 to work with them. That meant that 'every male between 15 and 55 is potentially against us', the Norwegian PRT concluded.[61] During the first half of 2010, Norwegian forces were attacked almost every day, encountering IEDs or direct fire.[62] Ghormach had really become 'a hornets' nest', the head of the Norwegian contingent in Afghanistan said. 'We have a difficult job and meet a lot of resistance. We are now being shot at in places where we earlier moved freely'.[63] It was a familiar pattern: expansion and action to root out the rebels sitting across the provincial boundary had provoked reaction and expansion in turn.

The British in Helmand: Fortifying the Insurgency

The British deployed to Helmand in April 2006 in what analysts in London described as 'a vast and unforgiving terrain, [with] a paucity of established infrastructure and a tribally fragmented population that has little experience of central government and who are xenophobic, conservative and largely predisposed to resist foreigners'.[64]

The insurgency, however, was still in its infancy. Taliban leaders, some of whom were originally from Helmand, had started returning from Pakistan to reactivate their local networks, asking their supporters who had hung up their weapons after 2001 to take them down and drive out the infidels. Gradually they succeeded in mobilizing discontent, fuelled by the predations of the local leaders who had taken power after 2001, the failure of the new order to deliver on the expectations for peace and economic prosperity, and 'aggressive search operations and aerial bombings by Western Special Forces on counter-terrorism missions', a British journalist wrote.[65] Nevertheless, by the time the British arrived a relative calm prevailed. The Taliban were there, General Richards said, but they had a 'marriage of convenience' with the Governor and his men, as well as with the drug lords who controlled Helmand's massive opium production.[66] A balance of power of sorts prevailed, with conflict over control of the poppy trade looming over the insurgency. A British journalist who visited the province just ahead of the British forces warned that the major fight would be against the drug mafias, describing a scene where 'at night the southern desert roars with the sound of high-speed convoys—Jeeps crammed with itchy-fingered gunmen and Class A narcotics—whizzing across the hardened sand'.[67]

The arrival of the British not only changed the local balance of power. Being British, they also evoked Afghan memories of British invasions during the nineteenth century that made them particularly attractive targets to the militants. The embittered Anglo-British history had been cited by international diplomats at the Bonn conference as an argument against asking the British to lead the ISAF contingent in Kabul; now British forces were deployed in the region where they had fought (and been defeated by) Afghan forces in memorable and celebrated battles of the Second Anglo-Afghan War in 1880. The former Taliban leader Mullah Zaeef was not the only one who thought sending British forces to the south was a strategic mistake.[68] Other Afghan analysts thought the same. 'The British are known as a defeated force here. Now people think the British are here to take their revenge', Professor Wadir Safi at Kabul University said.[69] A former Taliban official who had been reconciled with the Karzai government feared it would be counter-productive. 'Every year we celebrate Afghan independence from British... In school history books and in tales, people are told of the bravery of empty-handed Afghans against the well-equipped British army. This can harm the counterinsurgency', Waheed Mujda told AFP.[70] But no other US ally stepped forward, and the British deployed—perhaps in a spirit of imperial hubris, as Anatol Lieven later claimed.[71]

Spreading Out in Helmand

The initial deployment in 2006 was light—3,100 troops, of which only 700 were infantry, and the rest support and logistics. The Defence Secretary sent the troops off saying he hoped no shots would be fired, although he added that the mission was 'complex and dangerous'.[72] The plan was to concentrate the forces in a triangle around the provincial capital district, Lashkar Gah, which included Helmand's major population and administrative centre as well as some of the most fertile areas of the province. From this 'inkspot' of security and development, the government's authority would spread outward on the Helmand blotting paper. The plan, produced by a joint civil-military process in London in late 2005, was explicitly modelled on the Malayan counterinsurgency campaign of the 1950s and streamlined with NATO's evolving 'comprehensive approach'.

The troops were deployed in April 2006. By May the fighting had started. It soon turned into the most intense fighting involving British forces since the Korean War. Reinforcements of 1,500 troops were rushed in but casualties mounted and the entire British mission came close to collapse.[73] During the summer months alone, 33 British soldiers were killed and more than 100 injured. The civilian development component barely got off the ground and was 'severely, and continually, restricted by the security situation'.[74] Quick Impact Projects that were started in lieu of more ambitious development plans also stalled as local contractors were intimidated or killed.

What sparked such ferocious fighting? For a start, the British were vulnerable. The Task Force Commander had dispersed his force in small outposts, including Sangin, Musa Qala, Kajaki and Now Zad in the remote northern corner of the province, rather than concentrating them in the triangle as planned.[75] Not surprisingly in view of the outcome, this 'platoon house strategy' caused much controversy and a blame game. According to the Task Force Commander, he merely responded to a request from the Helmand Governor; the Governor later denied this, claiming it was truly a joint decision.[76] Whichever the case, the background facts are not in dispute.

Insurgents had burned a clinic built by American soldiers, who had been in the area before the British arrived, and taken over a village in the upper Baghran valley. The Governor raised the issue with the Task Force Commander as soon as he arrived: would he send his troops to retake the village?[77] A couple of weeks later British troops were on their way to Sangin in the Baghran valley and, soon afterwards, to other district centres in the far northern part of the province to extend the authority of the central government. Unfailingly, the units came under fierce attack. To defend themselves, British troops called in 'astonishing amounts of airborne ordnance, alienating the locals by destroying their homes and, sometimes, accidentally killing their children', as Fergusson's close account of events notes, and the violence widened.[78] Military analysts agree on this decision sequence. 'Political considerations forced the British to deviate from [the original plan] and establish platoon houses', Marston writes, citing pressure from both the Governor of Helmand and President Karzai.[79]

A different analysis is offered by the sociologist Anthony King. Blaming the political context 'falsely absolves commanders in theatre from responsibility, robbing them of the agency which they have clearly exercised', he writes.[80] The Task Force Commander acted in line with the operational autonomy traditionally accorded British field commanders, in this case reinforced by the 'lack of strategic political guidance' that enabled the Task Force Commander to depart from the initial plan.[81] The organizational culture of the military and institutional incentives 'to act' and demonstrate a 'can-do' attitude did the rest. When faced with requests to show the flag and deploy his newly arrived force, the commander—and certainly some of his men on the ground—seemed eager to get an opportunity to go and fight. This was what they had trained for and were sent to do, King argues.

Both perspectives overlook the more fundamental point that ISAF's core mandate was to extend the central government's authority, and therefore had a huge built-in potential for conflict. It may be questioned whether the initial provocation by Taliban (burning down a clinic) justified the immediate deployment of British troops—if, in fact, they were Taliban and not drug smugglers or just a rival faction challenging the new Governor—or whether a village of some 14,000 inhabitants in the remote Baghran valley was an important strategic goal. Sangin, where the trouble started, did have some strategic properties. The district was located on the crossroads of the opium trade and close to the huge Kajaki hydroelectric dam that the international forces later made great efforts to repair and guard. Either way, if the British troops were to provide 'security assistance' on behalf of the central government, it did not seem odd to insert forces in disputed areas to plant the flag of the government when requested by the provincial Governor who was appointed by Kabul. 'Political considerations' in this sense were at the heart of the mandate.

Whether the force was adequate for the mandate is another question. As it was, the British forces were deployed in small and isolated outposts that were quickly surrounded by well-organized, courageous fighters, apparently instructed by trainers familiar with British military tactics.[82] The debacle led to requests for more troops to boost the contingent, but when these arrived, the insurgents adapted as well by moving towards greater reliance on guerrilla tactics. A larger initial force might well have produced a similar response.

Deposing the Governor

Another challenge buried deep in ISAF's mandate was managing the relationship with the local power holders. Tribal politics in Helmand had long and complex roots, shaped by issues over land (especially after some older khan families had been weakened during the Communist period), control over opium production and trade, and patterns of alliances and hostilities formed during previous conflicts—the *jihad* against the Soviets, its chaotic aftermath, and the Taliban regime that followed.[83] In the northern part of the province, a sub-tribe of the Alizai, the Akhundzada clan, had developed its power base for over three decades to achieve a dominant position but lost out to the Taliban. In exile in Pakistan, the Akhundzada had aligned with Karzai and were rewarded with the governorship of the province after 2001. The Governor, Sher Mohammed Akhundzada (called SMA by the British), did not rule by the dictates of narrow clan politics alone. While securing significant power for his own clan, he distributed the important offices of police and internal security across tribal lines to ensure broad cooperation. Other factions were excluded—especially a rival sub-clan that had sided with the Taliban (Abdul Wahid)—but the system established by Sher Mohammed produced considerable order and stability. In late 2005 US forces raided the Governor's compound and allegedly found a large stash of opium. The raid created considerable embarrassment for the British. Britain was the lead nation for counter-narcotics activities in Afghanistan, according to the division of labour established by the major donors in Geneva in 2002, and one task of the contingent dispatched to Helmand was to address the province's burgeoning opium problem. The adverse effect on Sher Mohammed's reputation was therefore serious, even though in some respects he was more acceptable than other high officials of the post-Taliban order who had appalling human rights records. Before deploying to Helmand, the British asked Karzai to remove Sher Mohammed as Governor. Karzai complied, but was more conscious than the British of the dangers of alienating a powerful local clan. To sweeten the dismissal, he appointed Sher Mohammed to the Upper House of the Parliament, and his brother Amir Muhammad Akhundzada to the position of Deputy Governor. As befitted the member of a powerful family, Sher Mohammed placed key allies and relatives in other positions in the provincial administration.[84]

His dismissal nevertheless disturbed the balance of power he had carefully erected and opened a new round of making and unmaking alliances. In the process, the Taliban came out stronger than before, and the British certainly had fewer friends. Combined with the platoon-house strategy, it made the British dangerously exposed. Karzai later said he warned them:

Before [the British came] we were fully in charge of Helmand....They came and said 'your governor is no good'. I said, 'all right, do we have a replacement for this governor? Do you have enough forces?' Both the American and British forces guaranteed to me they knew what they were doing and I made the mistake of listening to them. And when they came in, the Taleban came.[85]

While Karzai in 2008 had reasons to say 'I told you so', there is no reason to doubt that this consummate player of tribal politics saw the risks at the time. A British journalist, Tom Coghlan, who followed Helmand politics closely, came to a similar conclusion: 'While the control of the province by the former Jihadi leaders appears to have been often divisive and their control far from comprehensive, their abrupt removal in the absence of significant government or foreign forces to fill the void seems to have been a still larger error of judgment'.[86]

The deeper reasons for this error of judgment might lie in the interventionist zeal that marked the Blair government. Yet when the decision to sack the Governor was made in late 2005, the British did not have a mission on the ground in Helmand and had little knowledge of local politics. The Task Force that later arrived had no Pashto speakers, and only one fluent Dari speaker seconded from the Foreign Office. The British 'did not know friend from enemy', as a woman parliamentarian from the province later said.[87] Much later British generals acknowledged the importance of understanding the nature of tribal politics and the relationship to the insurgency. Understanding why various groups made life difficult for British battle groups, General Nick Carter noted in 2010, 'will define a different strategy in terms of ... how you will defeat the problem, than if you simply labelled them as Taliban'.[88]

Knowledge might have prevented errors of judgment but did not remove the basic dilemma posed by ISAF's mandate. The Akhundzada Governor was an ally of Karzai, and as such certainly an extension of the authority of the central government. But he was a poor instrument for the implementation of most other aspects of the Bonn Agreement and the liberal internationalism it represented. If that mandate were to be taken seriously, the international forces needed counterparts in what Bertrand Badie has called 'importing elites'—local leaders committed to the reformist agenda.[89] Lacking such counterparts, the British brought in outsiders to perform the task, yet these were invariably weak, dependent on British support, and so unable to effectively function as an 'importing elite'. The result was a threefold power structure: the formal but weak new government appointee, the informal power structure controlled by the deposed, but still present, former Governor, and, when the insurgents flexed their muscles, a Taliban shadow governor on the provincial and district level.

The new Governor, Mohammed Daoud, fitted the bill nicely in terms of formal qualifications. He spoke impeccable English, had previously worked with the UN as a development expert and had an engineering degree. As a technocrat from outside Helmand, he had no local tribal ties. But that was also his weakness as a powerbroker. 'He has no personal militia, no private source of income, and no tribal links with village elders', a British source conceded.[90] His only coercive power derived from the newly-arrived British Task Force, which he requested should be placed throughout the province to extend the government's authority. Daoud lasted less than a year as Governor. His successor, Assadullah Wafa, was considered obstructionist and ineffective by the British and was replaced after two years. The next Governor, Mammed Gulab Mangal, was still in the post by mid-2010.

Path Dependence: Escalation and Deepening of Commitment

The circumstance of the initial deployment created a 'path dependence' of escalating involvement and deepening commitment. The immediate British reaction to the attacks on their exposed forces was to send more, on the grounds that 'the main reason why this [platoon house] strategy almost went so badly wrong was... a lack of manpower'.[91] The deployment steadily increased, from the initial 3,100 in 2006 to 6,500 the following year, and close to 10,000 in early 2010.[92] The military repeatedly asked for more troops to increase security and carry out the mission more effectively. The Task Force Commander in 2008 called for a doubling of his forces; the call came as the Taliban switched to new methods, particularly extensive use of IEDs, which caused high British casualties. NATO's leadership and the US reinforced the demand for more troops, particularly in 2009 and 2010, as discussed above. Institutional interests were involved as well. A former British Ambassador to Afghanistan told the Foreign Affairs Committee of the House of Commons that the war in Afghanistan had given the army reasons to claim resources 'on an unprecedented scale' and to shield it from budget cuts. The head of the army was reported to be afraid that he would lose the battle group returning from Iraq in a future Defence Review unless it was deployed to Afghanistan. A supply-side strategy, said Ambassador Cowper-Coles.[93]

Negotiate to Withdraw? Musa Qala

On the ground, the dynamic of deployment reinforced the logic of staying the course rather than pulling back. The dispersed British force was vulnerable, but withdrawal even as a tactical adjustment could be interpreted as a defeat. The first—and by early 2011 the only—attempt to negotiate withdrawal from a precarious outpost had ended badly, setting a negative precedent.

Musa Qala had been one of the districts chosen for British deployment soon after the Task Force arrived in April 2006. Fighting had earlier flared in the Musa Qala district between Akhundzada's men and a rival faction belonging to Abdul Wahid, who had controlled the area under the Taliban but had retreated after 2001 to a neighbouring district. When Sher Mohammed was ousted, the Taliban sensed the opportunity for a comeback. They were reportedly welcomed by the population of the district centre, who resented the abusive practices of Sher Mohammed's police force, but the district authorities requested the British to send troops to restore the authority of the government.

The British arrived in May 2006 with a small unit later supported by Danish ISAF troops. The Taliban kept up the pressure, however, surrounding the district centre and making resupply difficult.[94] The garrison was repeatedly on the point of running out of water, food and ammunition. Several attempts to break the siege over the summer failed. An additional complication arose when the garrison suspected the local police chief of collaborating with the Taliban. The British-Danish leadership of the garrison dismissed the police chief and a new police force was brought in from the outside. As outsiders they did not have direct ties to the local conflict, which was a plus, but as non-Pashtuns dispatched into the Pashtun heartland by the central government's Ministry of Interior they were part of a much larger conflict. It was the same scene recreated four years later in Marjah, the nearby cluster of villages targeted by General McChrystal to receive a 'government in a box'.

The difficulties of holding Musa Qala had by September led the Task Force Commander and author of the platoon-house strategy, Brigadier Ed Butler, to favour unilateral withdrawal. In London, the army chiefs deferred to his judgment in line with the autonomy traditionally accorded the field commander. In Kabul, however, General David Richards, the newly appointed head of ISAF, was sceptical. A unilateral withdrawal could be a political and propaganda success for the Taliban and appear to the Afghans as another Maiwand, the disastrous defeat of the British in the Second Anglo-Afghan War in neighbouring Kandahar. With only a handful of British survivors (along with the regimental dog Bobby), that 1880 defeat (though Britain eventually won the war) carried great political-emotive significance among both Afghans and Britons. In Britain, the battle was memorialized in a poem by Kipling, and in Afghan folklore it was remembered as the scene where the young woman Malalai urged her Pashtun menfolk to resist the invaders.

In Musa Qala the impasse was solved by a proposal from the elders for a cease-fire and withdrawal of both Taliban and Western forces.[95] The town had suffered severe damage from the fighting, including allied air strikes that had destroyed the local mosque. The elders now proposed that the district centre (the town of Musa Qala) should be demilitarized and ruled by the *shura* of elders, who would oversee development assistance and fly the Afghan government flag. Negotiated in cooperation with Governor Daoud and British officers, the 14-point agreement enabled the British to leave the town without being attacked. In December 2006 they piled into gaily decorated Afghan trucks and were driven out of town while the Taliban quietly observed.

For a short while, the Musa Qala agreement appeared as a model for local conflict management and a way to deal with the insurgency. Yet three months later, in January 2007, a US air strike targeted a Taliban commander who entered the town in an apparent violation of the cease-fire agreement. Although it is unclear whether the commander was inside or outside the town boundaries, the attack occurred the day after the American General Dan McNeil took over as ISAF commander from General Richards, and McNeil let it be known to Western reporters that he did not favour making deals with the Taliban.[96] The air strike triggered a chain of events that wrecked the agreement. Forces loyal to the commander who had been killed (led by his brother) entered the town in clear violation of the agreement. This was followed by more US air strikes, including one that killed a major Taliban leader. Taliban forces then stormed the town, executed some of the elders who had signed the agreement, hoisted the Taliban flag and established Taliban rule. Their regime in turn lasted only a few months. A massive force of some 4,000 US, British and Afghan forces, supported by heavy air and artillery power, retook the town in December 2007. A new district Governor was installed, this time an ally of Sher Mohammed and a former Talib who had repented.

To the British, the costs and the eventual futility of the Musa Qala solution left a bitter aftertaste. A Pakistani journalist who visited Musa Qala in December 2006, well into the cease-fire period, reported that the 'first thing one notices in the village of Deh Zor in the Musa Qala district is bits of British army equipment hanging from trees'.[97] Possibly, as the locals claimed, these were the remains of a convoy of British troops that had been sent to Musa Qala earlier to break the siege, but had been ambushed and hanged by Taliban fighters. Casualties on all sides were high. For both opponents and supporters—and there were Afghans and internationals on both sides of this issue—Musa Qala became emblematic of the difficulties of negotiating a local peace agreement. Above all it demonstrated that to endure, such agreements required firm support from the top of the NATO command as well as local restraint.

After Musa Qala, the British did not attempt similar initiatives. Staying the course now appeared the only alternative, only with stronger commitment and with a more comprehensive approach.

A More Comprehensive Approach

Soon after the 9/11 attacks on the United States, Prime Minister Tony Blair had formulated the British objectives in Afghanistan as defeating international terrorism, providing humanitarian assistance, and helping the Afghan people to create 'a better, more peaceful future, free from repression and dictatorship'.[98] Six years later, the Cabinet had redefined the list, which had now grown to six items: (i) reduce the insurgency on both sides of the Durand line, (ii) ensure that core Al-Qaeda does not return to Afghanistan, (iii) ensure that Afghanistan remains a legitimate state, becomes more effective and able to handle its own security, and increase the pace of economic development, (iv) contain and reduce the drug trade, (v) provide long term sustainable support for the Afghan Compact goals [adopted at the London conference in 2006] on governance, rule of law, human rights and social/economic development, and (vi) keep allies engaged. For bureaucratic purposes, these objectives were translated into 'nine interdependent strands' according to function (security; politics and reconciliation; governance and rule of law; economic development and reconstruction; counter-narcotics), geographical areas (Helmand, regional engagement, international engagement) and, to keep it all together, 'strategic communication' to generate 'public support for a peaceful and stable Afghanistan'. Reviewing this list in July 2009, the Foreign Affairs Committee of the House noted a distinct 'mission creep'.[99]

The expanded list reflected in part the growth of the international project itself, which conferred roles and responsibilities on the UK as one of its major sponsors. Internationally assisted national development strategies and plans for Afghanistan (ANDS) were part of an increasingly fine-masked net of goals and principles for the country's development that also entailed obligations on donors. Other donors and agencies involved in Afghanistan adopted similar policy agendas. But goal expansion also reflected lack of progress in the initial core mission of defeating Al-Qaeda and the Taliban. The House Foreign Affairs Committee approvingly cited Lord Ashdown's admonitions: the government's 'answer to the fact that we are close to losing one war in Afghanistan is to fight lots more: a war against the Taliban; a war against drugs; a war against want; a war against Afghanistan's old traditional ways'.[100]

To members of Parliament, this form of goal expansion made for confusion, lack of priorities and an impossible mission. In a classic counterinsurgency perspective, however, it made a great deal of sense. Since defeating the enemy means winning over the people, several wars had to be fought simultaneously. This had been the premise of the Joint UK Plan that framed the deployment to Helmand in April 2006. That strategy did not work, nor did tactical innovations that followed the abandonment of the platoon house strategy—fighting the Taliban was like 'mowing the grass', a British commander said.[101] To compensate, an even more comprehensive strategy was embraced.

The Helmand Road Map developed in 2007 was a more elaborate version of the 2005 plan and had a bottom-up approach. The two-year plan prioritized five geographical and district centres that the British still controlled (Lashkar Gah, Gereshk, Sangin, Garmser and Musa Qala) to launch a 'politically-led counterinsurgency campaign' structured around the nine interdependent strands.[102] The planners envisaged six to eight civilian advisers per strand per district, which meant that some forty specialists were required. The job-description was certainly demanding. According to one of the co-authors of the plan, the 'stabilisation and political advisers' would be deployed into forward areas, 'working with district authorities and local communities to build their trust in government and to sponsor the growth of community based structures with which formal government could link'.[103] At a minimum, the job would require trust, mobility, language skills and cultural knowledge—all of which were in short supply. Experts on Helmand were far and few between. The Foreign Affairs Committee was told that even by mid-2009 there were no Pashto speakers among the Foreign Office and DFID staff in all of Afghanistan, and only two Pashto speakers in the army. The civilian advisers, moreover, had limited mobility and rarely moved outside the garrison without armed escort. The Helmand Road Map was followed in 2009 by a new plan, more modestly and simply called the Helmand Plan and covering only one year.

In the meantime, the counterinsurgency campaign had produced few results. The British controlled a few district centres, but these appeared as the classic garrison towns that General Richards had observed when he commanded ISAF in 2006: '[W]ith British troops surrounded by the Taliban the moment they arrived in towns, the ink would not flow'.[104] In the northern area, the British sphere had shrunk altogether. In Musa Qala and Sangin the Americans had taken the lead after President Obama sent fresh American troops to the south. Even work on the prestige project of the Kajaki Dam had come to a standstill. In 2008 the British had taken the lead in the huge operation to haul a giant turbine up the Helmand River valley to the dam, the site of the hydroelectric power station serving Helmand and Kandahar. Some 2,000 British troops and an equal number of Afghan forces had protected the convoy. Yet work on installing it was put on hold owing to security conditions in the valley. With anti-government elements controlling the road and the countryside, all supplies had to be helicoptered in. The dam itself was protected by British Marines.

Another measure of the fragility of the mission undertaken by the British in Helmand was attacks on British soldiers by members of the Afghan police and the Afghan National Army, their ostensible allies and vital partners. In November 2009, an Afghan policeman in a team working with British soldiers turned and shot five of his mentors at a training base southwest of Lashkar Gah. In July the following year, an ANA soldier pointed his RPG towards the compound of his British colleagues just northeast of Lashkar Gah, killing three and wounding several. The incidents cut to the heart of the mission, further undermining the trust and cooperation which were essential if the British were to work with Afghan forces to extend the authority of the central state and permit the British military to exit from its twenty-first century campaign in Afghanistan.

* * *

Although the provision of 'security assistance' took different forms in the case of the Norwegian and British ISAF contingents, there are some common features. The presence of foreign troops acted as a honey pot to attract the attention of militants, rebels and other discontents. The international forces responded by developing pro-active strategies and/ or bringing reinforcements, but nevertheless faced growing resistance. Dealing with local power structures posed a different set of problems. Supporting reforms and merit-based appointments on the sub-national level were part of the spirit, if not the letter, of the Bonn Agreement that ISAF was mandated to implement, as well as being central to NATO's counterinsurgency strategy. Intervention to improve the quality of public administration was extraordinarily difficult, however, and—since the central government did not always support such interventions—potentially worked at cross-purposes with the other part of ISAF's mandate to help extend the authority of the central government. The British experienced all the problems typically associated with interventions of this kind when they demanded that the local strongman-Governor in Helmand be fired and a new, technocrat Governor installed. The reshuffle disturbed the local balance of power, creating new openings for Taliban to enter and mobilize support.

The experience of the two contingents is relevant to the broader discussion over ISAF's expansion that took place in 2002–03. The main argument for expansion, it will be recalled, was that an early and significant presence of ISAF beyond Kabul would help to create a secure environment and assist in the implementation of the Bonn Agreement. If the two case studies recounted here are representative, however, ISAF expansion turned out to be part of the problem rather than the solution. It is possible, of course, that an earlier deployment with great demonstration of force and resources would have cowed the nominally friendly warlords and nipped the insurgency in the bud, as the advocates of expansion argued. It is also possible that an earlier deployment merely would have introduced the present problems at an earlier time. Expansion at any point in time beyond Kabul would have confronted ISAF with the same problems that faced the later deployments—the honeypot factor and the dilemmas of accommodating or confronting nominally friendly local strongmen. A large and forceful presence, moreover, would rapidly take on the colour of occupation rather than liberation.

Ultimately, the successful execution of ISAF's mandate depended on the other half of the international project—the economic, political and social reform agenda and the tasks of statebuilding. Yet, as we shall see in the subsequent chapters, these parts of the international project also showed strains and tensions that set it back.

5

BUILDING THE STATE

The Taliban gave Afghanistan the dubious distinction of being a quin-
tessentially 'failed state'. Their overthrow left contested legitimacy, a
proliferation of armed groups, greatly weakened public administration
on the national as well as the sub-national level, enormous physical
destruction and social dislocation. In this situation, 'statebuilding'—
conventionally defined as establishing a set of public institutions
anchored at the central level that could provide security and basic services—soon emerged as a central task for the aid agencies. There was,
as noted in chapter 2, some concern that the goal was over-ambitious.
Sceptics pointed to the weak historical foundations of the Afghan
state, in addition to the evident obstacles of the day. On the other
hand, historical trends in Afghanistan during the twentieth century
had been towards the formation of an increasingly unitary state in formal, structural terms, with a national public administration, a national
army and police, and a uniform judicial system. The violent interval in
the 1990s, when civil war conditions and warlordism ruled, only
seemed to confirm that a strong central state was a prerequisite for
peace and development.

The international aid community had by this time developed significant confidence in its ability to assist statebuilding in post-war situations. It had, after all, been done before, most ambitiously and recently
in the Balkans and East Timor. A professional cadre of international
civil servants with experience from earlier post-conflict situations and
a large number of NGO workers had developed. Their role was
enhanced by a growing body of empirically based statebuilding litera-

ture which extolled the possibilities for social engineering. It is indicative that Francis Fukuyama, who had proclaimed the end of history when the Berlin Wall came down, now wrote a book on statebuilding and world order.[1] It was the latest in a growing list of how-to manuals which denied that knowledge was a limiting factor; capital could be safely invested if proper strategies and sequencing were followed. On top of the how-to list was the need to establish a monopoly of force, reform public administration, and secure and regulate the inflow of capital. In post-2001 Afghanistan, something as basic as currency reform, for instance, was urgently needed; the afghani was nearly worthless while several other currencies were in use, including one issued by General Dostum in the north.

The sense of confidence—verging on hubris—in the aid community was expressed by a high-ranking UNDP official who in January 2002 called in representatives of NGOs and international organizations and declared that this time it would be done right, down to details of salary regimes. There would be no more poaching of local, skilled personnel by well-funded international organizations, no more outlandish salaries for foreign consultants. Instead, a regime of strict salary control and genuine local capacity building would be instituted.[2] The official soon proved wrong. Hopes for a strict salary regime went out the window as soon as billions of aid money and international consultants started rolling in, although currency reform was indeed instituted fast and effectively.

Salary levels and currency reform constituted some of the nuts and bolts of statebuilding. In a macro-level perspective, the key words were capital, coercion and legitimacy. The contemporary literature on statebuilding drew from a broader analysis of how states had developed historically through accumulation of capital, centralization and control over the means of coercion, and the enhanced power of rulers to access both resources by appearing as legitimate. Exemplified by the work of the social historian Charles Tilly, this literature spoke of state formation as a broader historical process rather than statebuilding as a feat of social engineering.[3] Still, it offered something that could be mined.

The key issue for internationally assisted statebuilding was to what extent, and in what manner, capital, coercion and legitimacy could be effectively supplied from outside. A strong case could be made for the importance of technical assistance in areas such as demobilization, elections and human rights monitoring, as well as aid to sound recon-struction projects.[4] But this did not add up to statebuilding. Nor did it address the critical legitimacy component. Some analysts argued that international peace operations provided both external legitimacy (to the outside world) and internal legitimacy (within the country), as Bar-nett Rubin argued early and forcefully with respect to Afghanistan.[5] Other analysts were more sceptical. An intrusive foreign presence, Richard Caplan noted, could affront nationalist sentiments and weaken the internal legitimacy of the post-war order.[6] Over time, the general dilemmas and contradictions that accompanied external pro-vision of capital, coercive force and, above all, legitimacy became increasingly evident.[7] This was also the case in Afghanistan.

Capital

Of the three key ingredients of statebuilding, capital was plentiful in post-Taliban Afghanistan. The illegal drug economy generated income and foreign exchange, the value of which by mid-decade was com-monly estimated to about half of the (legal) GDP. The other main income, roughly in the same order of magnitude, was foreign aid, cal-culated more precisely by the IMF as the equivalent of 49.5 per cent of GDP in the 2009–10 fiscal year.[8] US assistance alone was just under $10 billion in the same year.[9] From a statebuilding perspective, both sources of capital were problematic. The sheer size of the aid sector created extreme dependence, weak local ownership and corruption. The drug sector represented a vast, illegal structure of power—a quasi-state of sorts—that undermined the legitimacy of the state.

The forces driving Afghanistan's drug economy were many and powerful. Ready alternative livelihoods were lacking, and eradication campaigns were counterproductive in the context of an insurgency that recruited among poor farmers and un- or underemployed youth. 'Narco-mafia' networks obtained protection from the international military forces by contributing intelligence or manpower to the war against the Taliban and Al-Qaeda. The networks extended into high levels of the Afghan government to give further protection, and were shielded by a mostly ineffective police and a weak judiciary.[10] With the international community firmly refusing to legalize poppy production, the wealth could not be harnessed by the state but remained in the 'shadow economy', as Jonathan Goodhand called it.[11] Hence it provided life-saving income to farmers and sustained trading networks, but also fed a political economy of crime, corruption and violence that undermined a statebuilding process designed to provide public goods and protect the rights of people.

As for foreign aid, it was evident already by the middle of the decade that foreign donors were creating a rentier state unparalleled in Afghan history and nearly unique in the world of international assistance. A rentier state is characterized by heavy reliance on income from foreign aid, or extraction and export of natural resources, rather than revenue from domestic production, trade and services. Rentier states have several weaknesses. First, they inhibit democratic accountability. With easy income from foreign donors or extractive industries (often run by foreign corporations), rentier rulers have few if any incentives to create long-term bargains with their subjects in ways that promote democratic accountability.[12] Where foreign aid is the source of rents, structures of accountability instead run towards the donors. Secondly, rentier rulers are unlikely to develop effective administrations; they do not need to 'bargain with their producers over taxes, establish fiscal accountability towards tax-payers or build autonomous capable bureaucracies...'[13] Thirdly, they are vulnerable to external shocks over which they have little or no control. If rents suddenly end, states constructed on such income are likely to implode and become genuinely 'failed states'. The Somalia of Siad Barre, where the entire state apparatus was based on patronage financed by foreign aid generated by Cold War rivalries, is a classic example. Closer to home, the same dynamic felled the last Communist government in Afghanistan in 1992.

Despite these well-known weaknesses, and the fate of Najibullah in fresh public memory, the post-Taliban order in Afghanistan soon acquired the essential features of a rentier state. Foreign aid totally dwarfed domestic sources of revenues, a situation that remained unchanged throughout the decade.

Building a Rentier State

In the beginning, aid flowed in at a relatively modest rate. In the first year after the invasion it was around US$1.5 billion, mostly in humanitarian assistance. The volume then picked up to about $2.5 billion (FY 2003–04), and by mid-decade had doubled to around $5 billion a year.

While critics argued that this was grossly insufficient, and later cited it as evidence for the lost opportunity thesis discussed in chapter 1, there were also voices of prudence. Given Afghanistan's low absorptive capacity and small domestic revenue volume, the World Bank warned that aid flows in the magnitude of $2.5 billion a year were already 'very high' in relation to GDP—a customary indicator not only of dependence and absorptive capacity, but also of rentier status.[14]

The diverse aid scene makes it virtually impossible to obtain exact figures—even the Afghan government has problems tracking the totals—but it is clear that from mid-decade onwards the aid volume increased rapidly. Of the total $46.1 billion delivered in aid and tracked by the Afghan government for the entire period (2002–09), it seems that around two-thirds was disbursed during the second half of the decade.[15] This amounted to around $8 billion a year for this period—a huge amount for an economy the size of Afghanistan's, even if the illegal sector is not taken into account. The Afghan government estimate, moreover, seems rather on the low side. The United States alone, for which relatively complete figures are available, committed an average of $7.3 billion per year in the period 2006–09, with the first major increase in 2007.[16]

By the standards of the day—which was before the Iraq war changed the scale of reconstruction costs—the first donor conference in Tokyo in January 2002 was a success.[17] A pledge of $5.1 billion was sizeable, in fact it was exactly the same amount planned by the World Bank and the European Commission for the reconstruction of Bosnia and Herzegovina after the 1995 peace agreement. Presented in a $5.1 billion Priority Reconstruction and Recovery Programme and described as 'massive', the Bosnia programme was fully subscribed by donors over the next four years. After that there were no more joint, massive lifts.[18] In the case of Afghanistan, by contrast, donors agreed only two years after Tokyo to add another $5.6 million for reconstruction.

The response indicated Afghanistan's special status. A total of sixty countries and fifteen international organizations had assembled to pledge their support in Tokyo (and more attended subsequent meetings). Afghanistan was the front line in the US-led 'War on Terror'. Numerous governments had rallied behind the American invasion, driven by strategic interests as well as the emotional impact of the attacks on New York and Washington. Afghanistan was also the place where the Taliban had suppressed women, blown up the giant Buddha statutes and staged spectacles of public executions; it was the home of the fabled *mujahedin* who had fought back the Soviets and, in much of the Western public discourse, a country with a whiff of Orientalist mystique. The objective needs, moreover, were undisputed. Afghanistan had been one of the poorest countries in the world even before it was stricken by two decades of violence and social dislocation. A needs assessment carried out for the UN humanitarian agencies in mid-2001, on the eve of the invasion, found that aid agencies had extreme difficulties prioritizing since everything—food, health, education, shelter—was critically needed in so many places.[19] With the state apparatus nearly in ruins, funds were required to create immediate capacity in public administration as well. The early pledging conferences took place amid a sense of starting from near zero.

Meeting again in Berlin in 2004, donors concluded that the situation was more serious than before and additional infusions were necessary. Earlier optimism had given way to a growing realization that statebuilding and reconstruction would be a long, hard slog. A sense of urgency was injected from another front as well. Just before the donors met, the Madrid train bombing had taken place, killing 191 and wounding around 1,800 persons. The event drove home the apparently growing threat of international terrorism and reinforced the original rationale for regime change in Afghanistan.

The aid organizations had by this time become a powerful lobby for more assistance. Afghan NGOs, which had rapidly grown in numbers, joined the large international organizations to call for additional funds to address the vast problems of destruction, dislocation, poverty, neglect and abuse. Yet the aid organizations appeared more concerned with maximizing funding than with ensuring that the funds were spent effectively and in support of the larger statebuilding agenda. For instance, one widely cited report issued by CARE argued that Afghanistan was receiving much less aid than other post-conflict countries, that it was in fact disadvantaged in the order of 1:20.[20] The claim was based on per capita comparisons with small countries like East Timor (population 0.9 million), Kosovo (pre-conflict population 2.2 million) and Rwanda (pre-conflict population 7.2 million), as against Afghanistan's estimated 24 million people in 2003, which raised issues of scale.

The more serious problem with comparisons like this was that they ignored issues of absorptive capacity. To efficiently spend foreign aid in the order of several billion dollars a year required an administrative infrastructure that was lacking in the early post-Taliban period. International aid organizations and consultants were consequently employed to manage the money flow; they soon formed the backbone of a virtual parallel administration. This did produce immediate results, although in the longer term it meant importing rather than building capacity that could support a national statebuilding process. In a more narrow organizational perspective, importing both capital and expertise was, of course, also in the interest of the international aid organizations and consultant firms.

There was also some hard lobbying and careful preparation on the Afghan side. In preparation for the donor meeting in Berlin, leading technocrats and reformers had worked with the international financial institutions and the UNDP to prepare a detailed framework for reconstruction assistance. The result—*Securing Afghanistan's Future*—was a comprehensive seven-year plan for development, complete with a costing estimate of $28.5 billion in aid requirement.[21] Massive infusions of aid were justified by what the report described as a critical turning point in the post-war order. Signs of a vicious cycle that could stall or reverse the reconstruction were already evident in the form of a fast-growing illegal drug economy, recalcitrant warlords, a weak state, and mounting popular disillusionment with a new order that had not delivered the expected peace dividend. Unless the international community came forth with billions of fresh capital, Afghanistan would turn into a 'narco-mafia state', the Finance Minister, Ashraf Ghani, warned, dismissing the previous $5 billion pledged in Tokyo as 'peanuts'. A massive inflow of capital, on the other hand, could kick-start a 'virtuous cycle' of growth and stability, supported by an effective but lean state, Ghani argued.

The government's plea for heavy external funding can also be understood as a variation on Jean-François Bayart's theory of *extraversion* as a political strategy. Developed with reference to the colonial penetration of Africa, Bayart's thesis is that aspiring African elites invited relationships of external dependence in order to collect rent to advance their position vis-à-vis rivals or population groups at home.[22] Similarly, the Berlin conference represented an opportunity for Afghan technocrats and reformers to stake their claim to shape the country's future and, in the process, secure their position vis-à-vis rivals at home—particularly the old guard of *mujahedin* and warlords, but also other reformers. Favoured technocrats could draw on their support in the donor community to build powerful bureaucratic empires and related political constituencies, and they needed to do so before the international community shifted its attention to another international crisis area, above all Iraq.

The Minister of Finance and the Minister of the newly-created Ministry of Reconstruction and Rural Development (MRRD) were especially well positioned in this regard. Both were technocrats who spoke the language of the donors and had gained their trust. Ghani had just returned from the United States and a long-time position in the World Bank. The MRRD Minister, Haneef Atmar, had an NGO background and a postgraduate degree in reconstruction from England. His first ministry had been created with the help of donors to circumvent the Ministry of Agriculture, which was run by a member of 'the old guard' and ineffective. The MRRD soon became the principal recipient for reconstruction and development funds; it stood to gain more if total funds increased. Large inflows of aid capital would significantly enhance the power of the Ministry of Finance as well, especially if channelled through the government, as Ghani strongly advocated. Both Ghani and Atmar had political ambitions, Ghani openly so by running for president in 2009.

The Berlin conference responded positively with pledges of $5 billion. That lasted two years. In 2006, a new conference was held, this time to mark the end of the transitional process outlined in the Bonn Agreement that had culminated with the parliamentary elections in September 2005. The London conference in January the following year was called to define the terms of the future relationship between the government and the donors. The conference reflected the changed situation. Given that progress on almost all fronts of the reconstruction project had been slow, and that a new war was developing in the east and southeast, the donors were anxious to prevent backsliding and wanted to set conditions to ensure progress in the future. The Afghan government, for its part, had an interest in maintaining the kind of external financial and military support on which its survival depended, but also in influencing the terms of the relationship. A measure of formal legitimacy bestowed by the elections served to enhance its bargaining power vis-à-vis the donors. The result was the *Afghanistan Compact*, a virtual contract between donors and the recipient that laid out mutual obligations with benchmarks and a timetable for achievement, and pledges of $8.7 billion in fresh money.[23]

By this time, as noted in chapter 1, a few aid workers and analysts were warning that the large aid presence raised troublesome questions of sustainability, accountability and legitimacy. The aid flow was destined to overwhelm local absorptive capacity and—combined with the parallel structures that followed in its wake to administer the money—would undermine the principle of local ownership. The project in this form did not seem sustainable and invited a political backlash among the Afghans.[24] International financial institutions had critical but more specific concerns. IMF reports on macro-economic developments noted the low ratio of domestic revenue collection to GDP. World Bank reports drew attention to problematic budgetary implications of the very large Afghan National Army being planned. Neither the general criticism nor the more specific concerns of the international financial institutions had much impact.

The international project to create a new, post-war Afghanistan had gathered a seemingly unstoppable momentum. Criticism and doubt were overshadowed by institutional interests in spending aid money and the competitiveness among aid actors; international public awareness of the sufferings of the Afghan people and the strategic imperatives of the 'War on Terror' continued to play a part. Their combined force brushed aside a sense of proportionality that was a well-known and accepted premise of aid. The importance of genuine local ownership that had framed the initial plans for a light footprint was gone. Even the American analyst Barnett Rubin, whose magisterial and widely read political history of Afghanistan had examined the problems of the rentier state in earlier periods of Afghan history under Daoud and the Communists, now adopted the opposite logic, publicly and repeatedly calling for more aid.[25]

The juggernaut moved on. Two years later, at the donor meeting in Paris, anxiety and conflict had deepened. The insurgency was growing at a fast rate, and so was corruption in the government. The two were linked insofar as corruption and poor governance weakened popular support for the government and strengthened the appeal of the insurgents. But new problems had also generated fresh approaches and initiatives on the governance front that seemed to suggest additional investment was warranted. The government was taking formal steps to address the corruption problems by ratifying the UN Convention against Corruption and establishing a High Office of Oversight and Anti-Corruption. Both events took place shortly after the Paris conference in June 2008. While evidence from other countries was that anti-corruption commissions had little if any value, it was a straw for donors to grasp.

Another initiative in the governance sector attracted donor support as well. A new agency to strengthen sub-national administration, the Independent Directorate of Local Governance (IDLG), had recently been set up and was led by a technocrat-reformer, Jelani Popal, who had the confidence of key donors. The agency was designed to improve the quality of sub-national administration and harmonized with the new donor emphasis on decentralization and bottom-up statebuilding, rather than the top-down strategies adopted after 2001 which had focused on creating administrative capacity at the central level. There was nothing *a priori* to suggest that state-building at the local level would be any easier or escape the tensions that plagued the process on the central level. On the contrary, working on the sub-national level would seem to require a great deal of knowledge of local conditions, including language capabilities. Even donors heavily involved in both the aid and military sectors had not made much investment in this direction, as noted above (chapter 4). Nevertheless, 'bottom-up state-building' seemed to offer fresh solutions to the increasingly complicated and troublesome Afghan venture. Another allocation of $14 billion was pledged. As in the military sector, new strategies seemed to offer fresh hopes and steady the project when it became mired in new and unforeseen difficulties.

The most significant actor that shaped the overall aid picture was the United States. American economic and military assistance represented about half of all assistance during the early years after 2001, but rose sharply towards the end of the decade. Most US aid was channelled bilaterally and military assistance was often not included in the biannual pledging meetings. Between half and two-thirds of all US assistance in the 2007–09 period was in the security sector, totalling $15.8 billion, which paid the salaries, equipment and facilities of the fast-growing Afghan army, police and other security forces.[26]

The Rentier State in Operation

Rentier states had existed in Afghanistan before, but on a distinctly smaller scale. Foreign aid had been important to the developmentalist state promoted by president Daoud in the 1970s, although it accounted for 'only' some 40 per cent of all expenditures.[27] The Communist governments that followed had initially received significant revenue from export of gas and other commodities and expenditure was limited. Compared with present donors, the Soviet government was quite tight-fisted. The Soviet military approach, for a start, had not been based on a counterinsurgency strategy that entailed large outlays for development and governance.[28] To the extent that such projects were undertaken, they were part of the 'political work' of government officials and not a major aid category.[29] Available statistics suggest that aid accounted for half of the government's total expenditure during the year of the Soviet invasion (1979), going down to one-third in the 1980s before Soviet troops were withdrawn.[30] By comparison, foreign aid financed around 90 per cent of all official expenditure in post-Taliban Afghanistan during most of the post-invasion years, declining only slightly towards the end of the decade.[31]

Foreign funds covered basic functions of the post-Taliban state—including salaries or salary support for senior civil servants and salaries of the army and police—as well as most development expenditure. Two-thirds of all aid money was spent directly by donors through subcontractors of their choice. Afghan authorities had no control over these funds and did not have full information about their magnitude and purpose. This so-called 'external budget' dwarfed the government budget. The arrangement was an extreme expression of the principle of 'shared sovereignty', advocated in some academic and aid circles as a means to rescue failed states and reduce corruption in post-conflict countries.[32] Yet it signalled a first-order dependence on external donors that mocked declared policies of local ownership and made basic state functions subject to the variable interests and funding capacity of foreign donors. Over time, a greater measure of government control was introduced as domestic revenue increased slightly and donors channelled more funds through the national budget. By 2009, 'only' half of the national budget (called 'core budget') was covered by foreign grants, but the bulk of the aid money still went through 'the external budget'.[33]

A second feature of the Afghan rentier state was its self-perpetuating dimension. Thus, although domestic revenue increased slightly and more aid money was channelled through the government budget, donors also spent more money directly through subcontractors. Similarly, international consultants had been ubiquitous in the national

127

administration soon after the invasion, but a new class of skilled Afghan government officials had come into being towards the end of the decade. Known as 'the second civil service', these officials received heavy salary support from donors. By early 2010, donors paid an estimated $45 million a year in salary support to some 6,600 Afghan officials in various ministries and government agencies. The main supporters were the World Bank, the United States, the United Kingdom and the UNDP.[34]

The large inflow of aid money in the second half of the decade set in motion a negative spiral that affected reconstruction and capacity building. With existing institutions unable to handle large and multiple contracts, corruption increased; this led to more fiduciary controls and slower budget execution, which in turn generated demands for more aid and consultants in order to produce results. The trend peaked with the US-led surge in 2010 in both the military and the civilian sector. While budget execution of some ministries around mid-decade had been around 40–50 per cent, by the end of the decade it had slowed to around 25 per cent for the core budget as a whole.[35] The government clearly had problems 'moving the money'. The overall result of this process was heightened bureaucratic activity that meant a lot of work for technical advisers and consultants of all kinds, while in the countryside ordinary Afghans were still waiting for the peace dividend.

The relationship between the donors and the Afghan government rested on an element of mutual dependence, which tended to perpetuate Afghanistan's dependence on foreign capital and expertise, but also represented a certain security for the future. The Western-led coalition and the major donors could not simply or easily abandon the project. A World Bank report on public administration reform in 2008 had concluded that 'many functions expected of government are still performed by the international community or not performed at all. Realistically, this will remain the case for many years to come'.[36] Yet, only two years later, underlying concerns about the vulnerability of public structures and services funded largely by foreign aid surfaced when the Obama administration led NATO into an exit-strategy mode scheduled to start in mid-2011.

If financial dependence were to be reduced, the most direct way of doing so would be to increase domestic revenue, as the international financial institutions had consistently urged the government to do. By mid-decade, domestic revenue was about 5 per cent of the (legal) GDP, a level well below that of even very poor countries, the World Bank had warned in 2005.[37] By the end of the decade, the ratio had grown only marginally to 8 per cent and the rate of change was then expected to flatten out; the increase reflected additional taxes in 2009 that were a one-time event.[38]

The problem of domestic revenue mobilization was not exclusively a result of the rentier condition. Early Afghan statebuilders had recognized the challenge. As Abdul Rahman Khan had lamented in the late nineteenth century, '[o]ne quarter of the money which is rightly mine, I get without trouble; one quarter I get by fighting for it; one quarter I do not get at all; and those who ought to pay the fourth quarter do not know into whose hands they should place it'.[39] Then, as now, the main problem was the weak grip of the central state on the provinces where wealth was created, in particular provinces astride the central trading routes. Local rulers in Herat, Kandahar and Mazar e-Sharif jealously guarded the customs collections. The Iron Emir nevertheless fought hard for 'his' money, in part because he received only modest subventions from the British in India and had strong incentives to raise his own revenue.

By contrast, the post-Taliban government had more generous international patrons as well as strong local adversaries, some of whom had been recently empowered by the US military to help fight Islamic militants. When Karzai in 2004 finally moved against the 'warlord' of Herat, Ismail Khan, the operation was remarkable in two respects. First, subduing the western strongman required a military operation involving the deployment of 1,500 government troops to the province, and Karzai only sent in army troops when assured of support from both local rivals of Ismail Khan and the US military.[40] Second, the objective was partly to access Herat's rich customs pickings but more generally to break Ismail Khan's powerful hold on the western region. As it turned out, the move against the long-time ruler of Herat was a singular event.

During the second half of the decade, the insurgency and related politics of co-opting local strongmen increased the difficulty of extending the taxation reach of the central government in the provinces. Smuggling and other forms of tax evasion were rife, while the fast increasing aid flow reduced the political incentives to collect revenues. With these constraints, it is noteworthy that the Ministry of Finance could point to any increase in tax collection at all during the second half of the decade. The achievement was due to three main factors. First, provincial governors appointed by Kabul had an interest in funnelling revenue to the centre in order to maintain their bargain with the President. This did not prevent them from levying additional taxes and fees of various kinds that went into their own coffers.[41] Secondly, the growing professionalization of the ministry and its considerable staff of foreign-funded advisers were starting to show results. Moreover—and unlike rentier states based on natural resources extraction—the Afghan government was constantly pressed by donors and the international financial institutions to undertake reforms and willing to pay for 'a second civil service' to implement them.

The Second Civil Service

The development of the 'second civil service' illustrates the transformative but self-perpetuating nature of rentier dependence. Soon after 2001, foreign advisers had been ubiquitous throughout the national administration. Donors demanded quick and visible results for the benefit of their domestic publics and to show the Afghans that the new order could deliver both security and reconstruction. With aid inflows exceeding Afghan state capacity, which was nearly nil, capacity in the form of international consultants was imported on a large scale. At the same time, efforts were made to reform government ministries and make greater use of skilled Afghans in line with the principles of local ownership and cost-effective use of aid money. Under a programme started in 2003 (Priority Restructuring and Reform, PRR), special salary scales were introduced for merit-based appointment of Afghan nationals in ministries selected for reform. The aim was to establish a cadre of skilled technical and managerial staff which would progressively replace civil servants hired under patronage systems and lacking qualifications required for the post-2001 bureaucracy.[42] With skilled Afghans in huge demand by international agencies and organizations, and limited supply despite significant number of returnees, wages were immediately pressed far above regular civil service rates. The result was a two-tiered Afghan civil service with an upper tier of senior advisers and technical staff who were not part of the regular civil service and received donor salary support, easily running into $10,000 a month for a senior position.

The 'second civil service' thus became another thread in the web of Afghan dependence on external money. Moreover, the Afghan advisers did not appreciably replace the international consultants, but mostly added to them. The situation in the Ministry of Finance, considered the most restructured and reformed of all the ministries, is striking. In early 2003 the Ministry was given 30 international and 200 Afghan technical advisers under a programme financed by USAID and implemented by the consultancy firm BearingPoint. Six years later, in 2009, the Ministry had 70 international consultants and 300 Afghan technical advisers, with all the Afghans on salary support amounting to full salaries from donors.[43] In the Budget Office alone, the UNDP financed 70 out of 105 positions.[44]

Launched as a reform initiative, the 'second civil service' had by the end of the decade mutated into a creature with dysfunctional effects. Donor willingness to provide salary support was now driven by the deteriorating security situation and attempts to turn things around before transitioning to full 'Afghanization'. But the scheme reduced the incentives of the government to take budgetary responsibility for the Afghan advisers and integrate them into the regular civil service, which would have serious budgetary implications. When a programme was terminated, so often were the services of the 'technical advisers' who could readily find employment elsewhere in the national or international sector. In the Ministry of Education, for instance, the appointments of 490 Afghan technical advisers funded by USAID were terminated when the programme came to an end.[45] As a result, institutional capacity that could reduce long-term dependence was not being built.[46]

Another question was whether the salary support scheme tended to inflate rather than reform the state. The prospect of a generous salary created an obvious temptation to create positions regardless of need. A US government audit cited a case where 30 of 70 positions on international salary support in one government agency alone were assessed as superfluous.[47] More generally, *ad hoc* arrangements for employment contracts, competition among donors to get their pet projects adequately staffed, and a plethora of scales and rates led to waste, a conflictual working environment, poor organizational morale and invited corruption, a World Bank study concluded. Not only were favours traded for well-paid jobs, but petty bribery flourished: 'The wide variation in pay across comparable jobs ... creates a perception among the core civil service, that it is outclassed and out-paid, and that corruption is a valid means of levelling the playing field in this regard'.[48]

The capital-intensive approach to statebuilding did produce some relatively well-functioning government agencies, although within the long-term structural constraints of dependence on foreign funding. By the end of the decade, USAID rated five out of the nineteen government agencies that it supported as requiring moderate or little external assistance, largely because of the 'second civil service'.[49] The MRRD, the Ministry of Public Health and the Ministry of Finance were among the best ones. All had strong, professional leadership that worked closely with the donors. The MRRD, as mentioned, was a new entity, created by the donors. Its flagship programme, the National Solidarity Programme, was financed by the World Bank and initially managed by the German aid agency GTZ. The Ministry of Health delegated delivery of its primary health care units (Basic Package of Health Services) to NGOs and had a relatively small in-house administrative staff.

Corruption

Rentier states are not necessarily corrupt, but states with very high levels of foreign aid are likely to also have high levels of corruption, recent studies show.[50] Corruption in Afghanistan had caused concern already by mid-decade; during the second half it became 'pervasive, entrenched, systemic and by all accounts ... unprecedented in scale and reach', a report prepared for USAID concluded.[51] A major issue domestically as well as in relations with the donors, corruption ranged from petty daily occurrences to formation of dedicated networks that brought its members huge earnings. It came in many forms—bribery, extortion, rent-seeking through kick-backs, sale of office, patronage, manipulation of procurement processes and prevention of scrutiny. The police, prosecuting authorities and the court system generally failed to deal with the problem, particularly major cases. In this respect, some Afghans said, the legal system was like a spider's web: too thin to catch anything but the smallest insect. The extent of corruption was documented in several reports and regularly placed Afghanistan near the bottom of the list issued by Transparency International.[52] The magnitude was suggested by the arrival in the United Arab Emirates of one of the country's two Vice-Presidents, Ahmed Zia Massoud, reportedly carrying $52 million in cash, which he 'was ultimately allowed to keep without revealing the money's origin or destination.'[53]

Spectacular corruption was hardly surprising given that the country's wealth originated primarily from two sources—an illegal drug economy that required protection, and a vast, sudden influx of foreign aid and billions of dollars' worth of contracts issued by foreign organizations and militaries. The money flow simply overwhelmed the country's social and institutional capacity to deal with it in a legal and socially acceptable manner. This was not unique to Afghanistan. Underlying reasons for corruption are usually traced to weak formal institutions of control and the predominance of social norms and practices that favour patronage and clientelism in social exchanges and obligatios.[54] Societies in transition are particularly vulnerable insofar as norms and formal institutions that frame the social order are in flux. On all these accounts, Afghanistan fitted the bill. There was also a perception among many Afghans that the international presence itself entailed diverse forms of corruption, whether or not formal procedures were followed. Multiple sub-contractors, high overheads and large sums spent by donors in numerous and seemingly impenetrable ways through the 'external budget' appeared as so many ways for outsiders to enrich themselves on Afghanistan's misfortune.[55] The operations of the external sector muddied the waters about what was right and wrong and the appropriate definition of corruption. Was it merely the abuse of public office for private gain?

Aid flows were only one source of foreign-generated wealth in the post-Taliban order. The large international presence of troops, aid workers and consultants during the second half of the decade was another important source. Together, the inflows created an aid-and-war economy with an atmosphere of easy money that encouraged permissive strategies, reinforced by the prospect that the boom would not last. Huge contracts created a bidding frenzy among Afghans as well as international companies. The US Department of Defense, for instance, authorized work contracts in Afghanistan for $11.5 billion in two years alone (2007–09).[55] Not surprisingly, Afghans competing against established US companies like Louis Berger Inc. and large Turkish construction companies used whatever comparative advantage they had in the form of patronage and political access. One Afghan official explained to diplomats the 'four stages' for skimming money from American development projects: 'when contractors bid on a project, at application for building permits, during construction, and at the ribbon-cutting ceremony'.[57]

Donors tried to reduce corruption primarily through monitoring, liberalization procedures and capacity building. International staff or 'second civil service' advisers were assigned to improve Afghan public financial management. Efforts were made to liberalize the state sector and reduce bureaucratic regulations, largely a heritage from Daoud's state in the 1970s and the Communist period. Extensive regulation invited large as well as petty bribery; getting an electricity connection in Kabul, for instance, formally required twenty-three signatories. Assessing progress in 2009, a World Bank study found serious obstacles remained.[58] Improving the quality of the civil service through merit-based appointments, for instance, met with opposition from vested interests within the administrative apparatus and in political circles, which cited Afghan traditions and political culture. In one case, the Ministry of Interior in flagrant violation of all rules substituted its own list of district governors for a list developed by the Afghan Civil Service Commission bodies, criticizing 'the incompetence of [civil service] commissioners ready to appoint people no one knows about', particularly in politically sensitive areas.[59]

There were issues of scrutiny on the donor side as well. The diversity of funds and channels used by donors contributed to an opaque fiduciary environment. The 'external budget' financed relief or development projects executed through NGOs and other subcontractors, various salary support schemes, equipping of the Afghan army and the police, and related items in the aid-and-war economy. National ISAF contingents had discretionary funds for intelligence or development to 'win the hearts and minds' of the people. Discretionary funds available to US military commanders in 2010–11 alone were estimated at $1.5 billion.[60] The huge international presence meant funds were flowing in multiple directions—for rent of properties and lease of land for bases, for construction for the military, hire of private security companies and private militias and for sundry services. To what extent donors effectively monitored this money flow to prevent corruption involving Afghans, their own nationals, or other nationals was an open question. Recognizing the problem, the US Congress in 2008 established a Special Inspector General for Afghanistan Reconstruction (SIGAR) to track the spending of some categories of US funds. Within Afghanistan, security constraints increasingly prevented controls through on-site monitoring of projects. For instance, USAID was able to conduct on-site monitoring of only fourteen of forty projects in 2009, leaving it uncertain how the money was being used, and by whom.[61]

The magnitude of corruption in post-Taliban Afghanistan distorted the statebuilding venture in several ways. First, it contributed to a political economy that reinforced the rentier state and all its problematic features. The dynamic was simple. Political access gave privileged entry to bid for contracts from the foreign militaries, donors, international aid organizations and the government, or to obtain a government licence for businesses that served the international presence. Windfalls from contracts financed the politics of patronage that further enhanced the power and status of the agents involved, and bought further access. In this cycle, incentives were structured only one way—to perpetuate the system. Insofar as a large part of the money flow during the second half of the decade was spent by foreign militaries or for Afghan security forces, it also helped to sustain the war economy.

The pattern was evident on the national as well as the subnational level. One small but telling example from Kabul, for instance, involved the Defence Minister's son, Hamed Wardak. The younger Wardak was CEO of a company which obtained a licence to establish a private security company, enabling him to participate in a fast expanding and lucrative sector that protected military convoys, road construction, and foreign civilian establishments. The license was granted by a government board despite formal regulations on family relationships that made him ineligible.[62]

In the provinces, political access to foreign militaries or Afghan political strongmen likewise generated money. In Kandahar, for instance, key local strongmen and their families reaped immense economic benefits from the international forces' presence in the province, starting with the first Governor, Gul Aga Sherzai, who worked with the American Special Forces during the invasion, and prominently including Ahmed Wali Karzai, a half-brother of the president and arguably the single most powerful man in the province. The sprawling Kandahar Airfield with barracks and mess halls that in 2010 housed 15,000 troops meant huge construction contracts, lease of land, provision of services and the like. Local power brokers monopolized access to these contracts, which, next to drug smuggling, represented a major source of provincial wealth. Ahmed Wali Khan, for instance, provided rented properties and private militias to the Americans which significantly enhanced his wealth. In the district housing the Canadian base, the brother of the district Governor had secured a position as 'trusted local' to Canadian forces, which enabled him to 'control every aspect of development contracting' to maximize his profits and enrich the family, as an internal ISAF memo noted.[63]

The opportunities for enrichment were vastly expanded when the US forces in 2010 moved into a new offensive mode, accompanied by budget authority over millions of dollars in discretionary funds to rebuild areas destroyed during the fighting and win the population over with improved facilities. In Kandahar alone, the US military budgeted for $656 million for such purposes in 2010–11.[64] It was an astounding amount of money for a province with an estimated population of half a million people, equivalent to $650 per head per year if it were evenly distributed, which most certainly would not be the case.

Corruption also struck at the core of the statebuilding project itself. It undermined the internal as well as external legitimacy of the government, which was widely considered complicit, and raised questions among many Afghans about a social order where the newly rich could flaunt their wealth while unemployment and economic insecurity dominated the life of the majority. On this point, at least, the numerous opinion pollsters were unambiguous.[65] All the new wealth was not, of course, attributable to improper access to foreign aid or other income from the international presence—the drug economy was a major source of new wealth. But since nobody knew which sources of income accounted for what wealth, the aid-and-war economy and the drug economy seemed to come together and collectively define a social order marked by corruption and inequality. Popular anger over this state of affairs was behind the appeal of the populist politician Ramazan Bashardost in Kabul, and contributed to the riots in the capital in 2006, while widespread disenchantment with corrupt and abusive authorities in the sub-national administration limited support for the government and played into the hands of the insurgents.

Political Functions and Dysfunctions of the Rentier State

The Afghan rentier state had built-in sources of conflict over ownership and control. Essentially funding the enterprise and supporting it with a large military presence, the foreign patrons tried to establish a thick network of controls—in administrative and fiduciary matters, in political appointments such as governors and police chiefs, and through implicit conditionalities governing the progress of reconstruction and statebuilding, as in the *Afghanistan Compact*. The 'external budget' was an instrument of direct control. Funding a 'second civil service', including 105 positions in the Office of the President, and even the salaries of ministers were indirect instruments of control. Some foreign governments approached the control issue in a straightforward and rather patronizing manner, as reflected in a US embassy report from a meeting between a senior American official and Ahmed Wali Karzai (AWK):

AWK was eager to engage and rarely stopped talking in the two hour meeting. While he presented himself as a partner to the United States and is eager to be seen as helping the coalition, he also demonstrated that he will dissemble when it suits his needs. He appears not to understand the level of our knowledge of his activities, and that the coalition views many of his activities as malign, particularly relating to his influence over the police. We will need to monitor his activity closely, and deliver a recurring, transparent message to him of where[our]redlines are and what we expect of him in the months ahead.[66]

On different levels and in different ways, Afghan political and administrative elites fought back. Some did so openly, most famously the former Finance Minister Ashraf Ghani, who claimed ownership in line with the formal ideology of post-conflict statebuilding. In 2003, Ghani had evicted the consultants assigned to him under a USAID programme administered by the consultancy firm BearingPoint, forcing them to set up office outside the ministry.[67] Ghani also clashed with donors and UN organizations over aid modalities, demanding that all aid money, including relief assistance, be channelled through the government. He was mostly rebuffed, but the issue remained a constant thorn in the aid relationship. All subsequent finance ministers kept pressing the issue, and gained support from some European donors as well as the World Bank.

Ownership-versus-control issues in explicitly political matters came increasingly to be focused on the Office of the President, where Karzai struggled with the foreign supporters of his government on a range of political, judicial and military issues. Western donors intervened regularly in the appointments process, sometimes indirectly as part of civil service reform, sometimes more directly, for instance as part of police training programmes which gave donors a role in vetting appointments of senior police officers, or when a foreign government insisted on removing a governor as a precondition for deploying troops, as the British did in Helmand. Yet Karzai managed the appointment process to suit his own calculus of patronage. He removed some governors who were considered not up to the mark, such as the first Governor in Kandahar, Gul Aga Sherzai—who, however, was reappointed as a governor elsewhere. He agreed with the British to dismiss Governor Sher Mohammed Khan Akhundzada from Helmand, as described above (chapter 4), but placated the family with other important appointments. A similar strategy was followed in Uruzgan, where the Dutch made troop deployments conditional on the removal of Jan Mohammed Khan (called JMK by the foreigners) from the governor's position. JMK was removed, but made adviser to the President, and remained a major power-broker in the province.[68] As Karzai's relationship with his foreign patrons worsened towards the end of the decade and foreign, especially American, officials publicly rebuked him, Karzai seemed to pay even closer attention to appointment matters. He now micro-managed the process in an evident bid to strengthen his domestic base.[69] The predictable result was more conflict with donors.

Similar tension arose in judicial and legislative matters. Karzai used his powers of presidential pardon to interfere with the legal process in order to protect his own network even if it meant crossing important donors. A recent case that attracted much attention involved Mohammad Zia Salehi, a high-level adviser to the President who had been indicted for corruption in late 2010. It was initially an exhibit case for two American agencies, the FBI and the Drug Enforcement Agency, which had trained the special Afghan investigative units that collected the evidence against Salehi. When Karzai intervened, ordering the Attorney General's Office to drop the case, US officials responded with great anger but an even greater show of helplessness. In legislative matters, Karzai likewise balanced contradictory interests in ways to strengthen his domestic political networks. On the eve of the 2009 elections, for instance, he catered to conservative Islamic and Hazara minority interests by signing off a Shia Personal Status Law that had been denounced by Western governments and human rights organizations in the strongest terms, as discussed below (chapter 6).

Funding salaries for 105 staff in the Office of the President clearly did not mean that foreign donors could control Karzai. Disagreement extended to crucial matters of NATO strategy, relations with Iran and Pakistan, and negotiations with the Taliban. As noted above, Karzai had since mid-decade criticized NATO strategies that inflicted heavy civilian casualties and relied on night raids, both of which created deep popular resentment. The tempo of criticism increased during the second half of the decade, seemingly topped by a public rebuke of the strategy pursued by General Petraeus on the eve of NATO's Lisbon meeting in November 2010.[70] Karzai also struck an independent tone in relation to the Taliban and relations with Iran. Taken together, the moves signalled a distancing in his attitude towards his original patrons that a close observer like Ahmed Rashid described as a U-turn in policy.[71]

Dependence, in other words, did not mean ready submission to external control, but often resistance, evasion and lack of compliance. The elites of the rentier state were able to do this because the international project formally celebrated 'local ownership' and because the condition of sovereignty conferred a considerable measure of Afghan autonomy in the constitutional exercise of judicial, legislative and executive powers. Underlying this autonomy was the fact of mutual dependence. Afghan elites had significant bargaining power because of the country's strategic significance to NATO. Unlike rentier states based on natural resources, an aid-dependent strategic state had a major advantage: as with big banks, the patrons could not afford to let it fail.

Strategies used by the Afghan elites to influence policy vis-à-vis their international patrons did not include long-term political institution building by strengthening political parties and the parliament. Instead, the political and technocratic elites that formed the core of the rentier state engaged in short-term survival strategies. These were of at least three kinds. One strategy was to maximize political space for autonomous action by exploiting the many disagreements among donors, for instance regarding the external budget, the importance of merit appointments versus accepting local strongmen as allies in fighting the insurgency, approaches towards judicial reform, and, towards the end of the decade, negotiations with the Taliban. A second approach was to develop short-term bargains with other elite representatives, whether tribal notables, local commanders, former *mujahedin* leaders or religious leaders, in order to create political capital on particular policy issues and possibly longer-term support if and when foreign assistance were reduced. Karzai's appointment management was an expression of this strategy. A third approach was to accumulate capital, as international press reports of cash-laden government officials arriving in the United Arab Emirates suggest (see e.g. Wikileaks Cable reported in The New York Times, 29 November 2010). Capital could be used to trade favours, buy armed followers and obtain political support for the present as well as future contingencies, quite apart from the personal benefits of material gains.

The preference for personalized survival strategies over long-term institution building was partly a function of the rentier state. Dependent on foreign funds and international military forces for their survival, the political leaders had few incentives to develop long-term bargains with their subjects, for example through conventional instruments such as political parties and strong elected assemblies. This orientation was reinforced by the new Constitution, which established a strong presidency, and an election law that penalized the development of political parties, as we shall see in the next chapter. But the penchant for short-term survival strategies also reflected the origin of the regime. Having come to power as a result of the US-led intervention, the post-Taliban elites were diverse, representing exiles, technocrats and various *mujahedin* factions. None had a background in conventional political parties or experience in mobilizing people for social change. Possibly the only exception was the political factions associated with Islamist leaders, notably the Hezb-e-Islami, a wing of which had reconciled with the government, was represented in the Parliament and had adherents in the national and sub-national administration. Given its background in the Muslim Brotherhood and the role of its military faction led by Gulbuddin Hekmatyar during the civil war, however, the party was profoundly distrusted by both Western donors and Afghan reformers.

The contrasting behaviour of the last Communist government in Afghanistan under President Najibullah is instructive in this regard. A rentier ruler of a smaller magnitude, Najibullah was still heavily dependent upon Soviet military and financial assistance. His response to Soviet preparations for withdrawal in 1986–87 was in part to seek out short-term bargains with local leaders. But he also tried to rejuvenate the Communist Party and make it more acceptable by promulgating a new constitution in 1989 that recognized Islam, universal human rights, foreign investment and a neutral foreign policy, and permitted a plurality of political parties. The response was consonant with the regime's origin in a political party, the People's Democratic Party of Afghanistan, developed in the late 1960s and based on a theory of social change made possible by the mobilization and correct leadership of 'the masses'. Najibullah had joined the party's more moderate faction already in 1965, and spent his whole professional life steeped in party politics. When his patron prepared to disengage, Najibullah tried to create a long-term bargain of a different kind with the people and Afghanistan's neighbours. By then it was futile, a gesture that failed to save either the regime or himself.[72]

Coercion

The second constitutive element of statebuilding—coercive force in service of the central state—was initially provided by international forces. As discussed in the previous chapter, ISAF made an essential contribution during the early phase by providing the coercive power necessary to protect the capital, establish the apparatus of the central state, and enforce the political rules for access to power at the central level. In this respect ISAF and, indirectly, OEF formed the military muscle for the implementation of the transition agreement adopted in Bonn. Yet inability to create a monopoly of force was the Achilles heel of the statebuilding venture from the outset, and it became more pronounced over time.

The Elusive Monopoly of Force

The challenge to the state's attempt to establish a monopoly of force did not initially come from the Taliban but from a profusion of nominally friendly, armed groups existing in a shadowy legal zone. Some were part of the Northern Alliance forces that had joined the American forces during the invasion. They had a formal structure, appeared in the international project under the name The Afghan Military Forces, and were slated for demobilization and reintegration after 2001 (DDR).

The DDR programme launched in 2003 by the UN (called Afghan New Beginnings) was imperfect in some ways and subject to the customary forms of cheating—old weapons were turned in and numbers of combatants were inflated to collect more assistance. More important, it did not start until the end of 2003, owing to reservations from the US military, which claimed the forces were needed to fight the Taliban, as well as resistance from the Northern Alliance and a slow-moving UN process. Secondly, the programme targeted only The Afghan Military Forces, not the militias that were working with the US-led coalition, particularly in the south and the east, but were outside the

Northern Alliance structure. The UN official in charge of the pro-gramme put the issue bluntly in September 2003:

In terms of militias that are fighting with the Coalition .... at the moment I am not aware of anything that says that they will be targeted [for demobilization]. I suppose that could happen at a subsequent [time] when we go into the main phase. It all depends how the work with the Coalition proceeds and whether the Coalition is in a position to be able to allow these people to be demobilized.[73]

The dictates of war allowed the militias to firmly establish them-selves, casting a long shadow over the prospects for good governance and the public monopoly of force that was integral to the peacebuild-ing agenda. Recalling the violent years of the early 1990s, villagers in many places complained that 'the bad old militias' were returning. To Afghan and international reformers, as well as human rights activists, the empowerment of the militias was arguably the single most impor-tant flaw in the whole international project.

The DDR programme nevertheless served a critical purpose in the post-war transition by helping key military leaders shift into the polit-ical arena, but without their armed followers. More than 60,000 men were demobilized and given reintegration assistance, a similar number of weapons were collected and the Afghan Military Forces were for-mally disbanded. Solidarity networks remained, making it possible to reconstitute units if the need arose and resources were available. But for the time being, at least, the factional leaders moved into important positions in the national or sub-national administration as ministers, governors, or senior advisers. Political life had its rewards. The leader of the main Tajik armed faction, Mohammed Fahim, was appointed Defence Minister and his close associate, Bismullah Khan, became Chief of Staff of the new Afghan National Army. The Uzbek General Dostum was initially a Deputy Minister of Defence before moving on to other positions, the Hazara leader Muhammad Mohaqiq was dep-uty chairman of the Interim Administration, and so on.

Among the rank and file of combatants, only a very small number went into the newly-constituted Afghan National Army, mainly because they were too old (the upper age limit was twenty-eight). An undeter-mined number joined local militias and semi-private police forces. With roots in the anti-Soviet resistance and the subsequent civil war, these armed groups now reconstituted themselves as part of patronage net-works organized around leaders who had been appointed to key positions in the sub-national administration, particularly as governors and police chiefs.[74] The militias were formally illegal and in this respect on a par with criminal gangs and drug smugglers who preyed on businesses and ordinary villagers, and with whom they often overlapped. Both types were formally targeted in a new programme called 'disbandment of illegal armed groups' (DIAG), which started after the first demobilization programme was completed in mid-2005. The DIAG programme, however, made little headway and soon ground to a halt.

One reason was its administration. Unlike the early DDR programme, which had been designed, funded and led by the internationals, the DIAG programme was formally led by the Afghan government in line with the fast-approaching end of the Bonn transition schedule and the principle of Afghan ownership. The Ministry of Interior was central in the process, and many armed groups—whether linked to local government structures, the drug economy, or both—had protection networks that stretched deep into the Ministry, particularly the police department. Their leaders were often formally on the payroll of the Ministry as officials in the district or provincial administration.[75] Moreover, some armed groups had been or were useful to the coalition forces, and their value increased as the insurgency mounted during the second half of the decade. Already in 2006, the US command started to establish new, local militias to fight the insurgents. Members of the new parliament who had links to armed groups were concerned as well. The Upper House in May 2006 called for the programme to be terminated, citing the need for people to defend themselves.

Against such varied opposition, the DIAG process struggled. In November 2008, the UN estimated that 161 groups had been disbanded, 1,050 individuals arrested, and 5,700 weapons seized. That left an estimated 1,800 groups, with perhaps 120,000 members and 336,000 small and light weapons.[76] At the time, that was about twice the size of the new Afghan National Army, built up after the invasion to serve as the central apparatus of state power in domestic and foreign policy and secure a monopoly of legitimate force.

The Afghan National Army (ANA)

The importance of establishing a national army was recognized by all parties to the Bonn Agreement and even enshrined in a draft of the national development strategy (ANDS), which was prefaced by a line from the ninth-century Islamic scholar Ibn Qutaybah: 'There can be no government without an army...' At first, the build-up of the Afghan National Army (ANA) was slow, reflecting a modest investment and high attrition rates. The total force level in 2005 was only 22,000 men. Then things changed. By mid-2008, the army had tripled in size and the ceiling was set at 88,000. Already in late 2008, the goal was further lifted to 122,000, and, when that was reached in mid-2010, further increased to 171,600 to be reached by October 2011.[77] The targets were again revised upwards in January 2011.[78] It was an extraordinarily fast expansion by any measure, driven initially by the growing challenge from the insurgents, and increasingly by NATO's emphasis on an Afghanization of the war that would permit a drawdown of its own combat forces.

The rapid expansion raised questions about the quality of the new army, related to high illiteracy rates, short training, intra-army ethnic tensions, and ultimately, both fighting effectiveness and political loyalty.[79] Other issues arose from the ANA's dependence on the United States. US forces had already started training and equipping the new army in 2003. By mid-decade, the US funded over half of the government's defence budget, including salaries, logistics, training, construction of recruiting stations, rehabilitation of hospitals, construction of garrisons in the southeast and the south, the establishment and operation of four regional ANA commands (Kandahar, Herat, Gardez and Mazar-e-Sharif), and the formation of the central Army Corps of three infantry brigades in Kabul.[80] By the end of the decade, US military assistance to the ANA had grown to over $4 billion in one year alone (2009), not including the cost of foreign trainers and related items.[81] Funding was mostly channelled through the external budget, which gave the US additional discretionary power. The US in effect determined the size and composition of the Afghan army, although force ceilings were formally decided in cooperation with the Afghan government and, after 2006, by the Joint Coordination and Monitoring Board (JCMB) set up after the London conference to represent Afghan and donor interests.

The funding structure highlighted problems of sustainability. Without very substantial donor funding, the Afghan government could not possibly maintain an army this size. There were also other security forces to be funded, including the national police (ANP), which increasingly had taken on a paramilitary function. The ANP relied heavily on donor funding as well, initially drawing on a multilateral trust fund (LOTFA), but by the end of the decade primarily US bilateral funding.[82] The World Bank had already in 2004 drawn attention to what it regarded as disproportionately large expenditures on security, warning that it could bankrupt rather than support the statebuilding process.[83] Five years later the Army was almost exactly five times larger and the ANP had expanded marked as well, but domestic revenue, as we have seen, remained exceedingly small.

There were foreign policy implications as well. An Afghan army built, trained, equipped and financed by the United States was subject to American influence in numerous direct and indirect ways, from ideological formation to budgetary controls and supply of spare parts. For the United States it meant a proxy army—although of uncertain quality—to support its interests within Afghanistan as well as in the wider region. For the Afghan government, however, it significantly constrained its ability to pursue an independent foreign policy.

The military's role in domestic politics—and, more broadly speaking, the kind of state being built—was another matter of long-term concern. For all its shortcomings, the army was a far stronger institution than the main civilian branches of the state, above all the judiciary, the parliament and parts of the executive branch. There were general reasons for this. Building an army is comparatively easier than building, say, a judicial system, a point noted in a frank assessment by the UN mission in a mid-decade report to the Security Council. Most state institutions were 'extremely weak... only the Afghan National Army programme has been able to encompass the various dimensions of institution-building, from in-depth reform of the Ministry itself, to the vetting and training of officers and soldiers, to post-deployment assistance and mentoring'.[84] That report was made in early 2005. Developments since then showed little evidence of great strides in institution building on the civilian side, particularly those charged with oversight of the military. By contrast, the United States and its NATO allies invested heavily in building up the army.

The imbalance suggested the possibility of a strong military role in politics, perhaps along the lines of Pakistan, or in ways that will recreate Afghanistan's past experience. Although the Afghan military in modern times has not seized and retained political power at the central state level, it has twice executed coups that paved the way for regime change. Army factions played a significant role in both the overthrow of the monarchy in 1973 and the events that led to the April revolution in 1978. Whatever form a strong military role in politics might take, it would be contrary to the declared policy of the UN and the international community to establish a post-Taliban state founded on democratic processes.

(Re)building Local Militias

A more direct challenge to the official policy of building formal state institutions came from a different direction. During the second half of the decade, the Afghan government and its international supporters, particularly the US military, were 'giving in to a cyclical temptation of working with informal armed groups to provide security, particularly in rural areas where the Taleban [sic] are gaining ground', Mathieu Lefèvre wrote in a carefully researched report.[85]

Three types of programmes were started, all of them designed, funded and implemented by the US military; at times Special Forces on the ground took the initiative, with the result that 'practice preceded policy'.[86] The first programme, in 2006, established an auxiliary police force but was quickly abandoned. It was followed by a new pilot programme started in Wardak province just south of Kabul, but this initiative was also abandoned. A third initiative was started by American forces in a decentralized way and was scaled up under General Petraeus in 2010, inspired by the success he claimed to have achieved with Sunni militias in Iraq. The idea in all cases was to create locally recruited militias that were accountable to local councils of elders (*shura*). They would be financed by the United States and would constitute a local line of intelligence about the Taliban. In principle, some of the programmes were placed under the Ministry of Interior, but in design and policy implications they were at odds with the policy of establishing a monopoly of legitimate force, which had been the purpose of the previous DDR and DIAG programmes.

The problematic implications of creating local militias, related to vetting, control and loyalty, are well known, and examples were close at hand in Afghanistan's recent history. President Najibullah established village militias on a large scale to compensate for Soviet military withdrawal, but most crumbled or defected to the *mujahedin*. Two decades later, the US military command in Afghanistan went down the same path, driven by the growing insurgency and the short deadlines set by NATO and the US for showing results, by which measure establishing formal military institutions was too slow a process. As the succession of similar programmes indicates, launching a programme was also an opportunity for US military officials and advisers to demonstrate that new solutions were being developed, in particular on their watch.

The initiatives received some support among donors, who by this time were exploring possibilities for recasting the statebuilding venture towards greater emphasis on decentralization and bottom-up approaches. One result was growing interest in using traditional structures to improve governance and provide justice through informal dispute resolution mechanisms. Extending a neo-traditional approach to security matters seemed a logical next step to some, although European officials were generally more sceptical than Americans.

On the central level, support for the programmes among Afghan officials depended on the degree of consultation and how it affected bureaucratic turf. On the local level, there were different considerations. For ex-*mujahedin* leaders and assorted commanders whose illegal armed groups had been targeted under DIAG, it was an opportunity to regularize their status and get new weapons and salaries. Some of these groups had provided services to aid organizations and the international forces, typically by protecting roads and supply convoys. To some, joining a militia meant acquiring assets for use in ongoing local disputes. In Wardak, for instance, many Tajiks and Hazaras signed up for the evident purpose of strengthening their position in conflicts with Pashtun *kuchi* (nomads) over land and grazing rights. For local officials who acted as middlemen, it was an opportunity to build patronage networks. Some villagers among whom the early pilot programmes were established, however, feared they would bring back the 'bad, old militias' and increase insecurity.

Responding to such concerns, the latest version of the scheme introduced by US Special Forces in Kandahar differed in some respects. The men were not given weapons (they brought their own), and they were not paid on an individual basis. Instead, the community was rewarded with cash-for-work schemes and in turn were expected to keep out the Taliban. As before, the programme was funded and implemented by the US military and an American subcontractor. When General Petraeus arrived in Afghanistan in mid-2010, plans were made to scale up the programme with a target of 30,000 recruits (called 'guardians') within six months. Speed seemed to be of the essence. In the model programme established in Argandhab, Kandahar, General Nick Carter, the head of NATO's southern regional command, was observed asking a local commander 'how quickly' he could recruit men, and how many he could bring 'by tomorrow'.[87] As before, local commanders were catapulted into the role of power brokers, with little or no external vetting of recruits.

The village militias may or may not provide added defence against the insurgents, but their impact on the statebuilding venture was clearly negative. Like earlier schemes, the programme for village 'guardian' units empowered local commanders as powerbrokers and legitimized militias in the name of 'village self-defence'. It added to the existing myriad of armed groups, with or without uniforms—including the Afghan 'special forces' of 3,000 men trained and guided by the CIA—that were not in a command-and-control chain of the Afghan government and did not necessarily serve its interests. It represented yet another reversal of the early transition policy to disarm irregular combatants and illegal forces in order to permit the state to establish a legitimate monopoly of force.

Legitimacy

Statebuilding, as history has amply demonstrated, is a highly conflictual process. In Afghanistan, previous efforts to strengthen the central state invariably courted confrontation with vested interests, above all in the form of local, tribal authorities and large landowners who were faced with demands for taxes and manpower, and from religious leaders who guarded their role in administering justice. Statebuilders who had modernizing visions to radically reform social, economic, legal and educational structures met additional resistance and, invariably, political defeat, as happened to King Amanullah in the 1920s, President Daoud in the 1970s, and the Communist party (PDPA) in the 1980s.

Statebuilding with an ambitious modernizing agenda places particularly great demand on the three foundational pillars of capital, coercion and legitimacy. Of these, legitimacy is particularly valuable because it facilitates non-coercive compliance by generating normative support. Some modernizing statebuilders have drawn on 'traditional' or charismatic sources of legitimacy in Weberian terms. In modern history, feats of active statebuilding have usually had a public purpose that lent added legitimacy to the venture, often couched in nationalist terms. That was above all the case of the two classic statebuilding achievements in the non-colonized world—the Meiji Restoration in

Japan in the late nineteenth century, and the creation of Turkey out of the rump Ottoman Empire in the early twentieth century.

Sources of Legitimacy in National Statebuilding

Both the Meiji leaders and Kemal Ataturk led nationally-driven state-building projects. Western technology and advisers were sought, but on terms that today would be called 'local ownership'. In Japan, the Meiji rebels started the process of transforming Japan from a weak, feudal society into a strong, centralized state; in Turkey, Kemal Ataturk instituted radical reform across the board to create a state with an effective army, a modern public administration and an independent economy. In both cases, sacrifices were made and resistance overcome in the name of saving the nation from foreign threats. In Japan, the arrival of US warships concretized the threat of foreign imperialism; the restoration of the young Emperor to his 'rightful place' gave added legitimacy to what is often described as the Meiji 'revolution'.[88] Similarly, the successor state of the Ottoman Empire was faced with Western occupation, onerous demands imposed after military defeats, and prospects of renewed war. Radical reforms were justified by the need to save the state, adorned with a legitimizing nationalism that rejected everything associated with the disastrous Ottoman past. The Kemalists rewrote history, introduced secular reforms, imposed Western dress codes and calendar and Latinized the writing of the Turkish language.

Foreign threats and impositions, coupled with an acute sense of national weakness, were important driving forces of early Afghan statebuilders as well, and justified in those terms. The two equally classic cases here are Abdul Rahman Khan in the late nineteenth century and King Amanullah in the early twentieth century.

Abdul Rhaman Khan legitimized his reforms with reference to nationalism and Islam. Afghanistan at the time was organized in semi-feudal fiefdoms, divided by tribal wars and weakened by foreign invasions. Imperial powers were pressing in from all sides—the British from India and the Russians from the north—and both were also competing for access from Persia on Afghanistan's western border. While the rivalries of the Great Game could be exploited to Afghanistan's benefit, Abdul Rahman Khan also recognized that he had to strengthen the state. His most important achievement in this regard was to create a standing Afghan Army, thus reducing his dependence on tribal *lashkar*s. To finance the expanding state structure he established small state industries, built infrastructure to promote trade, and introduced tax and currency reforms.

The Iron Emir's ruthless use of power and skilful political tactics accounted in part for his statebuilding achievements. In addition he deftly invoked Islam and appealed to nationalism. He legitimized his control over the courts by making Islam rather than customary law the basis for adjudication, thereby reducing the role of local authorities in the settlement of disputes and to that extent their overall power. The reformed courts thus became 'the basis for the amir's policies of centralization'.[89] Unlike previous Pashtun rulers whose authority had been conferred by tribal assemblies (*jirga*), Rahman Khan invoked Islam to legitimize his rule and defend the nation against foreign threats:

As God wished to relieve Afghanistan from foreign aggression and internal disturbances, He honoured this, His humble servant, by placing him in this responsible position, and He caused him to become absorbed in thoughts of the welfare of the nation and inspired him to be devoted to the progress of this people...for the welfare and true faith of the Holy Prophet Mahomed.[90]

The next great reformer, Amir Amanullah, was acutely aware of the country's weakness. His first priority after becoming king, as he announced in the Royal Manifesto when acceding to the throne, was to revoke the onerous conditions imposed by the British after the Afghan defeat in the Second Anglo-Afghan War (1880). The British at that time had gained control over fiscal, defence and foreign policy, in return for subsidizing Afghan rulers and promising protection against Russia. One of Amanullah's first actions was to launch a surprise attack on the British in what became the third Anglo-Afghan war (1919). An Afghan victory forced the British to end their formal encroachments on Afghanistan's sovereignty, but the Durand Line remained, famously imposed by the British in 1893 to separate the Pashtun population in what was then British India from their Pashtun kin in Afghanistan.

A sense of vulnerability to foreign imperial powers inspired Amanuallah's subsequent reforms. To maintain Afghanistan's independence and enable it to take its place among the modern nations of the world, the King and his mentor, Mahmud Tarzi, envisaged sweeping reforms. While conceived in the spirit of Islamic modernism, the programme to modernize society and strengthen the central state apparatus borrowed heavily from the West and the Kemalists. In addition to constitutional reforms, Amanullah introduced legal and educational reforms, as well as public demonstrations of modernity in the private realm through changes in dress code. Plans to expand and modernize the army and the national administration were under way when the opposition gathered. The ambitious, Western-inspired reforms had alienated a wide range of power holders—'religious, ethnic-tribal, military, administrative and professional notables—who grasped the reforms' objectives and found them threatening to their individual interests in one way or another', as Amin Saikal writes.[91] The King had failed to build a political coalition around the reform programme beyond a small group of modernists. When the *ulama* turned against him he lost religious legitimacy. The army that he had planned to strengthen was still small, poorly paid and disorganized. Amanullah now paid the price for having disregarded the advice he received from Kemal Ataturk when visiting Turkey earlier: If you want to reform the country, first build a strong army.[92] Even the ever-present threat of the British was at this point not enough to save him. On the contrary, the eastern tribes that rose in revolt were evidently ready to cooperate with the arch-enemy to bring down Amanullah. British support for the tribal uprising marked the beginning of the end of the King's brief rule.

Sources of Legitimacy in Internationally Assisted Statebuilding

The reform agenda introduced by the post-Taliban government and its international supporters was more ambitious and radical than Amanullah's policies, and in its modernizing intent resembled that of the PDPA. As before, resistance formed along two main axes. Centre-province relations were shaped by the interest of local power holders in maintaining or increasing their autonomy from the centre, but also in gaining a greater share of power at the centre and influencing national policies. At the centre, the main concern was to extend state control over the provinces in order to extract resources and influence local administration and politics. Centre-province relations were partly cast in terms of identity politics, a result of the greater political saliency of ethnic identity after years of fighting where Tajik, Uzbek, Hazara and Pashtun militias had fought each other and subjected their respective populations to vicious violence. A second and more consistent line of opposition to the modernizing agenda came from conservative, traditional and religious leaders, particularly in ex-*mujahedin* circles, who feared that many of the intended reforms would undermine their status and power, as well as changing Afghan society in un-Islamic ways.

In this contested situation, what were the sources of legitimacy for the new political order? The question went beyond the legitimacy of particular individuals such as Hamid Karzai; it concerned the broader edifice erected with much international support to replace the Taliban regime in order to reconstruct and reform Afghan society.

The main justification for the new order was to establish at least a minimally effective state out of the chaos left by revolution, invasion and civil war. This was implicit in the popular aspirations for peace and security that followed the fall of the Taliban, captured in surveys, public opinion polls and much anecdotal information. The broader rationale was laid out in the preamble to the Bonn Agreement, where the Afghan parties expressed their determination to 'promote national reconciliation, lasting peace, stability and respect for human rights' and embraced 'the principles of Islam, democracy, pluralism and social justice' to guide the future political order.[93] The international project was formally premised on these ideals as well, which were validated in UN resolutions that endorsed the Bonn Agreement and authorized multilateral assistance.

By implication, a state that provided a measure of security, justice, basic social services and 'good governance' would carry its own source of legitimacy. That belief was increasingly expressed in the aid community and other supporters of the government, as well as among Afghan reformers. The problem with a utilitarian source of legitimacy, however, is that it exerts no normative force merely by virtue of its ideational existence; the state has to actually deliver in order to cash in on its legitimacy potential. The same applies to elections. In order to legitimize a political contest, elections have to be seen as reasonably free and fair.

On the whole, the Afghan state did not deliver. True, significant strides were made on the educational and health fronts. Many people prospered, particularly in the northern and central regions, and some individuals became fabulously rich and powerful. Yet the government and its international supporters failed to provide the basic elements of human security in many parts of the country, failed to halt the growing abuse, corruption and incompetence in public administration, failed to stem the mounting insurgency and the perception that the international forces were responsible for excessive or unjustly inflicted violence, and failed to provide a political exit from the war. The liberal democratic vision initially promoted by international and Afghan reformers and supported through numerous governance projects was overshadowed by the daily realities of violence, inequality and corruption, and was fading even in the declaratory policy of donors. Whatever legitimacy was bestowed by the first presidential and parliamentary elections, it seemed lost in the violence and fraud that marred the second round in 2009 and 2010.

That left religion and nationalism as possible legitimizing ideologies. The only Afghan governments to have openly discarded both—the Communist ones—did not long survive. The post-Taliban authorities were careful to recognize the centrality of Islam in law and society in the new constitution and other instruments of authority, but the uneasy balance between state and religion that has shaped the history of modern Afghanistan resurfaced and was sharpened by the reform agenda, particularly in the legal sector (see chapter 7 below). The relationship between the Karzai government, its foreign supporters and Afghan religious authorities remained complicated and at times strained. Invoking Islam to legitimize the Western-supported order was certainly possible, but difficult—the insurgency had appropriated its militant forms and fought to expel the US-led forces, while internationally the West and militant Islam were locked in a wider war. Nationalism was clearly out. A state heavily dependent upon international capital, consultants and foreign military forces to survive could not credibly invoke nationalism as a legitimizing ideology. The only effort in this direction was the government's consistent accusation of Pakistani support for the insurgents, which possibly gained it some nationalist credentials.

For some Afghans, the promise of a liberal order remained the principal source of legitimacy for the post-Taliban order. For others, legitimacy was linked to utilitarian values, in particular the ability of the regime to provide individualized benefits in the form of protection, political positions and economic resources. Vast networks of patronage that delivered such benefits in return for political support became a principal safety net for the governing elites on both the national and the sub-national level. While helping to sustain the regime and the political order it represented, the patronage system was a fragile and fickle source of regime legitimacy. First, it was dependent on continued access to resources through the aid-and-war economy. Secondly, the strategy of co-opting local strongmen has a built-in self-defeating tendency, as Abdulkader Sinno points out.[94] To maintain their loyalty, the central patron must dispense money and weapons.

The main objective of local power holders, however, is to maintain and enlarge their own autonomy. The more they are paid in order to be loyal to the centre, the greater capacity they accumulate to break away from or challenge the centre. 'The currency to buy the short-term loyalty of Afghan local leaders, weapons and money, has always been the means to strengthen their long-term independence', Sinno concludes.[95]

*　*　*

The obvious but important lesson from Amanullah's ill-fated reforms is that ambitious reform of a statebuilding kind requires equivalent power. To the Kemalists, that meant a strong, centralized army, a vanguard party, a nationalist ideology and a popular movement. With those elements in place, capital could be generated domestically, as the new Turkish government succeeded in doing. The statebuilding venture in Afghanistan after 2001, by contrast, had ample capital and armed force, but both elements were provided by external powers. That created a deficit of legitimacy. The Kemalists dealt with that by creating a political party that mobilized people and sustained their ambitious agenda. The Afghans in the post-Taliban order formed neither conventional political parties nor social movements that could sustain an equally ambitious agenda. While the Kemalist model of national statebuilding may belong to an earlier historical period, the heavily internationalized statebuilding project in Afghanistan had elements of colonial practices that were equally out of step with the present, post-colonial era.

6

DESIGNING A DEMOCRATIC TRANSITION

The political transition to establish a new, representative and legitimate government in Afghanistan was in formal terms a success. All the steps outlined in the Bonn Agreement were carried out, on time, and mostly according to prescribed process. Culminating in the parliamentary elections in 2005, the completed transition was a cornerstone in the peacebuilding process and probably the greatest achievement of the international project. By establishing a constitutionally based political democracy with popularly elected government, the transition put in place some principal institutions for resolving social conflict in the political rather than the military arena.

This chapter first looks at the transitional mechanism and the forces shaping it, and then examines the workings of two principal institutions of liberal political democracy—the parliament and elections. These institutions were not, of course, introduced *de novo* in Afghanistan after 2001. From the early 1900s and onwards, constitutions had been promulgated and deliberative assemblies established for a variety of purposes. A brief examination of their history is a useful starting point for understanding the potential and limitations of the post-2001 reforms in this area.

Earlier Reforms: Constitutional Frameworks

The Constitutional Monarchy

Wracked by a turbulent history, modern Afghanistan has had an unusually large number of constitutions. The one promulgated in 2004 was the seventh, not counting the Fundamental Principles by which the early communist regimes ruled.

The first Constitution (1923) was inspired by the constitutional movements in the non-colonized Muslim world of Southwest Asia and the Middle East in the late nineteenth century. Seeking to strengthen their societies against the more powerful Western states, the movements not only borrowed from the principles of the Enlightenment to promote science and education, but also to liberalize the state. Essentially, this meant constitutional restrictions on the power of the ruler. The rulers, on the other hand, looked to Western military technology and public administrative practices as the means to strengthen the state, in the first instance as defence against encroaching Western power. Typically, the short term result was a mixture of state empowerment and liberalizing constitutional reforms.

In Afghanistan, the reforms were spearheaded by King Amanullah and his influential adviser Mahmud Tarzi, who had attended school in Damascus and Constantinople. Their aim was to strengthen and unify the country, particularly against the British threat. Tarzi despaired over the disunity and backwardness of his countrymen—village against village, clan against clan, and all against the city.[1] This virtual anarchy reflected the Afghan addiction to 'negative freedom', he wrote; it was freedom *from* law and common discipline, rather than freedom *through* adherence to law. To ameliorate this condition, Tarzi advocated education and social modernization. As part of this larger vision of progress, Amanullah proclaimed a constitution that turned Afghanistan into a constitutional monarchy.[2]

Modernity and nationalism, and not liberal democracy, framed the Tarzi-Amanullah vision of the future. The Constitution was drafted by the King and his advisers (including a Turkish expert) and prominently included provisions for social and legal reforms. But it also established checks on the monarch by introducing a national assembly (*shura-e melli*) founded on the Pashtun tradition of the deliberative assembly of tribal leaders (*jirga*). The assembly was partly elected, partly appointed and assigned three main functions: (i) *to advise* on matters of what today would be called development policies ('make suggestions to the government for the improvement of industry, commerce, agriculture and education'); (ii) *to petition* regarding irregularities in public administration or taxation, such petitions to carry quasi-judicial force; and (iii) *to complain* about violations of 'basic rights', rights conferred by the Constitution. The assembly was also empowered to review foreign treaties and the national budget. To assist the assembly and ensure what today would be called 'transparency', Article 61 provided for the establishment of an auditing office. For its time and place, it was a liberal document.

The King's modernizing agenda rested on a slim social base and mobilized a wide range of enemies. The combination undid his constitutional reform; only five years after the National Assembly held its first meeting, the King was overthrown and the reform movement ground to a halt. The purpose of the next Constitution (1931) was to legitimize the conservative reaction led by Nadir Khan, a relative of Amanullah who seized power after a brief civil war. The new king called a special deliberative assembly—a *loya jirga*—to approve his accession to the throne, promised to share some power with a national assembly and issued a constitution. The new constitution, duly approved by another *loya jirga*, granted the king extensive powers, but provided for an assembly with an elected and an appointed chamber as Nadir Khan had promised tribal notables and religious leaders the previous year. The rights of the assembly were defined at length in over forty articles that elaborated the advisory and legislative functions introduced by Amanullah.

While having limited power, the assembly was useful for all parties concerned.[3] A seat in the national assembly conferred some status and ensured close proximity to officials whose hands were on the levers of state power. In a tacit bargain, tribal leaders were allowed considerable autonomy in local affairs, but having the *khan* in the capital benefitted the king since his police could keep an eye on those same tribal leaders. More generally, the assembly served as a vehicle for the king to co-opt, isolate or reward persons of power and authority on the local level. The king and his ministers needed assistance from local notables and religious leaders in matters such as tax collection, recruitment of soldiers and manpower for the state administration, the maintenance of law and order, and obtaining local acceptance of the expanding web of central state administration. As Amanullah's fate had demonstrated, without the legitimizing force of Islam no government could long survive. Nadir Shah's Constitution prominently invoked the sacred principles of Islam and the King honoured religious leaders by appointing them to the Upper House.

Nadir Shah's Constitution survived for more than three decades. In this period, the balance of power between the executive and the legislative branch usually, and decisively, favoured the former. Only once, when the new King, Zahir Shah, was weak and his Prime Minister indecisive, did the assembly briefly demonstrate its potential to become 'more than an echo of the executive'.[4] Relatively free elections in 1949 and a new press law produced a parliament that 'broke the graveyard silence' of previous assemblies, as a deputy later proudly proclaimed. 'The deputies .... opened the floodgates and paved the way for those who will succeed them. They could not liquidate the arbitrary rule, but they threw a stone at it'.[5]

The outburst of activity by civil and political society reflected broader social change as well. Growing urbanization, education and commerce had created an emerging middle class of merchants, officers, civil servants and an aspiring and politically aware intelligentsia. These social formations gave rise to a variety of political movements that later formed into three main currents—Marxist, Islamist and ethno-nationalist.[6]

The new forces found an outlet during the period of the 'New Democracy', named after the reforms launched by Zahir Shah, in which the 1964 Constitution was the centrepiece. The reforms left some observers puzzled. What led Zahir Shah—known as a weak and indecisive king—to promote a basic law so liberal that it served as the model for the Western-supported Constitution adopted forty years later? Underlying social change had created demand for greater representation,[7] but the immediate cause was rivalry at the court.[8] The King's main concern at the time was to neutralize his former Prime Minister, Daoud Khan, who belonged to a rival lineage of the royal family. As Prime Minister, the elder and more assertive Daoud had dominated and patronized the King, marking himself as his ultimate rival. For Zahir Shah and his supporters, a constitution that empowered the parliament was a means to isolate Daoud, a man 'in whose blood politics had mixed', the historian Hasan Kakar writes.[9] It was a variation on the time-tested strategy of embattled monarchs to reach beyond the aristocracy to retain power. The King's strategy was encapsulated in Article 24 of the new constitution, which prohibited members of the royal household from holding high political office. That applied to Daoud, a cousin of Zahir Shah, but not to Zahir Shah himself, who as king was 'above politics' and whose status and powers the Constitution recognized.

Constitutional Developments During the Republic

The 1964 Constitution framed almost a decade of relatively peaceful and relatively democratic politics until Zahir Shah was overthrown by Daoud in a coup supported by left-wing factions in the military. Daoud's principal objective was to create a strong, developmental state, which left little room for either a king or political pluralism. Constitutions had by this time become the instrument of choice for marking new departures in politics, and Daoud duly prepared a new constitution. Approved in 1977 by a *loya jirga* as customary law required, the new Constitution had novel features. The monarchy was abolished and Marxist language introduced ('subjective and objective conditions'). The Constitution established a presidential, one-party system based on 'farmers, workers, the enlightened people and youth'. For the first time in Afghan history, it consolidated power in the hands of the president by abolishing the position of the prime minister. This did not happen again until 2004, when, as we shall see, it caused considerable controversy.

The new constitutional regime lasted about a year. In 1978 Daoud was overthrown in a coup led by leftist factions in the military, enabling the People's Democratic Party of Afghanistan (PDPA) to declare the birth of the revolution. The communists ruled with reference to a set of Fundamental Principles for almost a decade. When the increasingly catastrophic course of the revolution and the war prompted a reassessment in both Moscow and Kabul, Afghan leaders again reached for a constitutional process. After the Soviet Union in 1986 prepared for withdrawal, President Najibullah called for national reconciliation, promulgated a constitution with conciliatory provisions, and assembled a *loya jirga* to approve it.

The 1987 Constitution changed the name of the country from the Democratic Republic back to the Republic of Afghanistan. The document emphasized reconciliation and national unity, restored the traditional principle of a neutral foreign policy and prohibited foreign military bases. In an opening for power-sharing, the position of prime minister was reinstated. While the role of political parties was limited, the powers of the assembly resembled the provisions of the 1964 Constitution. Three years later an even more conciliatory constitution was promulgated, reflecting Najibullah's increasingly precarious situation after the last Soviet troops had departed in 1989 and his desperate need for new supporters. The 1990 Constitution removed restrictions on political parties and welcomed private investors and foreign capital. Foreign policy was based on the principles of neutrality and demilitarization. For the first time in Afghan history, the preamble also included a reference to the United Nations Charter and the Universal Declaration of Human Rights.

Looking back at these six constitutions, we see that they originated in quite diverse circumstances and had different objectives. The first provided a legal framework for the king's modernization agenda. The second legitimized an aspiring king's accession to the throne. The third mobilized support for the king in his struggle with a rival branch of the royal family. The fourth legitimized the abolition of the monarchy and the rise of a one-party, developmental state, while the fifth and the last constitutions were designed to provide an exit from a disastrous war and compensate for the loss of a critical ally. Not surprisingly, the constitutions differed in several respects, but there were also lines of continuity regarding the form of government.

Provisions for a strong executive—whether king or president—are a continuous feature. In all cases, the most important power of the king/president was the right to appoint his prime minister (when the position existed) and the rest of the cabinet. He was also commander-in-chief of the armed forces. The king could initiate and veto legislation and appoint the justices of the Supreme Court. A strong executive, as we shall see, is a defining feature of the 2004 Constitution as well. Provisions for an elected, deliberative assembly reflected democratic ideas of popular sovereignty that merged with traditional Afghan practices of tribal assemblies. But while the traditional *jirga* was an *ad hoc* body of notables called by the ruler to deliberate on, and legitimate, decisions in extraordinary situations, the constitutionally-defined assembly took on modern, democratic forms with popular, direct elections to the lower house and long-term, regularized sessions for conducting the business of state. All constitutions recognized the right of the assembly to monitor the executive and to initiate and approve legislation, although under the one-party state this division of power mostly disappeared.

After the Taliban

The Post-2001 Context for Democratization

The Constitution promulgated after 2001 was patterned on the 1964 Constitution of Zahir Shah, and it was a liberal document. It recognized fundamental rights and freedoms and provided for the main political institutions of liberal democracy in the form of separation of powers of government and direct elections. The social and political context, however, was less conducive to the substantive realization of the Constitution than had been the case under the 'New Democracy' in the 1960s.

As 'social constructions', in the words of Andrews and Chapman, democratic institutions have developed historically in ways that reflect the formation of different social segments and their conflict over access to political power.[10] By 2001, the social landscape of Afghanistan had changed dramatically from the pre-revolutionary period when a tribal aristocracy, religious leaders and an emerging middle class were vying for power. Some twenty-five years of revolution, foreign invasion and war had weakened older power structures. Members of the *ulama* had fled or were overshadowed by new, more radical religious leaders. Tribal structures and local notables whose status rested on large land-holdings had been challenged by the reforms of the Communist period, or fragmented in the flight, chaos and violence of civil war. The urban middle class had been sharply reduced by death and exile. A new class of wartime leaders were poised to claim political power—above all the *mujahedin* who had gained power during the war against the Communists, whether by virtue of their facility with weapons, charisma, or political qualities as powerbrokers.[11] None had democratic credentials. Flourishing opium production provided resources for political entrepreneurs with strong solidarity networks. Altogether, it was not a promising social base for the kind of liberal political democracy that had started to emerge in Afghanistan in the 1960s and had developed and matured in other countries on the back of a rising middle class, whether in alliance with the aristocracy against rising farmers and workers, or in alliance with the latter against the former.

Ethnically defined politics had become more salient as well. Two decades of factional in-fighting defined by ethnic and religious identities had sharpened 'identity politics', and the ethnic balance had shifted. Minorities had gained political and military power, above all during the last phase of the war when Uzbek, Tajik and Hazara-led factions allied with the United States to defeat the Taliban, who had recruited mostly among the Pashtuns. The Bonn Agreement and the early transitional phase confirmed the new-won political power of the minorities in what was widely seen by the Pashtuns as a challenge to their traditional role as rulers. In this context, institutions that had ensured Pashtun dominance in the past—the formally unitary state and a strong executive—acquired new political significance.

Afghanistan in 2001 was a deeply divided society. Multiple wars and accumulated grievances placed heavy demands on the capacity of political institutions to promote reconciliation and address the competing demands and aspirations of the various groups. This situation arguably favoured a democratic design based on inclusive institutions and decentralization of power. But Afghanistan was also a 'failed state'. This suggested the recreation of a central state with a strong executive branch that could quickly establish a post-conflict order conducive to reconstruction, stability and peace. The tension between the two principles of organizing political power played out in full during the constitutional debate, as we shall see, and resurfaced at critical points later.

Another set of tensions arose from the inclusion-versus-exclusion dilemma that is often acute in a post-war transition.[12] Democratic principles and the need to steer military leaders and militants towards a democratic political arena favour a broadly inclusive process; protection of the institution of democracy and the demands of transitional justice require a guarded entry. In post-Taliban Afghanistan, the victorious war-time leaders and assorted lesser commanders were ready to participate in the political arenas opened up after 2001, and most did so enthusiastically. Yet some warlords and commanders-turned-politicians relied more than others on 'armed politics', including intimidation, harassment and threats or use of force. Election-related violence and threats to manipulate the vote occurred during the first parliamentary elections (2005), and were widespread in the second one (2010).[13] Many candidates lacked democratic and human rights credentials and some were accused of serious crimes, including war crimes. Strong Islamist forces among the *mujahedin* candidates created fears among Afghan and international reformers that anti-democratic, religious forces would capture elected assemblies.

The heavy international presence posed other problems. With the partial exception of the Communist period, earlier political reforms had been the work of Afghans. Foreign advisers and transnational movements had provided inspiration and technical expertise, but the constitutional agenda had been a national initiative. This time the constitutional agenda was shaped by both Afghans and international advisers, but the underlying structure of dependence of the Afghan state on international military and financial support, as described above, sharply limited the substantive meaning of political democracy. Foreign states and international agencies wielded decisive power in matters central to the state, above all in the determination of the national budget and the military forces. The very limited decision-making power of elected Afghan representatives in these areas radically reduced the significance of political democracy as an expression of the will of the Afghan people. For the same reason, the introduction of parliamentary democracy was an uncertain source of internal legitimacy for the new order, although it generated a measure of external legitimacy in the international arena.

Heavy dependence on foreign powers affected the balance between the branches of government as well. As the principal counterpart to foreign donors and NATO, the executive branch increased its power relative to the parliament. In theory a pillar of the democratization process, the parliament was in practice deprived of the powers of the purse and all that this entailed.[14] More directly, the main sponsors of the international project intervened at critical points during the transition process to favour inclusion over exclusion in the parliamentary arena (in the name of stability), but promoted a strong executive over the power of the legislature (in the name of repairing Afghanistan's 'failed state' condition). In the Bush Administration, the main concern was to establish institutions that would give Washington a reliable and cooperative partner in Kabul. US interests thus merged perfectly with Afghanistan's constitutional tradition of a strong executive and a weak parliament.

Overall, the apparent assumption among the government's international supporters that democratization and stability were inherently contradictory during a transition period of the kind Afghanistan was experiencing, and that a choice between them was necessary—was not unfounded. Democratization, as recent research has shown, is often an unruly and, in the short-term, violent process.[15] During the early transition period in Afghanistan, international awareness of the potentially destabilizing effects of political democratization was heightened by a parallel and nearly all-consuming concern with short-term stability and security. The concern was threefold: first, that the transition would unravel if the Northern Alliance leaders were confronted directly; secondly, that their support as well as that of lesser commanders was necessary to fight the US-led 'War on Terror'; and thirdly, that stability was necessary for the on-time, step-wise implementation of the Bonn Agreement, which was the key measure of progress.

Structuring Transitional Power

The Bonn Agreement was in all important respects drafted in the UN under Brahimi's leadership. With the Northern Alliance forces already in Kabul, and Colin Powell literally calling on the UN for speed, speed, speed! the Agreement was signed within a week after the parties assembled in Bonn in early December. The Interim Administration established in Bonn was therefore only the first step in the much larger process outlined in the Agreement to create a representative and legitimate Afghan government.

The next step—to occur within six months to prevent the Interim Administration from entrenching itself too deeply—was to call a *loya jirga* that would select a head of state to lead a transitional administration until a government formed through direct elections could take over. It seemed a nice match of traditional and modern forms of legitimacy and the *jirga*—known as the Emergency Loya Jirga—convened within the allotted time period. Over a thousand delegates assembled in Kabul in June 2002. The proceedings were, however, marred by breaches of both traditional and formal democratic rules.

Many Pashtuns had looked to the assembly as a means to redress the ethnic balance of the interim authority established in Bonn, which privileged the non-Pashtun, Panjshiri core of the Northern Alliance. One faction felt that for this purpose the ageing Zahir Shah who returned from his long-time exile in Rome was a better candidate for head of state than Karzai, although this was opposed by other factions. While the factions argued backstage, the US special envoy and influential adviser to President Bush on Afghan affairs, Zalmay Khalilzad, stepped in to cut the debate short and ensure that Washington's candidate would be elected. In a much cited event, Khalilzad announced to the press that the King had decided not to seek a position. The assembly then voted for Karzai, but many members were incensed. Having a non-*jirga* member and official of a foreign government make a critical decision on behalf of the *jirga* made a mockery of the process. The story rapidly trickled down to the countryside as evidence of the limited significance of elections. What is the point, villagers later asked when discussing the scheduled next presidential election, when 'they' had even stopped the King being selected by the *loya jirga*?[16]

Breaches of protocol and principle of a different kind occurred as well. One problem was the presence inside the hall of agents from the national security agency (NSD), as discussed in chapter 4 above. In another violation of the rules, about 100 government officials, including 32 provincial governors (self-appointed or newly appointed), were allowed to join the *loya jirga* as well, despite having bypassed the elaborate process of indirect elections that had produced the other delegates. Both developments served to empower armed groups and strongmen against traditional tribal notables, the re-emerging Afghan civil society, and urban professionals who were trying to reassert themselves in the newly-opened political space. To members of the latter, the incidents sent powerful signals about the future political order—the internationals would accept violation of the political rules to accommodate nominally friendly warlords and militia leaders.[17]

Khalilzad and Brahimi played key roles during the *loya jirga*. Khalilzad's actions made perfect sense in terms of US national security interests by maintaining a known client who at the time was weak and dependent—Karzai even had American bodyguards, as Afghans pointedly remarked—and accommodating existing military partners. Brahimi represented a wider constituency, but he too spoke the language of stability and order rather than peace and justice when the two discourses collided.[18] His decision to overlook the irregular seating in the *loya jirga*, and more directly to stop ISAF from evicting the agents of the secret police, as discussed above (chapter 4), was consonant with this broader concern with stability.

The legacy of the first post-Taliban *loya jirga*, then, was mixed. To those who had high democratic hopes, the compromises made and the heavy-handed foreign intervention were a source of disappointment. To the Pashtuns, it failed to restore their leading clans to a position of political primacy; the Northern Alliance secured two-thirds of the cabinet position during the first year of the transitional administration. Nevertheless, one more piece in the transitional architecture was in place to stabilize the new order.

Creating a Strong Executive

It soon became evident that the political system would be structured around the institutions of a unitary state with a strong executive. Three events were particularly important in this regard. A signal of things to come was the defeat of moves in the 2002 *loya jirga* to establish an advisory assembly in the transitional government. The trend was confirmed by the new Constitution, adopted in January 2004, which established a strong presidential system. And in advance of the parliamentary elections scheduled for 2005, an uncommon election system was adopted that hobbled the development of political parties, further limiting the potential of the parliament to move the democratization process forward. In all cases, international actors played a decisive role.

Squashing a Transitional Assembly

The mandate of the *loya jirga* that convened in mid-2002 had not only been to select the head of the transitional government but it also had the power to determine its structure. This opened the way for a proposal to establish a legislative assembly in the transition period. Two groups of delegates argued in its favour: conservative Pashtun *mujahedin* factions, which saw it as a power-sharing device and a check on the power of technocrats as well as Northern Alliance members in the government, and reformers for whom an elected assembly was the institutional hallmark of political liberalism. The proposed assembly was not approved, however. After two days of what was reported to be furious discussion, Karzai 'and his advisers succeeded in shelving the proposal, according to a well-informed report by the International Crisis Group.[19] As newly-elected head of the transitional administration, Karzai clearly had an interest in not being limited by a legislative assembly, but on his own he was still weak. Khalizad and Brahimi were his most prominent advisers, and a streamlined Afghan authority with powers concentrated in the executive branch held obvious attractions for both the UN mission and the US government.

For a start, it would make it easier to complete the transition according to the tight timetable specified in the Bonn Agreement. This was important to all its sponsors, and particularly its architects in the UN. There was another concern as well. Brahimi later explained his opposition to the proposed assembly by saying it would have given political space to Islamist *mujahedin* factions who were poised to make their mark on the post-Taliban order, particularly the one led by Abdul Rasul Sayyaf.[20] Brahimi was possibly influenced by the electoral victory of the Islamic Salvation Front in his native Algeria in 1991, which in stark terms had brought out the familiar democratic dilemma of inclusion (in the name of democracy) versus exclusion (to screen out non-democratic participants). As it was, Brahimi used his immense authority to help block the proposal. In the Bush Administration, at the time preparing for its more important engagement in Iraq, a swift and smooth transition was important as well, suggesting a strong executive lead. The case was put in more general terms by the International Crisis Group: 'While unfettered executive power is problematic in the long term, however, it is not clear that a powerful parliament would have benefited Afghanistan in the short term ... [T]he assembly was bound to be internally divided, and it might have hindered the Transitional Administration'.[21]

Promulgating a New Constitution

As at previous junctures in Afghanistan's history, a new constitution was promulgated to mark the dawn of a new era. Apart from an unprecedented nation-wide popular consultation process, the drafting process followed established traditions. A small committee of experts prepared the first draft, which was reviewed by a larger commission. Although offered advice by numerous foreign experts, of whom three worked closely with the committee, the Afghan members appeared reluctant to receive advice and the experts were described as 'extremely frustrated'.[22] Constitution-writing was an important and time-honoured practice in Afghanistan, and in this phase of the work, at least, jealously guarded by the Afghans.

Several controversial issues emerged during the early drafting process, including the role of Islam and the status of Afghanistan's several languages (and hence of the non-Pashtun minorities). As for the form of government, the main question was whether the constitution should provide for a purely presidential system or a mixed structure with a prime minister. The debate was quickly cast in ethnic terms. The minorities—mainly the Tajiks, Hazaras and Uzbeks—favoured a system with parliamentary features, above all a prime minister elected by the national assembly. Collectively constituting some 60 per cent of the total population, the minorities presumably would have a strong presence in the assembly. A presidential system, by contrast, was assumed to favour the Pashtuns. Since the president in all probability would be a Pashtun, and since the minorities were divided on many issues, he would be able to carry the parliamentary vote if he could mobilize all

167

the Pashtun members and win some additional support from among the minorities.[23]

As the drafting progressed, the document moved steadily towards a purely presidential system. The first draft provided for a prime minister to be selected by the majority of the lower house, a so-called mixed system patterned after the French system. In a later draft, the prime minister was appointed by the president, in line with previous Afghan constitutions. At that point, the process was removed from the larger drafting commission and continued in a 'secretive and unaccountable manner' in Karzai's office.[24] When the document emerged to be made public a couple of months later, in November 2003, the position of the prime minister had been eliminated altogether. Instead, two vice-presidents to be selected by the president were added. This draft was forwarded to a constitutional assembly that convened the following month to deliberate and approve the document.

In the meantime, a nation-wide hearing process had been undertaken, led by UNAMA, Western donors and international and Afghan NGOs. While it was called a 'consultation', the UN-led process was brief, lasting only two months, and seemed *pro forma*. Most of the country was still sufficiently safe to enable NGOs to hold local meetings nationwide to discuss the nature and functions of a constitution, but the hearings took place in a vacuum. Since an agreed version had not yet emerged from the drafting process, there was no document to serve as a basis for debate. In this situation, the consultation served mainly to secure external legitimation in the UN system and Western countries.

Internal legitimation required that the constitutional draft should be approved by a *loya jirga* in accordance with Afghan tradition, and some 500 delegates indirectly elected from the whole country duly convened in mid-December 2003. The assembly soon launched into a fierce debate and at one point collapsed in mayhem over the provisions for a strong presidential system. The non-Pashtun delegates were ready to walk out, and the deliberations had to be postponed. Karzai's followers used the delay to mobilize additional support and, in the end, the assembly approved a purely presidential system. There would be no prime minister selected independently of the president to give the political system a more inclusive character on the national level.

Karzai's ability to steer the constitutional process towards a strong presidential system reflected in part his political skills and growing political base. By the time the constitutional process got underway in mid-2003, Karzai was starting to develop a power base of his own through judicious distribution of patronage and cultivation of local strongmen and tribal notables. His political skills were now demonstrated. He and his supporters exploited the procedures during the constitutional *loya jirga* and appeared to independent observers and the minorities alike to be openly playing 'the Pashtun card'.[25] Yet Karzai's ability to defeat a diverse and collectively strong Afghan opposition during the constitutional deliberations owed much to the support of his most important patron, the United States.

As noted above (chapter 2), Washington was by this time taking greater interest in 'nation-building' in Afghanistan. Presidential elections were scheduled in both Afghanistan and the United States the following year, and it was important to be able to present the intervention as a success. A close personal relationship between Bush and Karzai was developing through frequent telephone conversations. In late 2003 Zalmay Khalilzad was again dispatched to Kabul, this time as Ambassador with special funding and a brief to conduct a more active nation-building diplomacy. A frequent presence in Karzai's office, Khalilzad quickly acquired a reputation as the President's *éminence grise*. To Washington, a purely presidential system was clearly preferable to a mixed or parliamentary system often associated with divisions, bargaining and immobilism. As Barnett Rubin later wrote, a fully presidential system 'showed there would be no uncertainty about who held legitimate executive power in Kabul, and Washington would retain the benefit of having a clearly identifiable Afghan partner whom it would know well and indeed preferred'.[26] A presidential system was welcomed in broader international circles as well. The prevailing theme in UN and donor circles at the time was that constructing an effective central government was a first-order reform in so-called failed states.[27] A strong executive that could overcome Afghanistan's past catastrophic divisions followed logically from this premise. The rationale had, of course, particular appeal among the Pashtuns given their traditional role as rulers at the central level.

Yet a parliamentary system had a stronger claim to foster unity in divided societies, and the issue did not go away. When the minorities by mid-decade started losing some of their power in the central government, prominent leaders in 2007 formed an opposition movement called the United Front, led by Marshal Fahim, General Dostum and Younos Qanuni. One of its principal demands was a constitutional amendment that would change the political structure from a presidential to a parliamentary system. Another was election of provincial governors rather than their appointment by the central government, which would weaken the unitary state.[28] Although the Front soon disintegrated, questions of power-sharing on the national level or—failing that—greater devolution of power to the provinces remained salient. The issue resurfaced a couple of years later when talk of possible negotiations to end the insurgency raised fears among the minorities of a deal between Karzai and the Taliban that would strengthen the Pashtun grip on the central state.

Weakening Political Parties

The election system adopted in advance of the first parliamentary elections in 2005 was an obscure and rarely used arrangement called the Single Non-Transferable Vote (SNTV). Mostly known as a mechanism for splitting voting blocs, it gave Afghan voters a choice only among individual candidates in multi-member constituencies. There were no party lists. Political parties were allowed and could register, and many had done so already. But they were not allowed to present the list of candidates, and individual candidates were not identified by party on the ballot. The more than 2700 candidates who competed for the 249 seats of the Lower House were identified only by a personal logo. The voters, many illiterate, had to manage a ballot several pages long. Quotas were reserved for women and *kuchi* (nomads, mainly Pashtun), but not for other groups. Provincial council elections were held concurrently, compounding voter difficulty in identifying their preferred candidates.

As an instrument of liberal political democracy, the SNTV was deeply flawed.[29] The system was likely to produce a fragmented parliamentary body with a reduced capacity to aggregate local interests, address national-level issues and provide clear lines of accountability to the voters, and thus, in the end, operate as an effective check on the executive branch. A parliament elected on this basis was destined to be a shadow of the weak national assembly that operated under the 1964 Constitution promulgated by Zahir Shah and for some of the same reasons: the King had not permitted political parties at all for fear that this would limit his own power.

For a plural society like Afghanistan, a party-based system with proportional representation was arguably more suitable, as foreign diplomats and experts in Kabul strongly argued. The UN mission, European diplomats, and virtually all resident international experts and civil society groups warned the government against adopting the SNTV. Two constitutional experts based in the eminent Kabul think-tank, AREU, distributed papers detailing its negative consequences. The joint Afghan-International Joint Electoral Management Board likewise advised the government not to adopt it. So did the resident representative of the European Union, and the Brussels-based International Crisis Group.[30] Yet Karzai resisted and, after a year-long debate pushed through the SNTV in a final cabinet decision in February 2005.

It was a remarkable choice and several explanations have been offered. A charitable interpretation saw it as a misunderstanding—'a path of muddled missteps'[31]—or more purposefully as an ethnic calculation. If political parties were weak, Karzai could count on mobilizing the Pashtun votes in the parliament as he had done in the constitutional *loya jirga* on the presidential-parliamentary question.[32] There was also the public argument cited by Karzai and his supporters. Political parties had played a prominent role in the political upheavals visited on the Afghan people during the previous two decades—the Afghan Communist party (PDPA) had left a devastating track of violence, as had the civil war of the 1990s fought by armed political factions defined by ethnic and religious lines. With political parties discredited, better to have an election system where voters would vote for individuals rather than parties, it was said. Increasing signs of politics of identity after the 1990s worked in the same direction. Adopting an election system that strengthened the role of political parties might institutionalize ethnic divisions and work against national reconciliation and unity.[33]

While superficially convincing, the argument had a strong self-serving element for those who stood to benefit from weak political parties. The SNTV appears in retrospect as a part of a strategy to streamline power in the executive branch by fragmenting the parliament and weaken the opposition. This was the reason why the SNTV was adopted in Jordan—one of only two other countries in the world that used it at the time; the King had introduced it to divide the power of the Muslim Brotherhood in national elections. A president with a strong political party of his own might face a party-based parliamentary contest with some confidence, but Karzai never seriously tried to develop a political party organization. He relied instead on external support and management of patronage networks domestically. This strategy had served him well so far, including in the presidential elections in October 2004. The opposition was mounting, however. New political parties were germinating in the relatively liberal climate provided by Afghanistan's new Constitution. As the elections drew near, a total of thirty-four parties representing the entire political spectrum jointly called for an election system based on party lists and proportional representation.[34] The United Front likewise called for proportional representation when presenting its programme two years later.

The United States again acted as a backstop for Karzai's campaign to press through the SNTV. While other international representatives came out in favour of an election system with party-based proportional representation, US officials were strikingly quiet in public. A USAID-supported paper was circulated by the Asia Foundation that argued strongly against proportional representation and in favour of the SNTV.[35] Out of the public eye, Ambassador Khalilzad made the US position clear. Intervening at a meeting of UN officials and diplomats in Kabul called to discuss the issue, Khalilzad said he had just spoken to President Bush, who had declared that 'SNTV is the choice. SNTV is going to happen'.[36]

Apart from Washington's interest in a strong executive to support its 'War on Terror', considerations of the inclusion-exclusion dilemma now played a role as well. American officials cited concerns that recalled Brahimi's apprehensions about a legislative assembly during the transitional administration.[37] In the short run, those most likely to benefit from a party-based election system were political factions led by the old *mujahedin* leaders. Not organized like conventional political parties, these factions were neither internally democratic nor externally transparent. Their leaders were virtually all implicated in war crimes or crimes against humanity. Their political orientation was mostly conservative Islamic or Islamist. Yet they possessed formidable powers based on patronage, intimidation and identity politics. By comparison, the newly established, more democratic and secularist political parties were quite weak. An election system that rewarded political parties would be likely to further strengthen conservative Islamic power holders and 'warlords'.

The Parliament: Finding its Way

As expected, the September 2005 elections produced a highly fragmented parliament. A very small number of votes could produce a winner; in Kabul, for instance, most of the thirty-three winners received only one to two per cent each of the total vote, and one was elected with less than 2000 votes—not much more than what a careful mobilization of an extended family or clan could produce. Whether despite or because of this, the *mujahedin* factions secured a strong foothold in the directly elected Lower House of the Parliament, the *Wolesi Jirga*.[38] Over half of the elected deputies were previous militia commanders or associated with the old *mujahedin* parties.[39] They rapidly made inroads in the parliamentary leadership and the committees. The newer, secular-democratic political parties did less well. On the local level, tribes fielded candidates and canvassed votes, functioning as *de facto* parties, especially in the southern provinces.[40] Yet localized sub-clans of tribes did not aggregate above the local level.

Once it assembled, shifting coalitions and *ad hoc* alliance building were the order of the day in the *Wolesi Jirga*. Underlying party structures were visible, and insiders and close observers knew which member belonged to which faction, but the transparency, accountability and discipline associated with formal party identification were lacking. Shifting or weakly enforced rules were part of the generally low level of institutionalization of parliamentary proceedings that further contributed to an opaque process and clientelist politics.[41]

The quality of the deputies was another matter of concern. The President had decreed laws to limit the right of criminals, human rights offenders and 'warlords' to run for parliament. The Election Law stipulated that candidates must not have been convicted of a serious crime, and the Law on Political Parties prohibited registration of parties that had links to armed factions. In practice, however, the internationally supported and scrutinized vetting process excluded very few candidates. The human rights record of leading *mujahedin* leaders was public knowledge and had even been documented in a major international human rights report published just prior to the elections.[42] But as there had been no accountability mechanisms for past offences, no individual candidates could be excluded on grounds of convictions for war crimes. As for links to armed groups, the Northern Alliance leaders had demobilized their armed forces in compliance with the UN programme started in 2003 and—while most retained the capacity to rearm—had no difficulties in registering. In fact, of all the 60 or more political parties that registered, only two had problems, and not on grounds of having links to armed groups. In this respect, the inclusion-exclusion dilemma of a democratic system was weighted in favour of inclusion. A UN source estimated that of the 249 newly elected deputies in the *Wolesi Jirga*, 40 were commanders still associated with armed groups, 24 members belonged to criminal gangs, 17 were drug traffickers and 19 faced serious allegations of war crimes.[43]

In formal terms, the parliament enjoyed significant powers similar to those under the 1964 Constitution. This included the right to confirm ministerial and Supreme Court appointments, approve the budget and pass laws. In practice, the assembly members exercised their power with growing determination and gusto, rising above forces of fragmentation to form *ad hoc* coalitions on larger issues of policy and principle. Coalitions were built around conservative Islamic or traditionalist value.[44] The *Wolesi Jirga* marked its conservative orientations early on by sacking two modernist-reformist ministers (one a Minister of Culture and the other a Minister of Foreign Affairs who stayed on despite the assembly's vote of no-confidence), and maintained the course by approving towards the end of the parliamentary term a Shia Personal Status Law that was totally at odds with liberal interpretations of Islam and women's rights, as we shall see below (chapter 7). The power to approve Cabinet decisions was used with abandon to make life difficult for Karzai, although rarely for reasons that were straightforward or self-evident. The appointed Senate occasionally took up matters of national security. A Senate resolution in May 2007 called for direct talks with the Taliban and, meanwhile, a moratorium on NATO military operations against the insurgents. It was a gesture of support to President Karzai, who by then had become openly critical of NATO operations, as well as a signal to the international community.

The most controversial legislative initiative by mid-decade—rivalling the stir caused later by the Shia Personal Status Law—was an amnesty bill. Approved by both houses in 2007, the bill gave amnesty from prosecution to all Afghans who had been involved in the wars of the past two and a half decades, provided they forgave each other and supported the government's reconciliation process.[45] The Taliban were invited to join as well. Pointedly setting aside international legal principles, the bill denounced a Human Rights Watch report that detailed alleged war crimes of prominent *mujahedin* leaders and called for their prosecution. To underscore their point, the *mujahedin* leaders called together some twenty thousand followers for a public rally in Kabul that celebrated their role in the *jihad* against the Afghan Communists and the Soviet invaders. Afghan reformers and human rights activists, along with some of their international supporters, were incensed. Karzai took a middle position. After modifying the bill slightly, he sent it back to the Parliament without signing, a procedure which ensured that after a fifteen-day interval it would nevertheless become a law.

In key policy areas, however, the Parliament had virtually no possibility to exercise its influence directly. Although it formally passed the budget, substantive decisions were made elsewhere. With foreign aid making up the bulk of state revenues, and the large opium sector not subject to formal taxation, all important budgetary matters were in practice decided by international pledging conferences and in bilateral discussions with donors. Budget discussions in the Parliament were perfunctory, and efforts by international advisers to increase parliamentary budget expertise did little to change the situation.[46]

The same applied to national security policy. The size and functions of the Afghan armed forces were in reality determined by the governments that paid and trained them, that is, the United States in cooperation with major NATO allies. Periodic announcements regarding the targeted size of the Afghan National Army and the Afghan National Police, as well as the establishment of village militias and auxiliary police units, came from the US command in Afghanistan, from NATO, or from bilateral meetings with the most important foreign allies. The executive branch of the Afghan government participated in these discussions and had at least the possibility to influence matters. The parliament was totally marginalized and invisible in these areas of decision-making. Even the status of foreign forces in the country was not regulated by a treaty that would require parliamentary approval. Instead, Presidents Karzai and Bush had in May 2005 agreed on a 'strategic partnership', details of which were not made public and which would not require parliamentary scrutiny when the first assembly met after the 2005 elections.

Against this background, it is not surprising that members of the Parliament concentrated on public issues where they could have an impact—such as matters of culture, justice and Cabinet appointments—and otherwise used their positions to promote narrower constituency interests or personal business. This had been characteristic of the earlier parliament under Zahir Shah in the 1960s as well. The only detailed study of parliamentary behaviour at the time, by Marvin

Weinbaum, found little commitment to national-level legislation and institutional development. Rather, the deputies acted as intermediaries between the centre and their constituencies, effectively serving as ombudsmen for the special interests of their communities, extended families and related solidarity networks. In this capacity, the legislators spent considerable time in Kabul to access government offices, and on the floor of the Parliament 'grasped the opportunity for uninhibited debate'.[47]

Heavy dependence on foreign powers cannot explain the behaviour of Zahir Shah's parliament, although the primacy of monarchical power and the royal prohibition on political parties did have a restrictive effect. More generally, the function of both the earlier assembly and the one operating under the 2004 Constitution must be understood in relation to social and economic structures and the social basis for parliamentary politics. As a rule, legislative assemblies in agrarian and plural societies also tend to be weak instruments of national policy-making and horizontal accountability—that is, holding the executive branch in check. Clientelist politics will prevail, as Joel Barkan has noted.[48] In the Afghan context, the executive branch exerted a strong gravitational pull in clientelist politics by virtue of its command of important access points to the international support structure, and hence political and economic capital. Individual deputies who wanted projects for their constituencies, government approval for business permits, or aid in matters of justice or insecurity, could find it difficult to take a strong position on executive branch accountability. Insofar as the Parliament provided a forum for doing so, however, holding the executive to account—by threatening to vote off ministers or call on them to defend their policies—became part of the bargaining process.

The parliamentary elections in September 2010 indicated that the parliament was becoming an increasingly important arena for political struggle, as well as a place to accumulate personal economic and political capital. The elections were fought intensely, leading to allegations of massive fraud, and the results were contested with equal vehemence. When the government-appointed but formally autonomous Afghan Independent Election Commission discarded some 1.3 million votes (out of 5.6 million in all), the losers fought on, in some areas with public demonstrations of protest. It was rumoured that some losers would resort to arms and block the roads to the capital. Karzai and his supporters, who were widely seen as being among the losers, turned to the

Supreme Court courts to ask for a total recount of the vote and a special court was established to examine the results. It was a novel procedure. But then the results were extraordinary as well. Over two-thirds of the incumbents appeared to have lost their seats after the Independent Election Commission had gone through the results and invalidated what they deemed to be fraudulent counts. Although no authoritative count by ethnic identity is available, the Pashtuns lost heavily and the minorities, particularly the Tajiks and the Hazaras, made significant gains. A count by a Kabul research centre found the Pashtuns had won only 96 out of 249 seats, which gave the minorities collectively almost two-thirds of the *Wolesi Jirga* seats. The largest winners were the Tajiks and the Hazaras, the latter gaining sixty-one seats, or eighteen more than in the previous election.[49] For a minority that is commonly estimated to constitute ten per cent of the population, it was an amazing victory.[50]

The reasons for the minority gains appeared to be several. The SNTV system of 'first-past-the-post' election in multi-member constituencies privileged well-organized voting communities that were able to unite around their candidates or form disciplined voter blocs to support particular candidates even in the absence of party lists. This might well account for the electoral gains of the Hazaras, a traditionally low-status social group that increasingly appeared as an 'advanced minority' in terms of political organization and education.[51] The Pashtuns, by contrast, were divided and in some areas could not vote at all because of security problems. The situation was exemplified in the heavily Pashtun populated province of Ghazni, where all of the eleven seats went to the Hazaras. In several Pashtun districts, polling states were not open or no votes were cast for security reasons.[52] It was a severe blow to the Pashtuns, explained by some as the result of fraud organized by the ethnic minorities in a bid to ultimately capture state power. As the analyst Martine van Bijlert wrote at the height of the post-election crisis:

The election outcome has been increasingly framed [among Pashtuns] as a political encroachment by the Northern Alliance aimed at marginalizing the Pashtuns on one hand, and by commissioners with PDPA [Communist] background against mujahedin personalities on the other. In this analysis the 2010 election is not just seen as a brief messy and fraudulent episode after which political life will continue as normal, but rather as a possible turning point after which anything could happen.[53]

Although it descended into internal bickering as soon as it convened, the parliament had become an important arena not only for pursuing personal and narrow constituency objectives; the 2010 elections had made it a vehicle in the most difficult and sensitive politics of all—to influence the power balance among Afghanistan's ethnic groups. The election results also set off an intensified struggle between the executive and the legislative branch of the government, as vividly demonstrated by Karzai's initial refusal to open the parliament.

Elections

A popularly elected government capped the transitional mechanism outlined in the Bonn Agreement. Direct, free and fair elections were to be the principal legitimizing instrument of the new order, and the first presidential election in 2004 passed the test reasonably well in this regard. The parliamentary elections in 2005 were more problematic, and large-scale violence and fraud were expected as the 2009 presidential elections approached. At that point, however, there seemed to be no way back. The elections could not be called off.

The large turn-out reported during the 2004 election (70 per cent) was a high point in Karzai's presidential career and for the electoral process in Afghanistan. Karzai's victory was buttressed with a great show of American support and largesse. Khalilzad had just arrived as ambassador with an additional $1.4 billion in aid, of which a significant portion was spent during the run-up to the election. School buildings suddenly sprouted throughout the countryside, constructed so quickly that many soon fell into disrepair, a subsequent U.S. government audit found.[54] The parliamentary election the following year attracted less largesse of this kind, but foreign donors covered a hefty bill for direct expenses ($163 million) and provided technical assistance. Some 40 million ballots printed in Europe and Australia were flown in on huge transport planes while international experts arrived to assist in preparing and monitoring the vote. Yet there was evidence of large-scale fraud (a huge surplus of voter cards was traded, some of it openly in the bazaar), and voters were subjected to intimidation and violence.[55] The turnout was estimated to around 50 per cent, well below the level during the presidential elections the previous year even though the Taliban at this time did not try to prevent voting.

To deal with some of these problems before the next round of elections five years ahead, the international community discussed reforms of the election system and voter registration. Recognizing the negative implications of the SNTV, international experts advocated the introduction of party lists and proportional representation, hoping this would enable 'younger and more obscure candidates with party backing to win seats based on ideas about policy and governance rather than wartime clout'.[56] The possibility for reducing fraud through a nation-wide system of voter registration was also considered. In the 2004 and 2005 elections, voter cards were issued that stated the name and home province of the holder, but since Afghanistan had not had a census since 1979, there was no reliable estimate of how many cards were legitimately required in the various election districts, and how many ballots should be shipped out in advance. A more accurate voter registration system would 'forego shipping unneeded ballots to poorly secured and thinly observed areas', as an international election official later commented.[57]

Both reform initiatives failed. Existing power holders who had benefitted from the system during the past elections were uninterested in reform. The donors were unable to agree on an effective and feasible plan, and at any rate unwilling to force it on the Afghan government; their overriding concerns at this time were issues of governance, corruption and the mounting insurgency. Instituting a proper voter registration system, moreover, was likely to impact on the political and ethnic balance among groups. To reopen this Pandora's Box in the middle of the insurgency was not an attractive donor option. As a result, voter registration before the 2009 presidential elections simply 'updated' previous lists, but in ways that produced 'an improbably high number' of voters (seventeen million in an estimated population of between twenty-five and thirty million) and a brisk trade in registration cards.[58]

The stage was now set for massive election fraud. The security situation made the prospects worse. Holding elections in the middle of an insurgency posed enormous security and logistical difficulties. In large parts of the south and the southeast, the Taliban had the capacity to enforce their threat to prevent voting. Basic fraud-prevention measures requiring voters to dip one finger in indelible ink after voting made their task easier. The population in this Pashtun heartland, with its presumptive vote for Karzai as president, was in effect disenfranchised. The incentives to cheat were obvious, and large-scale fraud was expected. The deputy head of the UN mission famously proposed closing a large number of polling booths where international observers could not be present. Closure would have formally disenfranchised a substantial number of Pashtuns, however, and was unacceptable to the head of the UN mission.[59] The elections went ahead in August as planned, but in an atmosphere of fear, violence, and mistrust. Estimated turnout on a national basis was about thirty per cent, and less than half that in much of the embattled south. The first results showed Karzai led nationwide with 54.6 per cent as against 28.3 per cent for the next candidate, Abdullah Abdullah, his previous Foreign Minister and once a central member of the Northern Alliance, who was mostly associated with the non-Pashtun minority votes. As expected, however, massive fraud had taken place. In Kandahar, the home of Karzai's Popolzai tribe, officials had stuffed ballot boxes to produce an astounding 60 per cent turnout, all in favour of Karzai.[60]

For the government's international supporters, it was a moment of clarity. Accepting the results would serve short-term objectives of stability but definitively expose the hollowness of elections as a tool of liberal political democracy; rejecting them would mean another round of elections and related problems of fear, fraud and violence, or invite a backroom deal between the two leading candidates. Complicating the matter further was the probability that a victory for Abdullah would bring deep-seated tensions between the Pashtuns and the other ethnic groups to the surface with unforeseen consequences.

There were other costs to consider. By this time the international community had invested almost a billion dollars in various forms of election support since 2001, as well as its own prestige and the status of elections as the hallmark of liberal democracy.[61] On the ground, countless lives had been lost in the pre-election military offensives to make the area safe for voting. In Helmand, the British had launched Operation Panther's Claw, the largest operation since their arrival in the province three years earlier. More than 3,000 British, Danish, Estonian and Afghan forces supported by a wide range of air assets moved into an area around Lashkar Gah to create a secure environment for an estimated 80,000 voters. After two months of fighting, in which some 2–300 insurgents and five coalition soldiers were killed, and large numbers of the local population forced to abandon their homes, the area was deemed safe for voting. As it turned out, the area was only safe enough for one polling station to open, where early returns showed around 150 votes were cast.[62]

Nevertheless, turning back from the electoral path after the polling had taken place was even more difficult than in the pre-election period. Patching up its internal divisions, the UN mission looked for a procedure that could give some legitimacy to the process and ended up by auditing a sample vote. The recount results only deepened the crisis. Karzai no longer had a simple majority (only winning 48.3 per cent), while the vote for Abdullah had risen to 31.5 per cent. Karzai continued to insist he had won, and did not relent until the prominent US Democratic Senator John Kerry flew into Kabul to persuade him to accept the revised result. With the senator literally towering over him, Karzai announced that he would accept a second round of election as required by the Constitution. A run-off election would merely prolong the farce, however. Abdullah's decision to withdraw resolved the impasse, and a relieved international community accepted Karzai as the duly elected head of state.

The 2009 elections had highlighted the limitations of a presidential system where winner-takes-all in a divided society. As the hub of a formally unitary state, and as the central point of contact with the international community and its vital economic and military resources, the presidency was the single most powerful political institution in Afghanistan. This was useful for foreign governments that had supported statebuilding and fostered a strong executive branch as a reliable partner in development. In Afghanistan's divided society, it appeared as a zero-sum game decided by decimal points on either side of the 50 per cent mark, a mechanism that invited fraud and generated conflict.

* * *

The political transition envisaged in Bonn did establish a political framework for governing that rested on both Afghan traditional and Western democratic legitimizing devices—the *loya jirga* and direct, popular elections—and the transition was completed according to the letter of the text. In this sense, the operation was a success, but it was not enough to save the patient. There were, of course, many reasons for this, some of which have been detailed in previous chapters. But even two principal institutions designed to promote 'a broad-based, gender-sensitive, multi-ethnic and fully representative government', as the Bonn Agreement stated, were in large part captured by forces that worked at cross purposes with this objective.

The Parliament did become more assertive vis-à-vis the executive branch and emerged as an increasingly significant arena for political contestation. Yet it laboured under the constricting conditions of clientelist politics, weak party structures, fraudulent elections, and an inclusive membership that did not vet members for past human rights violations and other crime. Its potential as an instrument for democratic reform was correspondingly reduced. Some of this was the making of the international project—the preoccupation with stability, the fear of giving Islamists a voice and the preference for a strong executive, as well as the *de facto* external control over national revenue and the military, which deprived the Parliament of a meaningful role in matters of critical importance to the state. Elections—another key political instrument in the transition and beyond—became increasingly violent and fraudulent. In part this reflected the social context, in part also the lack of a proper voting registration system, but most of all the mounting insurgency that effectively disenfranchised large parts of the Pashtun population and put Afghanistan's sensitive ethnic balance under enormous stress. Neither the Parliament nor the elections did much to strengthen the rule of law, an important objective in the spirit, at least, of the Bonn Agreement and to a society that for decades had suffered from arbitrary rule.

7

REFORMING THE LEGAL SYSTEM

'After 25 years of war and a complete change in the direction of its government, Afghanistan's legal system needs a complete rebuilding'.[1] The spirit in international aid circles during the early years of the Bonn process is captured in this introduction to a UNDP-sponsored strategy for justice sector reform.[2] Afghanistan was perceived as a legal *terra nullius*—an empty territory where legal institutions had either disintegrated or were useless for the new order. Bureaucratic imperatives to produce visible and rapid results reinforced this outlook, leading to reforms that often were imperious, insensitive to Afghan legal and social traditions, and as a result ineffective. At the same time, the right of Afghans to 'own' the process and the need for the Afghan government to take the lead were repeatedly and almost ritually asserted, producing a striking disconnect between the ideological framework for policy and actual practice. Afghan agencies, groups and individuals nevertheless asserted their claims to ownership in many ways, initially by slowing down or sidelining internationally-sponsored initiatives, and over time by issuing laws and decrees that in the first instance reflected their own constituencies.

Judicial reform in the early period after Bonn is of particular interest in relation to the argument discussed at the outset of the book: that is, the internationals invested too little in the early period of intervention and thereby missed a window of opportunity for creating sustainable reform. In fact, in the legal field a spate of early international initiatives occurred. International experts and foreign diplomats promoted new legal codes, intervened in the appointment of key legal personnel, pronounced on judicial decisions in important cases before the courts, and started large training programmes. In this area, the internationals hardly missed the window of opportunity.

The reforms raised difficult issues of ownership and sustainability, however, and, more fundamentally, the meaning of justice. This chapter examines the early reform period in some detail, and then presents a case study of two prominent Afghan-led initiatives in the second half of the decade to codify by law the rights and obligations of women. Finally, the chapter turns to a theme that emerged at the end of the decade and seemed to open new vistas in legal reform: building on Afghanistan's informal system of justice.

The Setting

By early 2011, a decade of investment in legal reform had produced an impressive array of concrete results. New courthouses had been built, laws decreed, legal personnel trained and sector strategy plans written. The United States alone had by 2009 renovated 40 provincial courthouses, trained 900 sitting judges, and its train-the-trainers programme had covered 1,900 other justice professionals.[3] Conditions of work and pay for key government agencies had improved. The Ministry of Justice had been among the first government departments to be assisted and upgraded under a preferential civil service reform programme (Priority Reform and Restructuring, PRR). The principal legal institutions were barely functioning, however. An authoritative survey of Afghan attitudes and behaviour in the legal arena in 2007 found that the formal court system was widely considered corrupt and little used: some eighty per cent of the population relied instead on the traditional system of justice.[4] Impunity prevailed for high-level officials and power-brokers suspected of corruption and involvement in the narcotics sectors. Alleged crimes were rarely prosecuted, or offenders were pardoned. Human rights violations were reported to the Afghan Independent Human Rights Commission (AIHRC) but state authorities rarely investigated. The Action Plan prepared by AIHRC to establish a transitional justice process that would hold individuals accountable for war crimes and crimes against humanity, and to vet new appointments to high public office, had been halted. The parliament had pre-empted further moves towards prosecution by issuing an amnesty, as discussed above (chapter 6).

This state of affairs reflected the pathologies of a divided society. Historically thin, the state justice system had been weakened by more than two decades of war and upheaval and, like other institutions, had come under enormous pressure from the mounting violence and military operations. A weak state, unchecked corruption, an unprofessional and often predatory police force, militia forces of uncertain accountability and a flourishing illegal narcotics economy further undermined the rule of law. Failure to institute a process of transitional justice weakened the force of basic legal norms, particularly in a society where demand for such a process appeared widespread and was kept in the public eye by the Afghan Independent Human Rights Commission and other activists.[5]

The international presence itself had in some measure contributed to these conditions. The US government and UNAMA had from the start discouraged any attempts to prosecute alleged war criminals among the Northern Alliance, including active investigation.[6] Flushing huge amounts of aid into a weak state apparatus encouraged corruption, and empowering militia forces to fight Taliban and Al-Qaeda increased the capacity to rule by virtue of armed force rather than law. Moreover, international forces or foreign-financed private security companies themselves behaved at times as if they were above the law. US detention policies in major respects violated international law and human rights standards, as the UN special rapporteur noted in his 2005 report.[7] Private security companies operated with minimal regulation and legal oversight.[8]

For the international aid community, the starting point for legal reforms was difficult for other reasons as well. Afghanistan presented a complicated and—to most foreign aid agencies—unfamiliar scene. The legal system was a mixture of Islamic law, customary law and Western-influenced codes. Legal reforms in the past had been a key strategy of statebuilding as the ruler sought to strengthen the central state by asserting his right to appoint judges and issue laws. This necessarily set the stage for conflict between the ruler and the religious authorities (*ulama*), who were the authoritative interpreters of Islamic jurisprudence (*sharia*), and the tribal leaders, who interpreted and dispensed customary law. Afghanistan's great 'state-builder' in the late nineteenth century, Abdul Rahman Khan, had weakened the independent power base of the *ulama* by confiscating the religious endowments and offering the clergy positions as salaried judges in the courts. In this system,

Islam was the foundation of law and superior to customary law, and the role of the ruler (Abdul Rahman Khan) was to uphold the sacred law.[9]

Subsequent legal reform followed this path. Islamic jurisprudence was the foundation of law, but a new body of statutory law was gradually introduced, starting under Amanullah Khan and continuing under Zahir Shah in the 1960s. Reforms were modelled on Egyptian law—itself a blend of Western (Napoleonic) and Islamic legal traditions—with some codes directly translated from the Egyptian version by Afghans who had studied at Al-Azhar University. The initially bifurcated court system divided between administrative and *sharia* courts was gradually unified, and legal personnel were increasingly trained in civil and criminal law. Still, by the time the 1978 revolution ushered in a period of prolonged upheaval, the majority of judges were schooled only in Islamic jurisprudence.[10] Decisions in the state courts thus reflected the weight of the training of the judges, even though most matters of criminal law and civil law were by then covered by statutory law. Outside the courts, *ulama* and other religious leaders remained an authoritative voice that pronounced on principles of justice and the legitimacy of the ruler.

Building in Terra Hullius *Mode*

The Bonn Agreement acknowledged the state of legal pluralism in Afghanistan by identifying four normative points of reference for legal reform: Islamic principles, international standards, the rule of law and Afghan legal traditions. Work to 'rebuild the justice system' would, under the agreement, be started by an Afghan Judicial Commission, while the international community would provide assistance. At a meeting of donors in Geneva in April 2002, it was decided that Italy would be 'lead-nation' for assistance in the justice sector.[11]

What did a 'lead-nation' role entail? In the absence of an authoritative definition, it was an interpretational free-for-all. The Afghan government defined it narrowly to mean coordinating assistance in a large and unwieldy aid scene, nominally organized in a fine-meshed structure of consultative groups established in early 2003. In this context, the task of Italy was to maintain contact with donors to sustain interest in justice reform, facilitate donor coordination activities and work with other agencies to identify international expertise.[12] The newly established UN mission, UNAMA, advocated a similarly narrow assistance role in the spirit of Brahimi's 'light footprint', discouraging donor discussion of strategy so as not to pre-empt the work of the newly established Afghan Judicial Commission. Donors and organizations with a more activist bent differed. A report issued by the US government-funded US Institute of Peace in March 2004 suggested the task of a lead nation was to develop a policy strategy for the sector.[13] Italy started out with a minimalist role definition, but then swung into a proactive and interventionist mode.

The Lead-Nation

The choice of Italy surprised many. The country's main—or only— claim to previous involvement in Afghanistan was the welcome extended to Zahir Shah when he was ousted in 1973. The King had remained in exile in Rome and became the hub of a pro-monarchy faction among the Afghan diaspora. That gave Italy a certain standing in relation to the Bonn process, but little else. In particular, Italy had little or no experience relevant to reconciling Islamic-based law with international standards. Egypt or other Muslim countries that had modernized their legal system would in this regard have been a more logical choice as lead-nation, but none of them were part of the coalition that supported the invasion and established the framework for the post-Taliban order.

Lack of local knowledge and experience at any rate did not appear as a particular disadvantage in the quasi-imperial mood that prevailed in the international aid community in the wake of the 2001 invasion. The emphasis was not on painstakingly building on what was already in place and could be adjusted to work in the new situation; new departures and radical change were the order of the day. In the justice sector, the apparent need for drastic change was dramatically underlined by widely publicized accounts of the dark days of the Taliban regime. Even as late as 2005, the ten-year plan for justice sector reform spoke of Western, 'modern, market-based democracies' as the appropriate model for change.[14] In this perspective, the role of lead-nation for assistance did not require a great deal of expertise on Afghan legal traditions, and Italy appeared to have readily accepted the offer. Afghanistan in early 2002 was at the forefront of international attention, and the place to be. Moreover, an Italian-based NGO (IDLO) had long been working to assist rule of law developments in developing

187

countries, and became the government's main implementing partner in Afghanistan.

Another factor was at work as well. The Italians initially seemed to assume that Afghan authorities in fact would be 'in the driver's seat', as the policy rhetoric proclaimed, and take primary responsibility for whatever needed rebuilding. The Bonn Agreement, it will be recalled, had established an Afghan Judicial Commission specifically for this purpose. The Italian government at first took a reactive, almost passive position, claiming it was awaiting the work of the newly established Judicial Commission. Its passivity—or caution—was soon criticized in international aid circles, however; the criticism was articulated in a scathing report by the International Crisis Group in January 2003 which concluded that so far Italy had done next to nothing.[15] The Italians responded that the Afghan Judicial Commission had made slow progress; in fact, it had only functioned for a few months when internal dissension made its work grind to a halt and a new commission was appointed. Nevertheless, other aid actors were moving into what appeared as a vacuum. The German government aid agency GTZ had already in 2002 started needs assessment for legal reform, and the Max Planck Institute, renowned for its expertise in legal matters, was ready to offer technical assistance. The UNDP was developing a project called 'Rebuilding the Justice Sector in Afghanistan'.

Stung by the criticism and conscious of the competition among aid agencies, the Italians shifted their position. A special office was established in Kabul in February 2003 to support the lead-nation function, called the Italian Justice Project Office (IOPJ) and headed by an ambassador, with an Italian magistrate and distinguished jurist, Giuseppe Di Gennaro, as chief adviser.[16] Over the next few years, the office launched a series of activities—three major laws were drafted and gazetted, programmes were established to train Italian legal personnel in implementing the laws, law studies curricula were developed, and a National Legal Training Centre was built. Yet the new activism generated more controversy than the previously cautious stand.

Legal Activism, Italian Style

Of the three codes promoted by Italy—the Interim Criminal Procedure Code (gazetted 25 February 2004), the Juvenile Code (gazetted 23 March 2005), and the Law on Prisons and Detention Centers (gazetted May 2005)—the first received a great deal of attention both at the time and later on.

Far from Afghanistan being a *terra nullius*, by the end of 2001 the Afghan legal landscape was in fact a veritable jungle of laws and decrees. There were two pillars—the general Criminal Code (1976) and the Civil Code (1977) promulgated under Daoud—but they were not necessarily commensurate with 'international standards', and they were certainly not exhaustive. Four very different regimes had issued laws in the past four decades—the monarchy under the 1964 Constitution, the republican regime of Daoud in the 1970s, the Communist PDPA governments that followed, and lastly the Islamic Emirate of the Taliban. It was unclear which of these laws were still technically on the books and how they related to each other. To complicate the matter further, several volumes of the Official Gazette had been destroyed by war and upheavals, leaving gaps in the documentation. At the time, some laws were available only in the Dari language.

Faced with this situation, Di Gennaro decided to start *de novo* soon after arriving in Kabul when he was asked to draft an interim criminal procedure code. There were alternative approaches; most obviously, the existing criminal procedure code of Afghanistan could have been modified. The law had been passed in 1965 as part of Zahir Shah's New Democracy reforms, and later amended in 1974 (under Daoud), and by the Communists (in 1979 and 1981). The amendments gave sweeping powers to the Attorney General and the national security agency that at least one European legal expert found 'most disturbing'.[17] Instead of changing these provisions, Di Gennaro put the Afghan law aside and produced a brief version of the Italian criminal procedure code.

The decision to write an entirely new code could have been due partly to trivial reasons the existing code was long (500 articles) and had not been translated into English.[18] Moreover, the Italian magistrate worked in isolation, without the benefit of assistants with knowledge of Afghan laws and legal traditions. A short-cut, quick-fix response was an easy way out, but was still a curious approach for someone like Di Gennaro—experienced in international legal assistance and highly respected for his professionalism, expertise and seriousness.[19] The most obvious explanation lies in the working environment of enormous pressure to produce visible results very quickly. As Hartmann and Klonowiecka-Milart argue, drafting laws is a relatively quick, inexpensive and high-visibility type of reform activity, and was much favoured with donors in Afghanistan.[20] The pressure in the aid community for results was palpable, and other aid agencies had already criticized Italy for being slow and passive. Producing a new law, moreover, reflected the prevailing sense among reformers that the country's laws, like its courthouses and ministerial offices, were in a shambles and needed radical overhaul rather than a modest face-lift.

Possibly for the same reasons, the Italian office did not engage Afghans in substantive and sustained consensus-drafting of the new code. Consultation would have been time-consuming and possibly inconclusive given the fractured nature of Afghan legal opinion, as evidenced by the painfully slow pace of the Judicial Commission and its successor body. Failure to consult, however, created other problems. When presented with the new code, President Karzai refused to sign it, insisting on at least a modicum of consultation to give it an Afghan imprint. The Italian diplomats in Kabul refused and threatened to withhold funds unless the government accepted the draft law as presented. In the end Karzai relented, but the story spread rapidly in both national and international circles in Kabul, giving the Italians a reputation for being 'condescending, colonialist, unilateral, and pushy', as a UN official working in the justice sector later put it.[21]

The interim criminal procedure code has since been heavily criticized on political as well as technical legal grounds.[22] Widely known in Afghan policy circles as a product imposed on the government by foreigners, the law lacked legitimacy for a start. For the vast majority of Afghan legal professionals who were trained in Islamic law, the legitimacy issue turned above all on the failure to consult with Islamic legal scholars and, to those of illiberal persuasion, the fact that the law was drafted by non-Muslims. Islam was the foundational element of law in Afghanistan; this had been confirmed in all of the country's six constitutions since 1923, as well as the new one being drafted at the time. Even the two constitutions promulgated towards the end of the Communist regime in 1987 and 1990 affirmed that 'the scared religion of Islam is the religion of Afghanistan, and no law shall run counter to the principles of Islam' (1987 Constitution, Article 2). The last point established the primacy of Islam as a source of law and made religious scholars the ultimate authority in its interpretation. The convention had been observed even by the leftist, modernizing President Daoud, who had been careful to include members of the *ulama* in the drafting process that led to the Criminal Code (1976) and Civil Code (1977). Both laws are built on *sharia* jurisprudence. The criminal code, for instance, makes explicit references to *tazir* crimes, an Islamic category of offences, which it then proceeds to regulate.

For Afghan legal professionals of all kinds, the new interim criminal procedure code was even in outward appearance entirely different (89 compared with some 500 articles) from the extant law, with which those trained in criminal law were familiar. Some provisions were unsuitable for conditions in Afghanistan where communication was slower than in Italy (for example, short time limits for police to turn an investigating file over to the prosecutor), or introduced institutions alien to the country (successive Afghan Attorneys General resisted the Italian model of judicial police). Western legal professionals found it contained serious technical flaws (ambiguities in relation to other extant laws, internal ambiguities and too much generality for consistent application). Given the nature and origins of the law, its proper application would require careful dissemination and training, yet these were lacking as well. It took three years for the new code to be translated and distributed, and the commentary written by Di Gennaro was never translated at all. Training was organized in an *ad hoc* manner with foreign instructors providing short-term courses that did not all follow the same curriculum.[23]

Transplanting criminal law is difficult even under the best of circumstances;[24] this one withered before its roots could take hold. Well into the second half of the decade, it was only partially and inconsistently applied, contributing to a state of legal confusion that undermined the rule of law itself. But other kinds of harm had also been done. The overall role of Italian leadership in legal reform was negatively affected. Italian-sponsored law training programmes had little credibility among Afghan authorities. The then Attorney General, Abdul Jabar Sabit, exclaimed that he would 'not have [his] prosecutors taught their criminal procedure and penal codes by lawyers from Australia and Argentina who fly in for six weeks and then fly out'.[25] Nevertheless, eager to maintain the momentum of reform, the Italians were pressuring the Supreme Court, the Attorney General and the Ministry of Justice to accept institutional reform and threatening to withhold money unless they cooperated.[26] The relationship deteriorated to the point where all three Afghan institutions withdrew from the Italian-sponsored training programme for legal personnel. The new National Training Centre

191

built under a joint Italian and US initiative at Kabul University, however remained, and was used for training courses for prosecutors and lawyers.

...and American Style

The case of the interim criminal procedure code left politically conscious Afghans with an early impression of arrogant and ignorant foreigners who were trying to change their country. Arrogance and ignorance were not, of course, confined to the Italians. Rather, the case was symptomatic of a larger problem of rushed legal transplanting. The US rule of law programme, which ran parallel to and independent of the Italians despite Italy's lead-nation role, was afflicted by similar weaknesses, only on a scale that reflected the much larger US programme.

Soon after the invasion, USAID and the US Department of Justice flew in prosecutors to draft laws on financing of terrorism, money laundering and corruption. Decreed by President Karzai in late 2004, the laws were drafted as 'stand-alone' codes, based on foreign concepts that took no account of the existing Afghan legal framework. Moreover, 'no serious attempt was made to explain them to Afghan jurists and police, much less to train these stakeholders in how to implement them'. As a result, the laws were 'effectively ignored' by the Afghans, Hartmann and Klonowiecka-Milart conclude in their carefully argued paper.[27] Similarly, American and British legal experts drafted the counter-narcotics law, which was rapidly pushed through to be decreed into law in December 2005, just before the newly elected Parliament convened. In 2006, US Department of Justice representatives in Kabul promoted a Law on Terrorism that incorporated verbatim large segments of the US equivalent (the Patriot Act), but was so blatantly unsuitable for Afghan conditions and legal syntax and culture, as well as conflicting in part with international standards, that it provoked a combined Afghan and international opposition. The US often stood by itself in advocating its adoption. After a two-year struggle, the opponents succeeded in defeating the effort, and a simpler Terrorism Law was adopted instead, based on the original Afghan draft that had been eclipsed by the Patriot-Act model.

USAID also financed a large programme to retrain Afghan legal personnel, sub-contracted to a US-based consulting company. Standard courses were short—running from two to four weeks—and reporting by both the consultant and AID emphasized numbers of judges and other legal personnel who had received certificates, rather than qualitative assessments of the results of the training.[28] Unless they were markedly different from standard judicial training programmes run by aid agencies at the time, the courses probably had limited impact. While 'understandably appealing to aid agencies', judicial training 'is usually rife with shortcomings and rarely does much good', a review that drew on US judicial assistance in Latin America concluded.[29]

In Afghanistan, the starting point for Western trainers was difficult given the fact that the vast majority of Afghan legal personnel had previously been trained in Islamic law only and most were unfamiliar with the concepts and reasoning in Western law. Five years into the post-Taliban period, a survey of the educational background of judges found that only 12 per cent had legal training from a faculty of (secular) law, as against 44 per cent who had graduated from a faculty of Islamic law. Of the remainder, about half were trained informally or in lower level institutions for the study of Islam (*madrasa*), and the rest had no legal training at all, only primary or secondary education.[30] At Kabul University, the two law faculties—the Faculty of Law and Political Science and the Faculty of Islamic Law—existed as two separate entities with little interaction; attempts in the 1960s and the 1970s to create bridges through exchanges and common courses had come to naught.[31]

Nevertheless, training programmes, like law-making by decree, responded to political and bureaucratic pressures to produce quick and visible results. Law-making was particularly convenient for this purpose in the years before the parliament was introduced. Foreign experts working with a few strategically placed Afghan officials could get a law through the Ministry of Justice and decreed by the President without much difficulty. In this respect, the executive branch indeed turned out to be the cooperative and effective partner that the US strategy for democratization had presumed, as discussed in chapter 6. The parliament was expected to complicate the decision-making process; hence the urge to get as many laws as possible in place before 2005 by working through the executive branch. The result was a large number of laws decreed in the first half of the decade.[32]

Law-making in the early years after Bonn thus became a foreign, supply-driven process, divorced from the major legal traditions of Afghanistan and with limited input from sources familiar with Islamic law. Not until mid-decade did the Italians involve experts from the Middle East in its rule of law programme. Even UNAMA's rule of law division initially had few international experts on Islamic legal traditions and law, although a senior position in the mission was at one time filled by an Egyptian jurist.

A Judicial Reform Strategy—The Struggle over Direction

International activism was also a response to the painfully slow progress of the Afghan Judicial Commission and fears that, unless pre-empted or checked, powerful conservative Islamic forces could stall the broader modernization agenda.

Judicial reform brought out longstanding, deep divisions over the nature and directions of social change that in the not-so-distant past had violently divided the Afghans. In the past, Islamic modernism, Marxism and Islamist doctrines had inspired Afghan reformers and revolutionaries to embark on social change. By 2001, both Communist and Islamist regimes had been defeated; the main ideological divide in the new political elite now ran between Islamic modernists and reformers, on the one hand, and conservative religious leaders on the other. The division was deeply felt in the justice sector, virtually paralyzing the work of the Judicial Commission. There was also a new element in the legal landscape arising from demands of Afghanistan's Shia population, mainly the Hazaras, for recognition of Shia jurisprudence alongside the Hanafi school accepted by Afghanistan's majority Sunni population. The Hazaras had emerged as powerful military and political actors during the past two decades of warfare and were now vocally pressing their claims. One immediate consequence was that the Judicial Commission, which had no Shia representation, was dissolved, giving way to the more inclusive Judicial Reform Commission. Ethnic and religious divisions also shaped the competition for control of the country's permanent legal institutions. The divisions were so deep that when the three main institutions—the Ministry of Justice, the Attorney General's Office and the Supreme Court—presented a joint strategy to the London conference of donors in 2006, the document had no common vision of reform, only a list of infrastructural priorities.

The turf competition among the legal institutions was particularly intense in the early years when their respective mandates were defined, a new constitution was in the offing, and abundant donor funding was available for those adopting a reformist profile. The Ministry of Justice, for instance, opposed the establishment of a separate office of the Attorney General, insisting it be part of the ministry.[33] All three institutions fought over influence in the Judicial Reform Commission, which continued in a state of paralysis and was soon marginalized. The turf battles were sharpened by political and ethnic divisions and different approaches to the law. The Attorney General was a Panjshiri Tajik and former legal adviser to the great Northern Alliance hero, Ahmad Shah Massoud. The Minister of Justice was an Uzbek,[34] and the Supreme Court Chief Justice was a Pashtun religious leader from the eastern border province of Nangarhar and a close associate of Abdul Rasoul Sayyaf, the powerful head of an Islamist *mujahedin* faction. While distributing offices among competing political constituencies made sense in a calculus of equity, it also made cooperation difficult.

Most debilitating for legal reform was the clash between conservative Islamic leaders associated with the Supreme Court and Islamic modernists and their international supporters. The conflict in effect reopened fundamental issues concerning the nature of *sharia* in relationship to statutory law. An understanding of *sharia* that emphasized its literal meaning and unchanging nature, as well as its foundational role for statutory law, would be considered 'conservative'. The contrasting position, which held that Islamic jurisprudence was varied, permitted considerable room for interpretation, and could coexist with other sources of law, would be marked as 'moderate'. The two perspectives were only partially reconciled in the new Constitution which held that no law could be contrary to the principles of Islam; this still left a lot to be settled. In an international context where substantial aid resources were available for 'moderate' reforms, the legal-theological discourse had a financial edge that intersected with the turf war. The Minister of Justice in 2002–04, Abdul Rahim Karimi, early on flagged his profile as a moderate by stating that the *sharia* left considerable room for interpretation (*itjihad*), adding that Afghanistan could learn from other countries in the development of law.[35] The ministry, as noted, was rewarded with preferential administrative reforms that included higher salaries and enhanced facilities.

The Supreme Court, by contrast, was for the first five years headed by the powerful and controversial Chief Justice, Fazl Hadi Shinwari, and established itself as the locus of conservative legal thinking. Shinwari's formal sources of power were formidable. The Constitution gave the Supreme Court responsibility for appointing and administering judges in the entire court system. One of Shinwari's first acts was to fill the Supreme Court with a large number of like-minded judges. Shinwari was also head of the National Council of *ulama*, and thus at the apex of the institution conventionally vested with authority to assess whether a law was contrary to the principles of Islam, whether a given interpretation of the *sharia* was authoritative, and, in the last instance, whether the government applying the law was legitimate.

During his four years on the bench, Shinwari set the tone of the public discussion of law and morality. He wanted to restrict the role of women in the public sphere, did not appoint female judges to the high court, sought to ban cable TV, supported the reintroduction of the Ministry for the Promotion of Virtue and Prevention of Vice—an older institution that became infamous during the Taliban regime—and sent a clear signal about the limits on freedom of speech by agreeing in 2002 to hear a charge of blasphemy. The accused was the well-known reformer and outspoken Minister of Women's Affairs, Sima Samar, and later head of the Afghan Independent Human Rights Commission. Although the case was dismissed, it cast a chill over the public debate.

Another blasphemy case reached the courts in late 2005, and now members of the *ulama* publicly called for the death penalty. The accused, Ali Mohaqiq Nasba, an editor of a women's magazine, had been arrested at the request of the Supreme Court and charged with blasphemy for having written articles claiming that: (i) conversion from Islam to another religion was not a crime; and (ii) harsh corporal punishment was inconsistent with the principles of *sharia*; and (iii) Islamic law in some respects discriminated against women. The case caused an international outcry of protest, and within Afghanistan mobilized key institutions and individuals in the reformist landscape— the journalists' association, the government-appointed but independent Media Commission, the Afghan Independent Human Rights Commission and the (then) Minister of Information and Culture; all spoke strongly in defence of Nasba. Recognizing the limited room for safe protest, though they chose not to fight the Supreme Court on substance, which could have opened themselves to charges of blasphemy, but claimed that the process was flawed.[36]

A few months later another controversial case appeared. This time a charge of apostasy was laid against Abdul Rahman, who publicly (on TV) had renounced the faith. Even more than the prosecution of Nasba, this case raised fundamental issues about the boundary between statutory law and Islamic jurisprudence. Like earlier liberal constitutions, the 2004 Constitution held that if a matter is not addressed by statutory law, the courts shall rule 'in pursuance of' *sharia* jurisprudence (Hanafi school), but—to complicate the picture— 'within the limits set by this Constitution', which also has several references to international human rights, and 'in a way that attains justice in the best manner' (Article 130). In Hanafi jurisprudence apostasy carries a mandatory death penalty, and in this framework Abdul Rahman's transgression was an open-and-shut case. In Western countries supporting the Afghan government, however, Abdul Rahman became a *cause célèbre* and a symbol of everything that was at stake in the international effort to create a new and better order in the country. Abdul Rahman even featured in a popular vote question on a widely used American internet server (aol.com).

International organizations, rights activists and diplomatic missions in Kabul called for leniency in both cases and put considerable pressure on the government. It worked. Nasba was given a slight sentence and later pardoned, while Abdul Rahman was spirited out of the country and given asylum in Italy to avoid court proceedings. Yet *ad hoc* and high profile international intervention in individual cases was cumbersome and costly. International pressure to remove Shinwari and speed up general reform of the courts mounted. The International Crisis Group had already advocated his retirement in early 2003; the call was now taken up by more powerful actors. When Karzai in early 2006 was preparing to re-nominate Shinwari for a second term as Chief Justice, a group of European embassies in Kabul protested, stressing the urgent need to 'professionalize' the judiciary—a code word for removing conservative Islamic forces.[37] In the United States, the influential Council on Foreign Relations joined the lobbying effort by releasing a report that contained stinging attacks on Shinwari and called his attitudes towards women 'offensive'.[38]

In the end, Karzai did re-nominate Shinwari, but opposition to both Shinwari and, for unrelated reasons, to Karzai converged in parliament to defeat his candidacy. The judge who replaced him, Abdul Salam Azimi, was trained in both Islamic and statutory law, and had been a professor at Arizona University. To the international and Afghan reformers, it was a comforting change. Shinwari remained head of the

National Council of *ulama*, however, and continued to be an influential voice of conservative Islam. The margins for public dissent on matters that touched on Islam remained quite narrow, and the case that erupted next year sent a chilling message. In October 2007, a blasphemy case was brought against a young northern student, Sayed Pervez Kambaksh, who was charged with downloading an allegedly offensive item from the internet. The Council of *ulama* called for the death penalty. A huge international outcry, and a more cautions protest from Afghan reformers, again followed. After two years of intense international lobbying, Kambaksh was released from a twenty-year jail sentence and given asylum in Canada.

Within Afghanistan, high-profile international intervention in matters of law sharpened the divisions over legal jurisdictions and interpretations of the *sharia*, making a syncretic approach to judicial reform more difficult. Even more problematic for conservative religious leaders was the fact that non-Muslims were playing a high-profile role in the formulation of law and its application. This most basic issue of legitimacy was raised by learned clergy as well as lesser religious authorities. A survey of attitudes among religious teachers in Wardak province just south of Kabul by mid-decade is instructive on this point. The general profile of the *mullah* was that of rural, conservative Pashtuns, educated for the most part in a *madrasa* in Pakistan or in eastern Afghanistan. The older ones had been associated with conservative *mujahedin* factions in the 1980s and the 1990s. In other words, their educational background was similar to that of a sizeable portion of the country's judges as well as more ordinary *mullah*s. Asked about foreign assistance in the justice sector, the answer was virtually unanimous: it was quite acceptable provided the aid came from Muslim countries.[39]

Diagnosis and Remedies

By mid-decade, the transitional period defined by the Bonn process had formally come to an end. In the justice sector, as in other areas, the terms and ambitions for the internationally assisted reform process were adjusted. According to the *Afghanistan Compact* adopted at the London conference in January 2006, the goal in the justice sector was now to have institutions of justice 'fully operational' by the end of the next ten-year period.[40]

The immediate result of the London conference was the establishment of an elaborate Afghan-international coordination mechanism, the Joint Coordination and Monitoring Board (JCMB), with dedicated subcommittees to coordinate reform and assistance activities in the different sectors of reform. The justice sector alone had seventeen subcommittees. Although later pared down, it was a cumbersome, time-consuming and increasingly irrelevant structure. The largest donor in the justice sector by this time was the United States, which ran its programmes on a bilateral basis with minimal coordination or even information-sharing with other donors. Italy's role as lead-nation was still formally in effect, but was politically compromised and financially overshadowed by the US programme. Between 2002 and 2007, the US State Department alone spent around $110 million on rule of law programmes, while Italy's contribution was in the order of $60–70 million.[41] Other US agencies were running programmes as well, including the Department of Justice.

To comply with the programme of the London conference, work on a ten-year development plan for the justice sector moved forward. Preliminary planning had started already in 2004, arising, it was reported, out of a dispute between the Italians and the UNDP over their respective roles.[42] The Afghans were barely involved in preparing the first version of the plan, which appeared in early 2005, a point readily acknowledged in the text of the plan itself: The permanent Afghan institutions of justice at the time were 'not well established, and were often not able to be fully active participants in donor-led justice reform initiatives'.[43] The plan was later fleshed out as the justice sector contribution to the overall Afghanistan National Development Strategy (ANDS), but found little support in the Ministry of Justice. Asked about it later, a senior ministry official brushed it off as something that was over and done with.[44] The ministry had even signalled its disagreement with the planning process by refusing to prioritize items as demanded by the London conference and written into the *Afghanistan Compact*. The main drafting was done by foreign advisers.

The document was initially drafted by a dedicated working group whose participants were almost all international except for a representative of the ANDS Secretariat.... [T]he second [part] was finalized with major contributions from a representative of a foreign Embassy. The third part was...drawn up by the World Bank, and then amended after requests made by donors. The fourth part was prepared by UNAMA, with relevant inputs ...from contributing states.[45]

There may have been good reasons why the Afghans stood aside during the drafting process, as Tondini notes.[46] Short of manpower skilled in the international aid process, Afghan officials may have decided to focus their efforts on the negotiating stage after the plans had been drafted. Nevertheless, the planning process recalls the metaphor of parallel ball games familiar in policy analysis—the internationals were in one arena, drafting plans according to their objectives, resources, comparative advantage and a competitive aid framework; the Afghans in their arena were doing likewise, although in pursuit of different objectives and following different rules. At times the two games intersected and the ball would stray from one arena to another, but there was no truly joint game, and no coherent strategy, let alone a common vision, of judicial reform.

The Rome Conference

At the Rome conference in April 2007 called to assess five years of attempted judicial reform, the problem was frankly diagnosed. A team of legal experts led by the eminent lawyer Cherif Bassiouni, a former UN Special Rapporteur for Afghanistan, took stock of developments. Yes, there had been progress after Bonn. The foundation for peace had been laid although planning had been difficult when the availability of funding was uncertain. Afghans did not know how much they could plan for, and donors did not want to commit funds without a detailed plan.

In spite of this progress, the Bassiouni team rendered a devastating verdict. The sector strategy prepared for ANDS and designed to guide ten years of future development of the legal system had huge gaps. Key substantive areas were not addressed at all—the role of informal or traditional structures of justice, corruption, legal aid and access to justice, legal education, oversight of the secret police (the National Directorate of Security), women's rights and gender equity, land issues, administrative justice, transitional justice, and public awareness of the law and access to institutions of justice. More fundamentally, the plan failed to engage with Islamic law which, as stated in the Constitution, was the foundation for law in Afghanistan:

Most structural reform efforts addressed in this [plan]... do not involve substantive questions of Islamic law. Instead they deal with matters...such as: increasing salaries, supporting infrastructure, improving institutional communication and enabling monitoring and evaluation. Substantive legal issues directly linked to Islamic law include reviewing new legislation, establishing legal curricula and creating appropriate training and capacity-building programs. Internationally supported rule of law programs tend to ignore or avoid issues of Islamic law. This negatively impacts the acceptance of these programs by Afghan society. It is therefore necessary that rule of law programs openly engage Islamic law as well as Islamic legal authorities as a means of ensuring their success. It is important that programs are sensitive to [these] consideration ...by seeking formal links with Islamic legal authorities and involving international experts familiar with Islamic law.[47]

It was as much an indictment of past reform efforts as a platform for the future. International assistance programmes, as we have seen, had been oriented towards rebuilding and 'professionalizing' the judicial system according to Western models. The qualifying epithet 'according to Islam' was usually added in the international discourse, but mostly appeared to be tokenism. The London conference had done the same. In fact, the sections on the justice sector in its final document, *The Afghanistan Compact*, made no reference to Islamic law and principles at all. Instead, the operative paragraph pointedly described the overriding objective of reform as providing 'access to justice for all based on *written* codes'.[48] This represented a clear departure from Afghan legal traditions that include both Islamic jurisprudence (*fiqh*) and statutory law (*qanun*), over time bringing them together into a finely woven single texture. The message of the Bassiouni report on this point was clear: while the relationship between the two is 'complex and evolving', failure to engage with the Islamic jurisprudence will render judicial reforms illegitimate and ineffective, it warned.[49]

To 'engage' meant above all involving the National Council of *ulama* as a partner in the reform project. The report's recommendation in this respect reflected the main lesson of past reforms—the failure of Amanullah in the 1920s to bring the religious leaders on board, leading to failure, and the relative success of Daoud half a century later when he brought in the *ulama* to participate in the drafting of the civil and criminal codes that remain the principal legal texts of the country. Engaging the *ulama* in the post-2001 reform project was more difficult. The *ulama* were divided, and some international analysts advocated coopting the more progressive ones to make them 'allies of the [reform] process'.[50] But the bruising fight between the reformers and Shinwari had left a bitter legacy on both sides, followed by the high-profile blasphemy cases where the internationals stood on the frontline of protest.

The war between the US-led coalition and the forces of militant Islam—fought both in Afghanistan and internationally—further polarized the Afghan debate and narrowed the space for internationally-assisted reforms. This became more evident during the second half of the decade when the parliament asserted its legislative role, particularly in religious matters, and the insurgency spread. The government at that time tried to establish local pro-government councils of religious leaders, but those who joined in the contested areas risked being harassed or killed by the insurgents.

A Strategy of Consensus Formation

A cooperative approach that cut across different legal traditions was nevertheless tried out with some success. The coordination structure established by the London conference included a joint Afghan-international working group to review criminal law, chaired by the UN Office on Drugs and Crime (UNODC). Over a period in 2008–09, the Working Group reviewed the formulation of a new criminal procedure code to replace the Italian import in a process that entailed consensus formation across legal, political and national divides. It was a counterpoint to the earlier, flawed process and appeared to be a more promising way of reforming the law.

The draft code was prepared in the Ministry of Justice and then subjected to a long and rigorous review in the Working Group. Article by article, the code was examined. Participants on the Afghan side included officials from the Afghan Ministry of Justice, the Supreme Court, the Attorney General's Office, and the President's Office, members of parliament and representatives from the Bar Association and the Afghan Independent Human Rights Commission. The international side included officials from the UN agencies, UNAMA and the main diplomatic missions. The review started in April 2008 with a conference in Syracuse in the United States; the revised draft that emerged a year later was discussed at another international conference in Vienna in May 2009. This draft was further revised in Kabul. Reflecting on the process, participant-observers Hartmann and Klonowiecka-Milart found that reason, patience and expert interpreters made it possible to produce a consensus acceptable to all. '[A] humble international approach based on unrushed discussion and patient two-way explanation reveals far-going similarities in Western and Islamic procedural institutions and often removes points of contention, despite initially remote position'.[51]

Yet the process had limitations. First, like all genuinely deliberative processes, the consultation process was costly and time-consuming. Reviewing only one code took over a year. Funding for the process came from UNODC and the United States. Although the Afghan Ministry of Justice and participating members of Parliament requested that the Working Group continue, its future by 2010 was uncertain. The mounting sense of urgency and fast approaching deadlines that now gripped the international aid community left little space for slow-moving reforms dictated by patience, reason and fine-tuned legal discourse. Second, and more important, there was still a question whether this process was on balance more beneficial than a process genuinely initiated and directed by the Afghan institutions of justice, with foreign expertise invited at their discretion. An Afghan-initiated process of this kind might well pick up the historical trend in legal reform, interrupted by years of violence and extremism, to move the courts and the legal texts in the direction of Islamic modernism. It would certainly have stronger claims to national ownership than a joint process initiated and funded by foreign donors. A mark of national ownership was particularly important given a strong Western presence that polarized and politicized the legal discourse. One consequence of this, as we shall see, was to make joint advocacy coalitions of Afghan and international reformers vulnerable to political attack.

Afghan-Led Initiatives and Women's Rights: Two Case Studies[52]

The role of women has long been a significant symbol of the social order and, in Afghanistan as in many other countries, has been a canary in the mine for social change. The Taliban's treatment of women, Juan Cole wrote, signalled their 'quest for a pure Islamic counter-modernity'.[53] The quest entailed restricting the public presence of women and thus their access to health services, education and employment in ways that were unprecedented for urban Afghanistan, unusual in much of the rest of the country, and widely condemned in the West. In the post-Taliban atmosphere of liberation and new opportunities, the demand for greater rights for women moved to the forefront of the aid agenda, carried by Afghan reformers with strong support from international organizations, foreign governments and

203

NGOs. Internationally, women's rights were even cited as a reason for the 2001 invasion and a justification for continued presence to support the reform agenda. International aid agencies launched a huge number of projects to educate, train, and economically empower Afghan women, and provided institutional support to establish a ministry of women's affairs.

Legal reform to strengthen women's rights was arguably a priority given the historically weak protection for Afghan women in both the formal and informal justice system. Yet change in this area was difficult given the sensitivity of the matter and the conservative make-up of the parliament. True, after 2005 there were more women in the parliament than ever before in Afghanistan's history: 68 out of 249 members of the *Wolesi Jirga* (Lower House), and 23 of the 102 members in the *Meshrano Jirga* (Upper House). The women did not form a coherent group, however, and were certainly not united on a pro-women agenda.[54] Among the male parliamentarians, clerics and ex-*mujahedin* commanders likely to be conservative in religious and social matters were in the majority, totalling three-quarters of the male members of the *Wolesi Jirga*, according to one careful estimate.[55] Religious conservatives chaired five central committees in the House, including the Justice Committee which in this case was central.

Foreign governments and international organizations that wished to support women's rights took their stand on international norms, stressing the government's international obligations under the Universal Declaration of Human Rights and the Convention on the Elimination of all Forms of Discrimination against Women (CEDAW, to which Afghanistan had acceded under a Communist government), as well as references in the 2004 Constitution to international norms governing the rights and needs of women (Articles 44, 53 and 85). More ambitiously, Afghan women activists took the initiative to judicialize the rights of women beyond the Constitution in one major area: protection against violence. The consequent Law to Eliminate Violence Against Women (EVAW) was an Afghan women's initiative, and the sponsors carefully protected their claim to ownership.

Eliminating Violence Against Women

The draft law originated around mid-decade in an Afghan commission established by the Ministry of Women's Affairs with the support of

UNIFEM to address violence against women, called the EVAW Commission. The Commission was inspired by international norms of women's rights, particularly their codification in CEDAW, and, possibly more important, the personal views and experience of the founding members. Many of them had worked as lawyers, doctors, or aid workers for NGOs. They had seen first-hand violence against women at home or in refugee camps. They were committed, capable and ready to seize the opportunity to limit such violence by law. A draft was handed to the Ministry of Justice for technical review on 8 March—International Women's Day—in 2006 amidst much public fanfare. The initiative received so much positive attention that other members of the rapidly growing and internally competitive network of Afghan women activists wanted to be part of the process. In short order, two other versions appeared on the desk of the legal drafting department (*taqnin*) of the Ministry of Justice. For about three years, the *taqnin* laboured to shape the three drafts into one code. During this time, there was little or no involvement of international organizations or the caucus of diplomats and UN officials stationed in Kabul who met regularly to monitor events in the human rights sector. By early 2009, however, a sense of urgency developed.

In a separate initiative, a law that severely limited women's rights had been promoted by religious clerics and was about to be passed by Parliament. The law affected only the Shia minority, but among that population imposed extraordinary restrictions on women. It provoked determined opposition from a core of Afghan reformers, who were supported by the human rights caucus of international officials in Kabul, as we shall see below. To counterbalance this development the EVAW law now seemed even more important, and the joint national-international advocacy coalition that had monitored the Shia law took up the EVAW law as a cause as well. To please all sides, President Karzai signed both laws on the same day, 19 July 2009.

The EVAW law was gazetted on 1 August 2009 and thus enforceable as law, but—in a move symptomatic of the prevailing confusion regarding constitutional requirements—neither the women sponsors nor their international supporters were certain whether it needed to return to parliament for ratification. Ratification was treated as an option, and the odds were not good. The atmosphere in the relevant parliamentary committees was becoming hostile, with members accusing the women activists of being under the influence of foreign powers and working against the good of the family. International supporters from foreign embassies in Kabul had quietly lobbied key members of parliament to support the law, but to no avail. By mid-2010, the sponsors had the law taken off the parliamentary agenda.

The women activists had welcomed quiet international lobbying on behalf of the EVAW law in Parliament. Their encounter with another segment of the international presence was less constructive. The joint, UN-led Working Group established to streamline the development of criminal law, discussed above, wanted to review the EVAW law as well. Initial scrutiny led the international experts to point out several technical weaknesses, including lack of coherence with the broader legal framework and confusion over legal categories. The women sponsors protested, arguing that the purpose of the law was primarily political. They wanted to bring the problem to general attention and signal an end to impunity for violence against women. They also feared that introducing changes at this late stage would complicate an eventual passage in Parliament. Some of the comments from the international experts, they said, were based on limited understanding of Afghan terms and cultural concepts. Perhaps most of all, the women resented unsolicited advice for a bill on which they had worked for several years, and which they regarded with a sense of personal ownership as *their* law.

Unlike the case of the last criminal procedure code, opposing views were not reconciled in the Working Group and the review process was aborted. Possibly the gap between the requirements of legal professionalism and the logic of political action was too great, particularly on a subject of great political and cultural sensitivity. Perhaps personality clashes played a part. The timing was awkward; the review process was inserted at a late stage and when the sponsors were fighting for the life of the bill. Overall, the difficulties of rendering effective international assistance showed, even though the national and the international actors in this case agreed on the need and purpose of the law.

Forging a national-international front to *oppose* a bill that reformers considered detrimental and dangerous to women was even more difficult, as the case of the Shia Personal Status Law shows.

Legislating the Obligations of Women

For the first time in Afghanistan history, the 2004 Constitution recognized the legal status of the country's religious minority by granting the courts the right to apply Shia jurisprudence in family matters where both parties were Shia (Article 131). The change emboldened Shia clerics to draft a personal status law covering family affairs, inheritance and personal legal competence. The efforts were led by Sheikh Asif Mohseni, an ambitious and powerful religious leader. While most of Afghanistan's Shia minority are ethnically Hazara, Mohseni belonged to the much smaller community of Qizilbash. His sponsorship of the Shia law was seen by many as an attempt to enhance his status by shifting primary identification from ethnicity to religion.[56]

Mohseni sent a complete draft of the law to the Minister of Justice, where the Minister, Sarwar Danish, himself a Shia, shepherded it through technical review before sending it to parliament in 2006. Here, the draft was buried in committees for almost three years before being reported out to the floor. The delay was not primarily due to the determined opposition to the bill from a small number of female parliamentarians. More powerful forces were at work. Sunni religious scholars feared that a separate law for Shias would diminish the hitherto hegemonic position of Hanafi (Sunni) jurisprudence in Afghanistan. If passed, it would be the first law in the country's history based solely on Shia jurisprudence. There were also unrelated disputes between (Shia) Hazara farmers and (Sunni) Pashtun nomads over access to land, and disagreement over quota representation for Pashtun nomads in Parliament. The disputes brought the parliamentary proceedings to a standstill for almost one month. In this situation, the parliamentary leadership was reluctant to bring to the floor a bill that might accentuate ethno-religious divisions.

Meanwhile, a small number of women parliamentarians had got hold of the draft. Aghast at what they saw, they worked with civil society organizations to remove its most objectionable features. These were above all the provisions governing the legal age of marriage ('minor' was taken to mean nine years old for girls and fifteen for boys) and the age at which the father would have custody of children after divorce (two years old for boys and seven for girls), but also the restrictions on the freedom of the wife to leave the house (requiring permission of the husband), and the duty of the wife to submit to conjugal relations (at least every fourth night). The bill had numerous other provisions that regulated family life in a detail that many Afghan women and legal scholars felt was an excessive codification of personal life.

A politically visible opposition formed around a few women Sunni parliamentarians and a civil society organization that provided technical advice. They took their stand on grounds of human rights, children's rights and women's rights, and argued their case with reference to a liberal interpretation of the *sharia*. Legal scholars versed in Shia jurisprudence helped formulate proposed amendments consistent with liberal Islamic jurisprudence. Working through the committee structure of the Lower House and on the floor when the bill was reported out, they succeeded in modifying the law in three priority areas: the legal age of marriage (raised to sixteen for girls and eighteen for boys), the age limits for paternal custody (raised to seven for boys and nine for girls), and greater freedom of movement for the wife. The women had a much longer list of proposed amendments—a short list of seventeen and a wish-list of ninety-six changes, including the conjugal obedience item—but the powerful Sunni leader and ex-*mujahed* Abdul Rasul Sayyaf cut the discussion short. After his intervention, the Lower House voted to approve the bill as a package without further debate on 7 February 2009.

It was only a partial victory for the women activists, but not bad considering that powerful, conservative factions dominated the committee structure of the *Wolesi Jirga* and steered the proceedings in unpredictable ways. This could make access for the opposition difficult. At one point, for instance, the female parliamentarian who led the opposition, Shinkai Karokhail, tried to enter a committee meeting discussing the bill but met with a frosty reception: 'Why are you here? You are not a religious scholar, you are not a Shia, and you are a woman'.

Karokhail and the other opponents made little effort to solicit international support until the bill was nearing the final stages of approval. After passing the Upper House in February 2009,[57] the bill was on its way to President Hamid Karzai for signature. At that point, an *ad hoc* coalition of opponents was formed, consisting of the Afghan women who had originally led the opposition, concerned Western governments and UN organizations. Yet, while critical of the bill and endorsing women's rights in principle, most of the internationals hesitated to take a strong stance.

First, the politics of the case were complicated. The Shia elite, including the Minister of Justice, supported the law. In parliament, sectarian lines were firmly drawn. Some Shia members said, 'this is our law' and asked Sunni members not to intervene. All Shia women deputies had voted for it in the Lower House. More uncompromising members of the parliament had told the opponents that their views were un-Islamic—a serious charge that could imply blasphemy or apostasy.

The case was further complicated by tacit political understandings and bargains. It was widely rumoured that Sunni and Shia leaders in the parliament had agreed to recognize their respective authorities in jurisprudential matters and not allow debate across sectarian lines on laws concerning religion. In a rumoured bargain of a different kind, Karzai and Mohseni, the original drafter of the bill, had made a deal whereby the latter would 'deliver' the Shia vote for Karzai in the 2009 presidential election in return for Karzai's support for the bill.

Concerned internationals were uncertain how they should position themselves on this issue, if at all. Some donors did not want to be seen as opposing minority rights by standing in the way of Shia desires for a separate law. The UN was divided. In UNIFEM, some officials advocated a strong stance against problematic aspects of the law. Others within the UN system, including Afghan nationals, argued that the issue was too sensitive for a high-profile UN involvement. International officials on the Kabul human rights network were leaning in the same direction. They had earlier expended precious political capital by opposing verdicts on blasphemy and apostasy, each time provoking anger among conservative Islamic forces over foreign intervention in matters of religion. The last case concerning the young student Kambaksh, in which many European diplomats were engaged, was still unresolved at the time the Shia Personal Status Law was on its way to Karzai's office for his signature. The Supreme Court had just upheld a lower court conviction of twenty years' imprisonment for blasphemy, and the human rights activists and foreign diplomats working on behalf of Kambaksh were trying to secure a pardon from Karzai.

Lack of relevant knowledge was another constraining factor. UNAMA had made a preliminary translation of the bill, but there was no authoritative translation until April 2009, well after the law had been passed by parliament and signed by President Karzai. Indeed, translation was no simple matter. The bill was a complicated legal corpus of 249 clauses, with numerous terms and concepts in Arabic. USAID had a dozen experts working for two weeks to produce an authoritative English version.

The opaque and non-transparent nature of the parliamentary process made it difficult for outsiders to influence legislation. Even Afghan nationals and some members of parliament had problems obtaining information about the status of legislative drafts before the parliament. Several members of parliament later said they thought they had voted for an advisory opinion rather than a law. For foreign embassies and international organizations the process was even more impenetrable, compounded by the lack of language expertise and deep knowledge of Afghan affairs in most Western agencies. By late March 2009, when the EU-UN network of international human rights advisers had started discussing strategies for modifying the bill, they did not know which version of the law had been adopted by parliament. In fact, they did not have an authoritative translation, or even a copy of the law itself. They did not know whether Karzai had signed it or not, or even whether it was now a law (the chairman of the House Justice Committee said it was only an advisory opinion for the Supreme Court).

At this point, a UNIFEM document deeply critical of the law was leaked to the international press and the debate entered the Western public realm, with consequent loss of nuance. International headlines proclaimed that the law legalized rape in marriage, prominently citing the provision requiring the wife to submit to sexual intercourse every fourth night (Article 132). Information landing on the desk of a European foreign minister said the law sanctioned rape, house arrest and paedophilia. The document was leaked to coincide with the opening of a major international meeting on Afghanistan in The Hague on 31 March 2009, called by the US government to solicit allied support for more contributions to the counterinsurgency effort in Afghanistan. News of the law created public outrage in the UN system and in NATO member countries whose governments had formally committed themselves to promote democracy and human rights in Afghanistan. With the credibility of the international mission at risk of being undermined in domestic public opinion, NATO governments issued strong statements of condemnation and asked Karzai to rescind the law.

The stronger international stance emboldened some of the Afghan opponents of the law as well. Several Shia women not connected to the Parliament or the core opposition staged a public protest. They were supported by Hazara leaders opposed to Mohseni and his suspected ambition of taking credit for delivering the country's first law to recognize the status of the Shia. Mohseni struck back, however, and organized counter-demonstrations in the street. Surrounded by a hostile crowd who accused them of being anti-Islamic, Western agents and prostitutes, the women soon dispersed.

Karzai also stepped back. After a storm of public international protest, he ordered the Ministry of Justice to review the law and amend any articles that might violate *sharia* or the Constitution. It was a new opening for the national-international advocacy coalition. In the months that followed, Afghan women and civil society organizations, the UN and concerned embassies met repeatedly to agree on strategies to influence the review process. Afghan women's groups, civil society activists and members of parliament also met several times with government officials to keep an eye on the process. The government played its cards close to its chest, however, with the Minister of Justice reported to be managing the review in person. When the ministry in early July presented a slightly amended law, it was rejected by the core opposition from parliament and civil society organizations. The amendments, they argued in an open letter to Karzai, had failed to take their suggestions into consideration and remained problematic on many issues, particularly relating to polygamy, women's rights to work and sexual obedience. The President nevertheless signed the bill into law on 19 July and it was gazetted a few days later.

In retrospect, the Afghan opponents of the bill were divided in their assessment of the international role. It was self-evident that the Afghans had to lead; the sense of national ownership of the opposition to the Shia law in this group was as strong as the claim to sponsorship of the EVAW Law in the other group of women. The question was what kind of international support would be most helpful, or least harmful. Too close an association with Western supporters left Afghan women activists open to accusations of being Western agents, un-Islamic or prostitutes. Both the Afghans and the international members of the joint advocacy coalition preferred international lobbying in a *sotto voce* mode to public confrontation, yet it was also recognized that the first method was not effective and the second only marginally so. As it turned out, the major changes to the bill were those that the Afghan women activists had secured before they turned to the internationals for support.

Building on the Informal System of Justice

By the second half of the decade, the international aid organizations had become fully cognizant of the slow process of improving the formal justice system and were ready for new departures. At the same time, the deteriorating security situation had sparked the interest of the international military command in justice sector reform. The Taliban's growing appeal was now ascribed in large measure to the ability of the movement to adjudicate local disputes. Against this background, earlier calls for building on Afghanistan's informal or traditional system of justice received a sympathetic hearing among donors. Before long, 'traditional justice' was a major item in the US aid programme, the British had started preliminary projects, and the ISAF command embraced it as a tool of counterinsurgency. In their eagerness to try a new approach, however, they risked repeating the earlier mistake of international agencies that had hurriedly promoted their own legal reform agenda, overwhelming or sidelining Afghan institutions.

The idea of building on Afghanistan's informal system of justice—based on customary law, informed by Islamic principles, and administered by local councils of elders (*jirga* or *shura*)—had been advocated by some experts in the first phase of the post-2001 reforms. An early and quite developed proposal for a hybrid model that combined formal and informal mechanisms of justice was presented at a conference of experts in Berlin in 2003 by Ali Wardak, an Afghan professor of law based in England.[58] To Wardak, the informal system had a twofold advantage: it was a functioning mechanism widely used to settle a range of local conflicts; and, more important, except for some kinds of transgression it emphasized restorative rather than retributive justice by reintegrating the offender in the community. A main principle of customary law was to deal with crimes and disputes in ways that promoted conciliation among families and thereby restored the previous social balance. Wardak had himself been imprisoned as a young man during the Communist period and had become an outspoken advocate of a non-punitive system of justice.

The US Institute of Peace had around the same time started exploring the nature and function of traditional mechanisms of justice, but the aid policy of the United States as well as all major donors was still focused on the formal institutions of justice. It was not until the UNDP published its second Human Development Report (HDR) on Afghanistan in 2007—of which Ali Wardak was the principal author—that the role of informal justice moved to the forefront of the policy discussion. The report was devoted to the justice system and delivered a stinging critique of the state institutions. The problems were numerous: 'the lack of professional capacity and resources, inadequate physical infrastructure, relative lack of accessibility, institutionalized corruption, the continued strong influence of militia and factional leaders over justice institutions, lack of security, and low levels of confidence and trust in the justice system'.[59] The current reform policy held little promise. There was no 'single, coherent long-term vision for (re) building' the justice system and no coordination among donors and Afghan justice institutions. The alternative recommended by the report was to build on the informal system of justice and create a hybrid model. This would be cost-effective and also promote justice in line with Afghan expectations and needs.

The HDR report prepared by Ali Wardak and a team of national and international experts built on Wardak's earlier paper, but was filled out with surveys and other data collection undertaken specifically for the report. The new research documented critical weaknesses in the formal institutions of justice. Judges, in particular, were widely considered corrupt. By comparison, traditional institutions were more trusted, fair and accessible. As a result, the population rarely referred legal matters to state institutions, preferring instead informal assemblies constituted by village elders (*jirga* and *shura*). These councils dealt with an astonishing 80–90 per cent of all legal matters, it was estimated.[60] The report acknowledged negative aspects of the institutions of the local *jirga* and *shura*, above all their patriarchal nature that almost always excluded women from the deliberations. They typically operated in a normative framework of customary law and interpretations of the *sharia* that sanctioned violence against women and girls, and privileged the rights of male parties to a crime or civil dispute. Most notorious in this respect, some councils endorsed *baad*—the practice in some communities of offering a female into marriage as a form of compensation in a settlement.

Recognizing weaknesses in both the formal and informal system of justice, the report proposed a hybridization that would divide jurisdictions according to types of cases. Minor civil disputes and criminal incidents would in the first instance go to the local *jirga* and *shura*, while major incidents and disputes would be referred to the state institutions. Human rights violations would in the first instance go to a joint national/international body for oversight, and human rights workers would advise and oversee human rights compliance in the informal justice system. Links between the two systems would be established to facilitate referrals and transparency. In many areas, the report argued, 'multi-layered, practical collaboration' between the state and the informal system of justice was already in existence; the task was to develop and formalize hybridization. International aid agencies and human rights activists would be encouraged to work with the informal justice sector as well.[61]

The model was carefully justified with reference to Islamic law, international human rights standards and principles of cost-effectiveness, but this did not prevent a many-sided opposition from mobilizing. Insulted and threatened by the report, state institutions of justice went on the attack. Afghanistan's formal state institutions, it will be recalled, had been developed by Abdul Rahman Khan in the late nineteenth century as a means to curb the power of the tribal khan who administered customary law, as well as to make religious authorities more beholden to the ruler.[62] From this perspective, enhancing the status of local, informal bodies of justice was a regressive step that would weaken the power and legitimacy of the state. In addition, aid flows could well be diverted from the state institutions to the local *jirga/shura*. The Chief Justice of the Supreme Court was so incensed that he banned the report, claiming quoting or citing it was illegal. The principal author was called in before both the Ministry of Justice and Supreme Court officials, and reprimanded before leaving for England.

In the UNDP—which had sponsored the report and stood by it— some officials were strongly critical as well, but for different reasons.[63] To some, it represented 'a great deal of romanticisation of the informal system' of justice where women are systematically disadvantaged. Questions were raised whether the voices of the 'marginalized and vulnerable' had been adequately represented in the surveys. The idea that human rights workers would provide advice and oversight to the village *jirga/shura* was dismissed as 'simplistic', 'unworkable' and 'wishful thinking'. Similar views were common in circles of Afghan and international human rights activists and feminists, where Afghan traditional justice was seen to legitimize practices that entailed discrimination and violence against women and children. Its principal instruments—the *jirga* and the *shura*—were part of a tradition that was at odds with the promotion of human rights and social progress, the head of the Afghan Independent Human Rights Commission, Sima Samar, told an international conference in August 2007.[64]

Combined opposition from state and civil society effectively marginalized the main message of the report, although some international organizations and expert voices endorsed it. In contrast to Dr Samar, the Bassiouni team, writing a few months after the UNDP report was published, argued that local *jirgas/shuras* of 'respected elders' who applied 'their vision of law linking Islamic *sharia* with local customary law' were relevant to local society and culture and viewed as legitimate instrument of justice by the population. Recognizing the potential problems in relation to international standards of human rights, the Bassiouni team suggested that the role of traditional justice mechanisms in the first instance could be strengthened and linked to the formal system in areas such as adjudicating of land disputes.[65] A major World Bank report in 2008 concluded likewise.[66] The opponents remained determined, however. '[F]ierce opposition' from state institutions succeeded in preventing more than a passing reference to informal justice institutions in the National Justice Sector Strategy developed in 2007–08.[67] The reference obligated the government to develop a policy on the state's relationships to informal/traditional justice institutions and a joint national-international working group was duly constituted to draft a policy. The working group soon split along national lines. International members were trying to move the work forward, especially the semi-official US Institute of Peace, which had a long-standing programme on traditional justice and strongly supported enhancing the sector along the lines sketched in the UNDP report. Afghan human rights activists and officials from the Afghan permanent institutions of justice remained firmly opposed.

Little progress was made until late 2009, when the case for strengthening the informal justice sector received support from another direction. It was by then apparent that the administration of 'Taliban justice' in areas under insurgent control, while harsh, had some local appeal: it was swift, anchored in Islam, predictable, and its agents were not corrupt. To undermine this appeal, major donors and the coalition forces embraced informal justice mechanisms as a means of quick and effective of reform, a strategy endorsed in the communiqué from the international conference of donors and Afghan authorities held in Kabul in mid-2010.

The ISAF command had recognized the potential of developing the informal justice system for counterinsurgency purposes in mid-2009 when General McChrystal arrived in Kabul to lead the force, COIN manual in hand. His first major assessment to the US government of the military situation laid out a comprehensive counterinsurgency strategy; as part of this, the military needed to work with informal institutions of justice.[68] To bring home the point to the ISAF leader-

215

ship, he invited the US Institute for Peace to organize a seminar on the subject in November 2009, which he personally opened. The British had already started work on the ground in Helmand, organizing a 'prison *shura*' of elders who would decide on the release of suspected criminals, and encouraging the Governor to organize inter-district *shura*s to adjudicate disputes between districts.

With strong military backing, the informal justice sector became a priority programme in the US rule-of-law strategy for Afghanistan in 2010. Focusing on district-level projects, the programme announced a differentiated strategy corresponding to the military situation. Areas in the south and east where the Afghan government 'lacks credibility with a population that has lost (or never had) confidence in formal government' were defined as 'priority districts'. Here, 'increasing security and providing space for traditional dispute resolution mechanisms to re-emerge is the top priority'.[69] Military operations would 'provide security and space for traditional justice systems marginalized by the Taliban to organically re-emerge'. Simultaneous reforms of the government institutions of justice to fight corruption and crime and prevent radicalization of prisoners would create 'islands of success'. In a slight variation of the 'ink spot' concept in British counterinsurgency strategy (in which the ink was presumed to spread outwards), the islands were expected to attract people towards them by offering traditional, but non-Taliban versions of justice.

The entire rule of law sector was generously funded. The State Department components had a total budget of $336 million for 2010. Most of this was for International Narcotics and Law Enforcement, but USAID, which covered the informal justice sector as well as some parts of the formal sector, got a sizeable increase. Its budget more than doubled from 2009 to 2010, to $75 million dollars.[70] That was almost twice the amount spent by the agency on rule of law programmes for the entire 2002–07 period ($46.6 million).[71] Even allowing for inflation, it was clear that justice sector reform was receiving new attention as part of the Obama Administration's 'surge' in Afghanistan.

For the first time, moreover, the US government's programme for support to the rule of law sector was closely integrated with US military strategy. Even the language in the strategy document had adopted the 'clear-hold-build' terminology of the current counterinsurgency doctrine: '[T]he "clear-hold-build" sequence refers to focusing first on eliminating Taliban influence in the justice sector, improving access to traditional and state justice systems, and reducing official corruption and removing corrupt officials ("clear") while strengthening the entire sector and expanding access to it ("hold and build")'.[72]

The close integration between justice reform and military strategy showed in other ways as well. The strategy emphasized 'short-term successes' that would be publicized in order to create the anticipated 'islands of success'.[73] The US would be the principal agent, as pointedly conveyed by the language: 'Simultaneously, the U.S. will build the state justice system'.[74] In concept, terminology and tone this was quite different from the language of the Afghan national justice sector strategy laboriously produced by the international aid agencies in (at least some) cooperation with Afghan authorities, which had a ten-year framework for development and paid homage to the principle of Afghan ownership and leadership.

Integrating justice sector reform with US military strategy raised a host of political, practical and ethical issues. Unlike most of the earlier strategies in this sector, the new approaches could at least draw on a body of knowledge that had been accumulated by the United States Institute of Peace. The Institute advocated further studies of how the informal system of justice actually worked in order to 'build' in the relevant areas, although the use of such knowledge for military purposes was not unproblematic. The problems were old and familiar, in the Afghan context most acutely demonstrated by the recruitment of social scientists in so-called Human Terrain Teams developed by the US Department of Defense.[75] On another level, there was a distinct possibility that prioritizing the informal justice sector could lead to an overdose of aid money that would undermine its legitimacy, as the United States Institute of Peace indeed warned.[76] More fundamentally, by making assemblies of supposedly 'respected elders' into an explicit object of war, the strategy would further reduce their freedom of action. The space for informal judicial activities, like humanitarian space, seemed to be steadily shrinking.

* * *

Judicial reform is difficult under the best of circumstances, requiring time, patience, knowledge of local conditions and recognition that rule of law—however defined—in the end is reflective of a positive social order that cannot be easily or rapidly constructed. A World Bank report assessing legal reform in the former Soviet Union and Eastern Europe concluded that reform in this area was slower than in almost any other sector.[77]

Afghanistan was possibly the most difficult of circumstances. Time and patience on the donor side were in short supply. The meaning of justice was disputed. There was no inherent reason why Western legal norms and Islamic modernism should not interact positively in ways to enrich both. Islamic scholars with a modernist orientation have argued the point,[78] and reforms in many Muslim countries, including Afghanistan in an earlier period in its history, have shown it to be possible. But reforms of this kind require a favourable environment and an appropriate process. Such was not the case in Afghanistan, where reforms were launched in a context of violence used in the name of extremist ideologies—a global 'War on Terror' and *jihad*—and through an internationally-driven process that, with some exceptions, was short on time, relevant knowledge and readiness to explore areas of substantive and procedural agreement.

The result was that Western-initiative legal reforms were ineffective at best. At worst, they were counterproductive by weakening the reform process itself. Moreover, the bureaucratic and political demands for quick results had produced an early profusion of foreign-directed and largely uncoordinated reforms that had another and more deeply worrying effect. The 'bewildering speed and lack of coordination', two UN-appointed legal experts concluded, 'has only bred resentment of the law and created incentives and opportunities to operate in a large grey area if not entirely outside it'.[79] Poorly-conceived assistance, it seemed, had undermined the very concept of the rule of law.

8

CONCLUSIONS

SCALING DOWN

Looking back, the international project in Afghanistan appeared to be driven by two main forces—American militarism to assert strategic power[1] and UN-centred peacebuilding to create a less violent world. The latent tension between the two permeated the enterprise from the start and hindered its progress, but each represented a broader constellation of forces that simultaneously deepened the involvement.

The US invasion in October-November 2001 to bring about regime change triggered military contributions from Washington's friends and allies. Many were less convinced than the Bush Administration that international terrorism could best be fought in the mountains and deserts of Afghanistan. However, considerations of solidarity with the United States entered into their decisions. Furthermore, the Taliban were international outcasts, and the subsequent US invasion of Iraq reinforced the image of the Afghan conflict as 'the good war'.

Once troops were committed, the power and prestige of the US and its allies were on the line. This translated into demands for more troops and equipment, initially to protect the force and execute the mission. Over time, failure to secure a strategic victory and the possibility of a humiliating withdrawal came to overshadow the initial objective of defeating international terrorism. To gain at least tactical victories that could have a political impact in Afghanistan, and signal to all that an eventual military withdrawal would be on favourable terms, the US government led the alliance onto a sharply escalating course.

219

NATO's institutional involvement in 2003 worked in the same direction. A 'mission creep' of sorts resulted in the transfer of the ISAF command to NATO. This was an opportunity to make the alliance relevant in a world with new strategic challenges and affirm its significance in the post-Cold War era. NATO's prestige was now irreversibly invested in the Afghan venture. For the next seven years, pressure increased on members and associates to enable the alliance to defeat or decisively weaken the enemy.

After some initial hesitation, the military establishments in NATO countries responded positively. Deployment was an opportunity to protect their forces from budget cuts; the British Ambassador in Kabul later characterized the British strategy in Helmand as supply-driven.[2] It also meant practical experience in meeting unconventional threats. The German contingent in Kunduz, as we have seen, was chafing under restrictions imposed by the Bundestag to prevent it from engaging in combat. The Norwegian contingent in Faryab creatively circumvented NATO's cumbersome command structure that hindered it from going after the Taliban.

While the principal justification for the invasion and the subsequent military build-up was to eliminate the core of international terrorism, the peacebuilding agenda provided the normative superstructure for the larger project of creating a new, post-Taliban order in Afghanistan. Its promise of peace and security, human rights and representative government, relief assistance and economic reconstruction had a powerful legitimizing effect in Afghanistan as well as internationally, seemingly validating both the military and the civilian dimensions of the enterprise. The idealist element of peacebuilding was particularly potent because it contrasted so starkly with Afghanistan's recent history—the 'endless wars', the millions of refugees, the ethnic massacres, the widely vilified Taliban regime.[3] As the international project grew its achievements remained modest and the violence mounted but the moral imperative gave it staying power and was invoked to warn against a precipitate withdrawal.

There was also an organizational factor. The enormous challenges of building a peaceful post-war order in Afghanistan resonated in the international community of professionals engaged in peacebuilding. The international peacebuilding regime was by this time a formidable, multinational structure of aid organizations, aid contractors, experts, and international and national officials that stood to benefit professionally and organizationally from the huge reconstruction and peace-building contracts that the invasion of Afghanistan opened up. Throughout, this disparate but influential group remained an articulate lobbyist for greater and sustained international commitment to build a post-Taliban order. Vested interests and new interests developed on all sides of the project, often in joint Afghan-international alliances. Past commitments generated obligations on the part of the intervening powers to their presumed beneficiaries, as well as a desire to protect their own organizations, power and prestige.

These forces help explain why, for almost a decade, signs of mounting setbacks and greater costs in both money and lives on all sides only led to more determined efforts to succeed, rather than a critical scrutiny of the assumptions, structures and overall realism of the project. Yet it was hardly an unwilled and unaware descent into a quagmire. The process is closer to that surrounding American involvement in Vietnam four decades earlier, as discussed in chapter 1. Coloured by the ideology of liberal internationalism, the project was steeled by the overarching purpose of defeating international terrorism and creating a post-Taliban Afghanistan supportive of Western national security interests. It was buoyed by a solid dose of confidence in social engineering, and sustained by fears and hopes. There were fears that a turnaround would mean a repeat of the humiliating Soviet withdrawal of 1989 and its disastrous consequences, leading to a loss of power and prestige internationally, which would in turn give ammunition to political critics at home. Again and again it was hoped that the latest change in strategy and personnel or increase in aid would be the silver bullet. In these scenarios, specific Afghan individuals were assigned great significance. If only, for example, Karzai could restrain corruption in the government and among his own family, it was said, things would look up. Yet Karzai was essentially a product of the system erected in the post-Taliban years; another leader would be subject to similar constraints.

The Turning Point

If the forces supporting involvement were so strong, how do we explain the decision by the US and its allies to start withdrawing troops by mid-2011 and complete the process by 2014? For a start, the economic costs were staggering. The cost of the war to US taxpayers in

2009—the year of Obama's policy review and the global financial crisis—was estimated at $60 billion.[4] And the cost in human lives had an impact on public opinion; as had long been assumed, Western democracies had limited tolerance for fighting distant wars. Allies that had sent troops for reasons not directly related to Afghanistan were starting to ask if the costs were worth the objectives.

The loss of Western soldiers and the tenacity of the insurgents—who steadily matched the increase in international forces by changing tactics and expanding their area of operations—instigated a closer critique of the rationale for the war. Was the military purpose primarily to fight international terrorists, or was it to conduct a broad counter-insurgency campaign in Afghanistan? Did fighting the Taliban in remote provinces of Afghanistan help prevent terrorism elsewhere? Terrorist plots were being uncovered in Europe and Africa, suggesting a geographical spread and organizational diversification that made Afghanistan less central in a counter-terrorism perspective than when Washington had launched its 'Global War on Terror' after the 9/11 attacks. Increasingly, material was coming to light showing that the Taliban had been a reluctant host to Al Qaeda in the first place, and that the relationship throughout was strained by divergent interests.[5] While having transnational links and long-standing ties to Pakistan, the Taliban were focused on national goals, and possibly even narrower Pashtun nationalist objectives. No Afghan Talib had been found to be directly involved in acts of international terrorism. As a result, the basic reasons for the counter-insurgency campaign began to be questioned. What interests did NATO have in crushing this Pashtun-based Islamist movement?

By the end of the decade, moreover, the US military had concluded that Al Qaeda and the Afghan insurgents most closely related to them (the Haqqani network) had relocated to Pakistan's border areas where they worked with (and sometimes fought) Pakistani militant networks. The latter had originally developed with Pakistan government support to put pressure on Indian-controlled Kashmir, but had grown rapidly after 2001 when the war in Afghanistan spilled across the border into Pakistan and led to attacks on Pakistani civilian and government targets. In 2010, the US government authorized a sharp increase in drone attacks in Pakistan's tribal areas (FATA), and renewed its demand that the Pakistan army move in to crack down on militants of all shades. In Washington, the argument was increasingly made that Pakistan—with its much larger population, conflictual relationship with India, and a nuclear weapons capacity—was the principal area of concern to the United States. From this perspective, Afghanistan held a lesser significance as a piece in the regional balance of power.

Limited progress on the peacebuilding side of the ledger further cooled public and official enthusiasm for the Afghan venture in the international community. Indicators of improvement in the educational and health sector were repeatedly cited to show good progress was being made. But large reform projects to improve the police, the provincial administration, the ministerial functions at the central state level and the justice sector had almost stalled. Highly publicized problems of the opium economy, governmental corruption, and the flawed elections in 2009 and 2010 were a source of continuing embarrassment. Western officials started to pare down the original aims of statebuilding and democratization; now the criterion was 'good enough'.

Registering these doubts, questions and concerns, and adding a few of its own, the new Obama Administration ordered a basic review of policy in 2009. The unusually thorough high-level review laid bare the weaknesses of the strategy to date, but also the problems of extricating the US and its allies from the war. Obama announced that US troop withdrawal would start in mid-2011, but government officials later emphasized the end date for foreign troop withdrawal (2014) rather than the beginning. Nevertheless, the announcement signified a turning point that changed the parameters of the public debate about the future, both in Afghanistan and internationally. A flurry of discussion and unofficial ideas about possible negotiations appeared. Modalities of the 'transition' and transfer of security responsibility to the Afghan government were developed. To underscore the point, NATO appointed a Director of Transition and the Afghan government established an Office of Transition. Some allies had previously started to withdraw troops (the Netherlands) or had announced future withdrawal (Canada and Germany). Now more followed. The UK and Sweden announced that their troops would be out by 2014. To soften the impact, international donors stressed at their biannual conference in 2010 that aid commitments would be maintained in the future. Hovering over the 'transition' was the fear that, as during the 1990s, foreign troop withdrawals would lead to more violence in a thoroughly 'Afghanized' civil war.

The Limitations

Why did the international project as initially conceived falter? On the military side, the difficulties of fighting a protracted insurgency were becoming evident by the middle of the decade and even more so during the second half. The regional and international context played a part, including the militants' access to a sanctuary in Pakistan. But the critical factor was the tenacity of insurgents who fought in the name of Islam to repel the foreign invaders, while a weak and divided government struggled to find its footing. The peacebuilding agenda, in turn, was overly ambitious. Its transformational ambition of statebuilding cum democratization, with unstated but inherent donor requirements of rapid results, was a 'fantasy', as Ottaway and Lieven had warned in early 2002.[6]

Why was it a fantasy? For a start, the Afghan context was extremely demanding. The public infrastructure—including the state—was in a shambles, armed groups proliferated, the population was displaced and traumatized by war, the poppy economy was about to make a comeback after its prohibition in the last year of Taliban rule, and the Afghans were a proud people who did not like being ordered around by foreigners, particularly those in uniforms, as Brahimi had warned in late 2001.

In sociological terms, the problem appeared differently. Blaming 'the Afghans' for the mounting problems towards the end of the decade— as was increasingly done in the international community—is unjust and unfair, and also 'essentializes the locals'. Moreover, this line of argument overlooks the numerous problems that plagued the project on the international side, as demonstrated in this book. The point, rather, is that Afghanistan in 2001 offered a shaky social foundation for constructing the 'liberal peace' brought by the international aid community. Islamic modernism had framed past modernizing initiatives in Afghan history and was the most obvious doctrinal anchor for the post-2001 peacebuilding agenda. But much of the liberal residue, never strong, had been wiped out by wars and violence fought in the second half of the twentieth century in the name of Marxism and Islamist movements. The voices of Islamic modernism were killed, forced into exile or otherwise silenced. The core of the 'importing elite' after 2001, to use Bertrand Badie's term, consisted of returned exiles from Western countries, Pakistan and Iran.[7] Some had worked with aid organizations in refugee communities; others were experienced professionals or entrepreneurs. Many were highly skilled, modernist reformers whose technical capacity and political orientation made them essential partners in the project. But in Afghan society as a whole, they represented a small and mostly urban minority. The main, and more powerful, partners of the US-led coalition were neither particularly peaceful nor liberal, but the armed factions that had fought the civil wars of the 1990s or commanders who had been empowered by the US military to fight Al Qaeda and the Taliban.

After 2001, Afghans associated with Islamic modernism often found it difficult to tread a path between conservative religious leaders, who felt threatened by the Western-led reforms, and Westerners who focused on the most objectionable elements of Islam from a UN human rights perspective. The international context of a conflict between militant Islam and the West, and the evolving Taliban insurgency fought under the banner of Islam, further polarized the political discourse. In sensitive matters of rights and religion, Western diplomats and activists found it difficult to aid Afghan reformers effectively. Like schools built by Western aid agencies, Afghan rights activists were made vulnerable by aggressive Western support for their cause, as detailed in the case study on women's rights in chapter 7.

The international project itself was torn by internal contradictions that severely hampered its progress, above all the tension between building peace while waging war. The war had a corrosive effect on the entire peacebuilding project. Perhaps most important, basic policy priorities were skewed in favour of winning the war. When faced with conflicting priorities between peacebuilding tasks, such as promoting justice and good governance, on the one hand, and stability and pursuit of the war on the other, the US and its main allies generally favoured the latter. The results, as we have seen, were empowerment of unsavoury 'warlords', failure to institute transitional justice mechanisms, barriers to the development of parliamentary democracy, weak human rights policies, and tolerance of the narcotics economy, as well as corruption and other crimes or injustices committed by high officials and self-appointed power holders who represented short-term stability.

There were also signs that the international military presence had negative effects that reduced the initial, popular support for the post-Taliban order. Repeated coalition offensives—with their civilian casualties, detested night raids, detentions and the practice adopted by some US forces of bulldozing villages to create 'safe zones' around their forward bases—caused deep resentment among the Afghan people. Possibly this would have been easier to live with if the rest of the international project had delivered in terms of economic benefits and protection from arbitrary exercise of power. As it was, the benefits from the aid-and-war economy were extremely unevenly distributed, the administration was generally corrupt, and the legal system rarely offered a redress of injustice.

The escalating war ratcheted up the demand for rapid and visible results, which in turn sharpened the tension among the various components of the enterprise. Efforts to rapidly create Afghan military capacity by rearming the militias collided with the conventional state-building strategy initially pursued—that is, to establish a monopoly of legitimate force controlled by the Afghan state. The subsequent massive expansion of the Afghan army and the national police created problems of fiscal sustainability and quality control, arguably two central criteria for effective statebuilding. The creation of a rentier state was itself a pre-eminent example of how assistance modalities were adjusted to suit wartime imperatives even though they violated all sound principles of promoting sustainable development and accountable government. The rentier state had a self-perpetuating element; with aid transfers far outpacing absorptive capacity, international consultants and a foreign-financed 'second civil service' of Afghans was required to manage the money flow. Predictably, the rentier state also spawned corrupt and opportunistic elites, which the US and its allies were unable to reform and reluctant to remove lest this should endanger the war effort.

A second set of tensions arose from the operations of an intrusive foreign mission set in a broader discourse of 'local ownership' and the legal framework of Afghan sovereignty. Intrusive missions do not fit well with the ideology of self-determination and nationalism of the twenty-first century. The awkward ideological implications of the unequal relationship were partially masked by a language of 'local ownership' and 'partnership' and, in fact, Afghan influences on policy grew over time to be both diverse and significant. Increasingly, the Afghans came to 'own' a great deal of the politics unfolding in the formal as well as the informal institutions of power. Joint Afghan-international partnerships and advocacy groups formed on particular issues as well. Yet the heavy, structural dependence on foreign funding, technical assistance and international military forces was a continuous reminder of the quasi-imperial nature of the project that gnawed at its legitimacy. Externally generated initiatives and supply-driven projects—products of the transformational impulse and organizational interests embedded in the aid community—were typically ineffective or counterproductive, as seen in the case of legal reform. More generally, tensions between Afghan demands for 'ownership' and international efforts to control the process were ubiquitous, slowing the reform process and bringing it to a standstill when the conflict between President Karzai and his main international supporters erupted into public quarrels.

The legitimacy problem struck deeper. Afghan rulers have traditionally invoked religion, tribal lineage and nationalism to legitimize their rule. A government visibly and heavily dependent on Western aid and military forces had to develop an alternative legitimizing ideology. Hence the government, but especially its international supporters, looked to 'good governance' to legitimize the post-Taliban order. Unlike religion and nationalism, however, 'good governance' exerts no influence simply by virtue of its ideational existence; it has to deliver. In this case, it did not. As a result, the weak legitimacy of the government, as well as the post-2001 order which it represented, was a structural defect that foreign money, troops, or consultants could not repair, but typically made worse.

Other limitations stemmed from the organization of the project. Its multilateral character was a source of international legitimacy by demonstrating that the engagement had wide support in the UN system, in NATO and among other American allies. The downside was a large and unwieldy structure that was poorly suited to a demanding, transformational agenda. The UN and the Afghan government tried in vain to coordinate the aid sector where a huge number of civilian and military actors operated with a high degree of autonomy. Major non-Western economic and political players—China, India and Iran—had independent bilateral programmes that resisted coordination, as indeed the US and Japan did for the most part as well. The many governments and organizations involved pursued divergent and often competing national strategies on a range of issues, including aid modalities (direct execution or via the Afghan government), law enforcement (to be pursued or not), police reform (German versus American training models), statebuilding (top down or bottom up), political parties (to be supported or not) and—towards the end of the decade—the question of whether to negotiate with the Taliban, or not. When dealing with their Afghan counterparts, the large number of foreign diplomats, officials of international organizations, consultants and sundry experts that in effect staffed the international project had an additional handicap. Most lacked relevant language and country expertise. This was not surprising, given the suddenness of the international intervention and the vicarious reasons for the presence of many US allies and their assistance, but it made meaningful communication and effective action difficult. Only towards the end of the decade had a small cadre of international experts developed who knew an Afghan language and had accumulated experience in the country.

The Future

What are the implications of this analysis for the future of the international project?

By early 2011, developments in Afghanistan were nearing a crossroads. The first American troops were withdrawn in mid-2011, following the timetable announced by Obama in June whereby 10,000 would be out by the end of the year, and another 23,000 by September 2012. The initial withdrawals would bring the US troop level down to where it was before 'the surge'. That still gave the US forces two fighting seasons before the reductions would seriously bite into their combat capacity. The Americans also expressed longer-term interests in maintaining a military presence after 2014, including access to bases, under the terms of a 'strategic partnership' with the Afghan government. At the same time, the Obama Administration put new efforts into opening negotiations with the Taliban.[8] Preliminary direct contacts were made in 2011, and several Taliban officials were removed from the UN Security Council's list of international terrorists as a confidence building measure to speed the process.

The end game had started. But because nobody could say how it would end, as Ahmed Rashid put it,[9] the debate about speed, options and trade-offs intensified.

At one end of the spectrum, a few hawks were still calling for a greater US effort to 'win' the war, or at least to inflict such a stinging defeat on the insurgents that the bulk of the US-led forces could withdraw without risking the immediate collapse of the present Kabul government and its administrative infrastructure in the southern half of the country. In the United States, this view had support in the military and conservative political circles, and contributed to a modification of Obama's original timetable for troop withdrawal. Arriving in Kabul in mid-2010 to take command of ISAF, General Petraeus pointedly announced that he had not come to Afghanistan to preside over a withdrawal. Similarly, in the discussion of the White House strategy review in December 2010, military officials cautioned that it was too early to judge the effect of the 'surge'. By implication, the US needed to stay firmly on course to prevent the gains made so far from slipping. Civilian voices from conservative think tanks went further. A former National Security staffer of President Bush as well as President Obama argued in a *Foreign Affairs* article that in addition to more troops, a dramatic civilian surge of consultants and aid were necessary to fix the Afghan state and create good governance. With additional commitments of this kind, the job could be finished and the war won, he claimed.[10]

This recent restatement of the 'more-is-more' thesis rests on the argument that the US had not committed sufficient resources to develop a serious counter-insurgency strategy in Afghanistan until the second half of the decade. In this view, the war had just started. It is true that Western commitments increased markedly towards the end of the decade. But if the analysis in this book is right, on balance this made the situation worse by exacerbating the dysfunctional effects of an intrusive and dominating foreign presence.

The overriding lesson of the past as narrated in this book is that 'more' in this sense has been 'less'—whether in the legal and political field where early interventions after 2001 were direct, but ineffective or counterproductive, or in the economic and military area where the heavy footprint did not appear until the second half of the decade, but then likewise had multiple negative consequences. Future additions of troops, money and consultants will necessarily operate under the same limitations and be subject to the same internal tensions that impaired their effectiveness in the past. If this results in a 'victory' in the sense that the insurgents split over negotiations, the hard core is pushed further back into neighbouring countries and a Western client state remains in Kabul, the victory will be pyrrhic. The international enterprise fought in the name of creating a stable and friendly Afghan state would inherit a weak, corrupt and illegitimate rentier state. Ethnic divisions would continue to deepen. Society would become even more militarised, as sundry militias and auxiliary police formations as well as the state security forces would have been armed to the teeth to defeat the insurgents. The US-led alliance would be even less able to walk away from this Afghanistan with some honour intact than at the present time. And the intensified war would put Pakistan at great risk of further destabilization.

The hawkish option has other costs as well. By the end of 2010 NATO officials estimated that the insurgents had some 25,000 fighters.[11] They had established a strong foothold in the north where various militant factions (the Taliban, the Haqqani network, and Hezb-e-Islami) fought alongside the Islamic Movement of Uzbekistan. In the south, the Taliban were able to absorb huge casualties. US-led forces had switched to a 'kill-or-capture' strategy and reported killing some 2,000 insurgents in three months in mid-2010 alone, mostly in the south. Yet they kept coming back. In the Kandahar area, local Taliban commanders boasted that if the coalition withdrew they could take over the entire southern crescent stretching from Kandahar in the southeast to Badghis in a couple of weeks. Local residents who remembered the forward march of the Taliban 'caravan' after 1994 were inclined to believe the claim.[12] With an infrastructure of this kind, defeating the insurgents would be extremely costly in terms of lives, social dislocation, and material destruction. At that point, the question will be even harder to answer: What interests are being served by a prolonged US-led military campaign against a Pashtun-based Islamist movement in southern Afghanistan?

At the other extreme is a scenario of a rapid military withdrawal under conditions that lead to a collapse of the present government and a fight among various Afghan factions for power. If, in the process, foreign aid were drastically cut, the rentier state would probably implode, and with it the central state apparatus. There would be limited funds to pay the salaries and other recurring costs of the army and the police, as well as teachers, health workers and some 240,000 civil servants in the sub-national administration. These operating costs are today mostly covered by foreign donors, whether channelled through multinational trust funds (ARTF and LOTFA) or bilaterally. Thrown back on its own revenues, the Afghan state would be operating on about half of its current budgetary capacity for recurring expenses and development projects.

A mid-way alternative would be a gradual reduction of military forces and a gradual paring down of the rentier state, combined with efforts to negotiate a political end to the insurgency. The trick, however, is how to combine these. In the search for a position of strength from which the US can bargain for an acceptable exit, the US and its allies are in fact pursuing short-term strategies that increase the dependence of the Afghan state on foreign largesse and are likely to be destabilizing for other reasons as well.

Most problematic in this connection is the rapid expansion of Afghan armed forces. New targets were announced in January 2011, to be met in less than two years, for a combined force of 378,000 for both the Afghan National Army and the national police. This represents a 42 per cent increase over existing levels. An estimated 95 per cent of the cost would be covered by the US.[13] In a conventional national security calculus, the much strengthened Afghan force would permit a gradual withdrawal of coalition combat troops, while holding the insurgents at bay, maintaining a pro-Western government in Kabul, and providing a strategic foothold for the US in Central Asia in the longer run.

Even if these aims were achieved, the huge, foreign-financed expansion of the Afghan security forces has a negative impact on possibilities for long-term stability, political development and fiscal sustainability. As we have seen (chapter 5), even earlier plans for a much more modest expansion of the ANA and related military and para-military forces raised concerns about the imbalance between civilian and military institutions, sustainability, and skewed reconstruction priorities. Several years later, political institutions remain weak and are unlikely to provide effective civilian oversight over the military, whether the regular army or the militias. If the US and its allies do succeed in building a strong, pro-Western army, the military are likely to dominate politics. The prospect of a representative, accountable and democratic government will recede even further. More likely, the very rapid expansion of the army and the police will produce a large number of men with arms, but weak institutions liable to break into factions under stress. The result would be a further militarization of society rather than the creation of organizations for national security.

In terms of regional international relations, the build-up of a US proxy army in Central Asia signals a long-term strategic presence that is likely to increase regional tensions and make it more difficult for future Afghan governments to pursue relations with its neighbours—including Iran, Pakistan and China—independent of the United States.

The Afghan security forces now being built will continue to be totally dependent on foreign, mainly US funding. The rentier state is thus perpetuated and the donors have set themselves a nasty trap: unless they continue to pay the operating expenses of the army and the police, maintaining them will tend to trump all other public expenditure of the government and still be insufficient. In that case, members of the army and the police would need to look for ways to collect their salary through informal taxation, corruption or 'protection' schemes, or simply desert. The bill for the donors is large: the US budgeted $5.6 billion in the fiscal year 2009/10 to support the Afghan National Army and the Afghan National Police, not including the cost of US military personnel.[14] By the end of the decade, the Afghan military and police absorbed over half of the international aid money. Almost doubling the strength of the security forces by October 2012 will mean an even stiffer competition with development aid, especially if, as expected, the withdrawal of coalition forces has a knock-on effect on economic assistance.

The question then is what, if anything, can be done to soften the trade-off so that short-term measures to facilitate an exit acceptable to the US do not increase instability and dependence of the Afghan state in the slightly longer run. There seem to be two kinds of answers.

One is to speed up the search for a political solution to the insurgency that would permit the coalition forces to draw down and reduce the demand for a rapid expansion of Afghan security forces. Waiting to negotiate until the insurgents are decisively defeated carries the risk that defeat remains elusive, while Afghan society becomes more militarized and the political landscape more polarized—thereby making negotiations ultimately more difficult. The point had been increasingly recognized by the end of the decade, and by mid-2011 the signs of approaching talks were becoming stronger.[15] Reports from a blue-ribbon task force and various thinks tanks on possibilities and modalities of an eventual settlement started to appear.[16]

From the perspective of the international project as analysed in this book, three points are particularly relevant for eventual negotiations. First, and most important, a settlement will not work unless the major Afghans parties are on board. The principle of 'inclusive enough' may be the best one can hope for in this case, but a settlement must at least be acceptable to the Afghan parties who have a capacity to undo it. That is a principal lesson of the Bonn 2001 Agreement. Second, in line with the country's constitutional tradition, the constitutional question may be reopened to mark the dawn of a new era, and possibly to craft a political system that is more sensitive to a divided society than the present presidential system and centralized rule. This is particularly important for the non-Pashtun population which has benefitted considerably from the post-Taliban order, and where fear of a settlement that accommodates the Taliban runs deep. Third, a settlement may again require an international presence that could help secure Kabul as a neutral political space. If so, it should be recalled that a modest international force was sufficient for this purpose in the early post-Bonn transition. The operative factors, however, were political agreement among the Afghan parties, wide international political support and the US Air Force.

A second challenge is how to pare down the dysfunctional rentier state. The objective is implicit in the 'The Kabul Process' to establish Afghan ownership and leadership, formally announced by the international donor conference in July 2010. Yet, assuming that state revenue does not rise dramatically in the near future, the process will entail painful dilemmas in donor priorities and national budgetary allocations. The budgetary demands of the military sector have been noted above. By comparison, the education and health sectors are relatively small, have shown considerable progress to date, and could relatively easily be protected. The same applies to flagship projects such as the National Solidarity Programme (only $75 million in 2009). Highly paid foreign consultants on US$25,000-a-month salaries will probably be among the first to go, and rightly so, although retaining a core of international and Afghan advisers would help sustain donor contributions through good management and fiduciary control. Other examples could be cited. The problem for donors is that adjusting aid downwards before a political settlement is in hand seems counter-intuitive. Political and bureaucratic pressures to produce quick and decisive results are if anything likely to intensify during the transition in order to show strength, support exiting partners and create overall favourable conditions for negotiations that will permit an 'honourable' military withdrawal and a 'responsible' reduction of civilian assistance. Afghans, for their part, recognize that the aid-and-war economy in the not-too-distant future will shrink, and have reason to maximize aid while the going is good.

Good transitional policies will need to resist such pressures. The period up to 2014, when coalition combat forces are scheduled to be withdrawn, could be used constructively to recast the international project towards a less intrusive foreign role, in the process reducing in good measure its internal and dysfunctional tensions. On the aid side, it would mean truly reorienting assistance according to principles of sustainability and absorptive capacity, building rather than importing capacity, and listening to local priorities. On the military side, it would be particularly important to recognize that 'more is less'. Arming the Afghans to the hilt is neither a sustainable policy nor a plausible condition for a peaceful post-transition order.

By 2011, Western governments had tried unsuccessfully to defeat the Taliban militarily for almost a decade. In the process, they had been fighting a war that was enormously costly to the Afghan people and further divided the country. They had supported a government with weak legitimacy and empowered or permitted the rule of local strongmen who abused their positions. Political realism suggests that a transition needs to be accompanied by more modesty about the possibilities of the US and its allies to direct political change in Afghanistan. On the aid side, the equivalent would be to lower the level of ambition and adopt a longer time-frame in accordance with customary principles of aid. In 2011, this proposition is certainly not as controversial as it would have been a few years ago. Earlier idealism about the possibilities for external agents to create peace and build states in societies riddled by violence has given way to new thinking that stresses the need to work from conditions on the ground as they 'actually are' in order to nudge social change in desired directions.

NOTES

1. INTRODUCTION: THE LIBERAL PROJECT

1. UN Security Council, *Report of the Secretary-General on the Situation in Afghanistan and Its Implications for International Peace and Security*, 9 March 2011. S/2011/120, p. 24.
2. Leslie Gelb, 'Vietnam: The System Worked', *Foreign Policy*, no. 3 (1971). Gelb's conclusion that 'the system worked', that is, it met the test of intentionality instead of producing an unexpected and unwanted outcome, is deeply controversial. To most other critics, the system worked in a totally pathological way, representing a terrible 'march of folly', as the historian Barbara Tuchman wrote. Barbara Tuchman, *The March of Folly: From Troy to Vietnam* (New York: Ballantine Books, 1985).
3. United Nations, *Report of the Panel on United Nations Peace Operations* (New York: UN, 2000).
4. United Nations, *A More Secure World: Our Shared Responsibility*. High Level Panel on Threats, Challenges and Change (New York: UN, 2004).
5. http://www.un.org/peace/peacebuilding.
6. In Washington, the more archaic term 'nation-building' was used by officials in the Bush Administration, usually with negative connotations.
7. Roland Paris, *At War's End. Building Peace after Conflict* (Cambridge University Press, 2004).
8. David Chandler, *Empire in Denial: The Politics of State-Building* (London; Ann Arbor, MI: Pluto, 2006), and Mark R. Duffield, *Development, Security and Unending War: Governing the World of Peoples* (Cambridge: Polity, 2007) view the international peacebuilding regime as a deliberate and coherent strategy in service of quasi-imperial objectives. Elites in the world's powerful states, they argue, seek to maintain or expand their dominant position and this requires international stability of a certain kind. Above all it requires the existence of reasonably well-functioning states that operate according to the rules of the international system. 'Failed states', civil wars or similar upheavals threaten the international order by producing humanitarian crises, facilitating international terrorism and allowing trafficking of

illicit goods. In this view, the underlying rationale of peacebuilding is to maintain the dominant international order.

9. Roland Paris and Timothy D. Sisk, 'Introduction: Understanding the Contradictions of Postwar Statebuilding', in Roland Paris and Timothy D. Sisk, eds, *The Dilemmas of Statebuilding* (New York: Routledge, 2009), p. 1.

10. Charles Lindblom's well-known formulation in 1959 of course argues that 'muddling through' produces an optimal outcome.

11. James G. March, *The Pursuit of Organizational Intelligence* (London: Blackwell, 1999), p. 5.

12. Pledging figures varies due to different accounting procedures. Here and in chapter 5, figures are taken from the Afghan government, Ministry of Finance, *Donor Financial Review*, Report 1388 November, 2009, p. 9.

13. Ministry of Planning, cited at http://www.cmi.no/afghanistan/themes/ngos. cfm. The figure held steady in the following years. In 2009, 1,610 organizations were registered with the Ministry of Economy, Department of NGOs (http://www.ngo-dept.gov.af), although there had been a turnover as many organizations were delisted and new ones entered. Throughout, Afghan organizations were most numerous, but the international ones had the largest contracts.

14. Lord Ashdown, 'What I told Gordon Brown about Afghanistan', *The Spectator* (Coffee House Blog), 15 September 2008, www.spectator.co.uk.

15. http://andersfogh.info/2010/02/23/from-washington-a-flexible-nato-and-a-secure-afghanistan/

16. Diego A. Ruiz Palmer, 'Afghanistan's Transformational Challenge', *NATO Review*, summer 2005.

17. Catherine Lutz, 'Introduction: Bases, Empire and Global Response', in Catherine Lutz, ed., *The Bases of Empire: The Global Struggle against US Military Posts*, (New York University Press, 2009).

18. Prominent contributions include Doyle and Sambanis, who already in 2000 claimed that strong peacekeeping commitments enhanced the probability of sustained peace and democratic development: Michael W. Doyle and Nicholas Sambanis, 'International Peacebuilding: A Theoretical and Quantitative Analysis', *American Political Science Review* 94, no. 4 (2000). Fearon and Laitin argued for strong and long-lasting international deployments to create sustainable peace: James D. Fearon and David D. Laitin, 'Neotrusteeship and the Problem of Weak States', *International Security* 28, no. 4 (2004). World Bank research led by Paul Collier concluded that correctly phased-in aid and long-term peacekeeping forces could prevent a return to conflict: Paul Collier et al., *Breaking the Conflict Trap* (New York: Oxford University Press, 2003). The findings were echoed by the UN High-Level Panel on international security which warned that failure to invest adequately in peacebuilding increases the chances of

a return to conflict: (UN, 2004). The comparative case studies in Sted-man's edited volume on implementation of peace agreements pointed in the same direction. Indeed, Stedman's conclusion ends with a call for a stronger peacekeeping force in Afghanistan: Stephen John Stedman, D. Rotschild, and Elizabeth Cousens, eds, *Ending Civil Wars: The Implementation of Peace Agreements* (Boulder, CO: Lynne Rienner 2002). The authors of these works are all prominent academics with influence in pol-icy-making circles.

19. Published in the *The Hill*, a publication of the US Congress, 8 February 2006.

20. Barnett R. Rubin, 'Saving Afghanistan', *Foreign Affairs*', vol. 86, no. 1 (February 2007), p. 66.

21. 'NATO's Choice in Afghanistan: Go Big or Go Home', *Policy Options* (Ottawa), December 2006–7, p. 36. Roland Paris's book *At War's End* (2004) had won international awards for contributions to global order and multilateralism.

22. Seth G. Jones, 'Averting Failure in Afghanistan', *Survival*, vol. 48, no. 1 (March 2006): pp. 111–28. The benchmarks referred to ongoing work at the Rand Corporation on UN and US peace operations in the post-Cold War world (plus Germany and Japan after World War II). In fact, the pub-lished work of this study group, led by Ambassador James Dobbins, did not produce 'benchmarks' for stabilization and concluded that the smaller and lighter UN operations had been more successful than the heavier US-led ones. James Dobbins, *America's Role in Nation-Building: From Ger-many to Iraq* (Santa Monica, CA: RAND, 2003). James Dobbins, *The UN's Role in Nation-Building: From the Congo to Iraq* (Santa Monica, CA: RAND Corporation, 2005); James Dobbins, *The Beginner's Guide to Nation-Building* (Santa Monica, CA: RAND National Security Research Division, 2007).

23. Ahmed Rashid, *Descent into Chaos* (London: Allen Lane, 2008), p. 248.

24. Writing in *Foreign Affairs* in January 2011, a US analyst advocated greater involvement, citing Jones' development of the thesis in his 2009 book, *The Graveyard of Empires. America's War in Afghanistan* (New York: W.W. Norton). Jones argues here that the US had squandered an opportunity in the immediate aftermath of the invasion to decisively squash the enemy and stabilize Afghanistan. Paul D. Miller, 'Finish the Job. How the War in Afghanistan Can Be Won', *Foreign Affairs*, vol. 90, no. 1 (January 2011), pp. 51–65.

25. Niall Ferguson, *Virtual History: Alternatives and Counterfactuals* (New York: Basic Books, 1999).

26. Marina Ottaway and Anatol Lieven, *Rebuilding Afghanistan; Fantasy Ver-sus Reality* (Washington, DC: Carnegie Endowment for International Peace, Policy Brief no. 12, January 2002).

27. Author's notes from seminars at the Carnegie Endowment for Interna-

tional Peace, January 2002, and the Nixon Center, 8 August 2002, both in Washington, DC.

28. Astri Suhrke, Kristian Berg Harpviken, and Arne Strand, 'Conflictual Peacebuilding: Afghanistan Two Years after Bonn' (Bergen: Chr. Michelsen Institute, 2004). Astri Suhrke, 'Reconstruction as Modernisation: The 'Post-Conflict' Project in Afghanistan', *Third World Quarterly* 28, no. 7 (2007).

29. Chris Johnson and Jolyon Leslie, *Afghanistan. The Mirage of Peace* (London: Zed, 2004). Much later the theme was acknowledged in the mainstream media. See Rory Stewart, 'Where less is more', *New York Times*, 23 July 2007.

30. Peter Bergen, 'After the Taliban', *Washington Post*, 13 March 2005.

31. See e.g. William Maley, *The Afghanistan Wars*. 2nd edn (New York: Palgrave Macmillan, 2009); Jones (2009); Rashid (2008).

32. See e.g. Sarah Chayes, *The Punishment of Virtue. Inside Afghanistan after the Taliban* (New York: The Penguin Press, 2006). Afghan and international human rights organizations also stress this point.

33. Michael Mann, *Incoherent Empire* (London: Verso, 2003), Andrew J. Bacevich, *The New American Militarism: How Americans Are Seduced by War* (New York: Oxford University Press, 2005).

34. Roger MacGinty and Oliver Richmond, 'Myth or Reality: Opposing Views on the Liberal Peace and Post-War Reconstruction', in Roger MacGinty and Oliver Richmond, eds, *The Liberal Peace and Post-War Reconstruction* (London: Routledge, 2009), p. 2.

35. On the importance of taxation, see Deborah Bräutigam, Odd-Helge Fjeldstad, and Mick Moore, eds, *Taxation and Statebuilding in Developing Countries* (Cambridge University Press, 2008). On the role of perverse incentives, see Dominique Darbon et al., 'The Legitimacy of the State in Fragile Situations', in *NORAD Report for the OECD DAC International Network on Conflict and Fragility* (Oslo: 2009).

36. This finding holds across disciplines. See e.g. Douglass Cecil North, *Institutions, Institutional Change, and Economic Performance, The Political Economy of Institutions and Decisions* (Cambridge University Press, 1990), Michael Ross, 'Does Oil Hinder Democracy?', *World Politics* 53, no. 3 (2001), Robert H. Bates, *Prosperity and Violence: The Political Economy of Development* (New York: W. W. Norton, 2001).

2. THE POINT OF ENTRY: A LIGHT FOOTPRINT

1. Serge Schmemann, 'U.S. and partners quickly set sights on a post-Taliban Kabul', *New York Times*, 13 November 2001.

2. Diego Cordovez and Selig S. Harrison, *Out of Afghanistan:The Inside Story of the Soviet Withdrawal* (New York: Oxford University Press, 1995).

Najibullah remained in the UN compound until 1996, when the Taliban entered the city and killed him.

3. Maley (2009), Chps 8 and 9.

4. The six neighbours—Pakistan, Iran, China, Tajikistan, Uzbekistan and Turkmenistan—plus Russia and the United States.

5. Astri Suhrke, Arne Strand and Kristian Berg Harpviken, *Peacebuilding Strategies in Afghanistan* (Bergen: Chr. Michelsen Institute, CMI report, 2001).

6. Lakhdar Brahimi, Briefing to the Security Council, Tuesday, 13 November 2001 www.un.org/News/dh/latest/afghan/brahimi-sc-briefing.htm

7. Bob Woodward, *Bush at War* (New York: Simon & Schuster, 2002), p. 192.

8. Doug MacEachin and Janne E. Nolan, 'The US and Soviet Proxy War in Afghanistan, 1989–1992: Prisoners of Our Preconceptions?' Working Group Report no iv, November 15, 2005 (Georgetown University). http://www12.georgetown.edu/sfs/isd/Afghan_2_WR_report.pdf, p. 10.

9. Ibid., p. 7.

10. Condoleezza Rice, 'Promoting the National Interest', *Foreign Affairs*, vol. 79, no. 1 (2000), pp. 45–62. The essay was written while George W. Bush was a presidential candidate.

11. Justine Smith, 'War on Terror. Bush's Pledge: Smoke'em Out', *The Mirror*, 26 September 2001.

12. Woodward (2002), p. 195.

13. Press conference, 11 October 2001, http://www.whitehouse.gov/news/releases/2001/10/20011011-7.html.

14. Woodward (2002), p. 193.

15. In mid-October, Colin Powell appointed the head of the Policy Planning Department in the State Department, Richard Haass, to be special coordinator for Afghanistan policy and the counterpart to Brahimi at the UN. Similar reassignments were made in the National Security Council, where two persons were given special responsibility for Afghanistan, including the Afghan-American Zalmay Khalilzad, later Ambassador to Afghanistan. In early November, James Dobbins was appointed as 'ambassador to the Afghan opposition'. The main task for Dobbins, a career diplomat with experience from European affairs, was to bring the various Afghan factions to form a government.

16. James Dobbins, *After the Taliban: Nation-building in Afghanistan* (Washington, DC: Potomac Books, 2008).

17. Rice (2002), p. 53.

18. Ewen MacAskill, 'Special Envoy Arrives for talks in Pakistan', *The Guardian*, 27 October 2001. Haass had also favoured a large, joint US-NATO invasion force. James Traub, *The Best Intentions: Kofi Annan and the UN in the Era of American World Power* (New York: Farrar, Straus and Giroux, 2006), p. 163.

19. Jones (2009), p. 110.
20. UN (2000).
21. Astri Suhrke, Jolyon Leslie and Arne Strand, 'Afghanistan. A Snapshot Study', in *A Review of Peace Operations: A Case for Change* (London: King's College, 2003), pp. 325–68, http://ipi.sspp.kcl.ac.uk/index.html
22. Cited in Alfredo Witschi-Cestari, Paula Newberg and Michael Keating, *Coping with Complexity: Reforming International Assistance to Afghanistan, 1996–98* (UNCO, Islamabad, October 1998), p. 1.
23. BBC 'Hard Talk', 17 October 2001.
24. Simon Chesterman, *You, the People: The United Nations, Transitional Administration, and State-building* (Oxford and New York: Oxford University Press, 2004).
25. Brahimi, November 13 speech.
26. Richard Caplan, *A New Trusteeship? The International Administration of War-torn Territories* (Oxford University Press, 2002).
27. The importance of protecting the organization was strikingly evident in the response of the UN to events in Rwanda in 1994. See Michael N. Barnett, *Eyewitness to a Genocide: the United Nations and Rwanda* (Ithaca, NY: Cornell University Press, 2002).
28. Colum Lynch, 'Envoy urges UN not to send peacekeepers', *Washington Post*, 17 October 2001.
29. Declaration on the Situation in Afghanistan by the Foreign Ministers and other senior representatives of the 'Six plus Two'. Press release. 12 November 2001. Posted on www.reliefweb.int
30. Resolution 1333, 19 December 2000, the last one before the 9/11 attacks.
31. Brahimi's speech, 13 November 2001.
32. Lynch (2001).
33. The story as commonly told fails to mention that there were several other survivors. They had been taken prisoners at an earlier stage and were treated well.
34. Todd Diamond, 'UN Representatives focus on humanitarian efforts in Afghanistan', Eurasianet.org 10/19/01; see also Headquarters Press briefing by Special Representative for Afghanistan, 17/10/2001, http://www.un.org/News/briefings/docs/2001/brahimibrf2.doc.htm
35. Jonathan Steele, 'Turkey asked to lead Islamic peace troops', *The Guardian* 18 October 2001. Some independent analysts strongly supported the idea, e.g. Anatol Lieven, 'Only a Muslim UN Force can Secure Peace', *The Independent*, 14 October 2001.
36. Press briefing, 17 October, cited in Lynch (2001).
37. Brahimi, 13 November speech.
38. Agreement on provisional arrangements in Afghanistan pending the re-establishment of permanent government institutions. http://www.afghangovernment.com/AfghanAgreementBonn.htm

39. Dobbins (2008), p. 88. The foreign diplomats were not formally part of the Bonn conference and did not have access to the negotiations among the Afghans that Brahimi led. They 'worked' the Afghan delegates from the outside, in the corridors and in other common social venues.
40. Dobbins (2008), p. 103.
41. Robert Cooper, *Re-Ordering the World: The Long-term Implications of September 11th* (London: Foreign Policy Centre, 2002).
42. Michael R. Gordon, 'Afghans Block British Plan for Brigade Force', *New York Times*, 20 November 2001.
43. Dobbins (2008), p. 128
44. UN Resolution 1386, 20 December 2001.
45. Dobbins (2008), p. 88.

3. AMERICAN BOOTS ON THE GROUND

1. Woodward (2002), p. 167.
2. T. Franks, *American Soldier*, New York: Regan Books, 2004, p. 324.
3. S.M. Maloney, 'Afghanistan: From here to Eternity?', *Parameters*, Spring 2004, p. 7.
4. R.B. Andres, C. Wills and T.E. Griffith, Jr., 'Winning with Allies. The Strategic Value of the Afghan Model', *International Security*, vol. 30, no. 3, Winter 2005/6, pp. 124–60. The term 'Afghan model' was developed by Stephen Biddle, *Afghanistan and the Future of Warfare*, ed., Strategic Studies Institute (Carlisle, Pennsylvania: U.S. Army War College, 2002).
5. This account and citations in this paragraph are from Andres et al., pp. 147–8.
6. Ron Synovitz, 'Afghanistan: U.S.-led Commando Teams Fight Taliban With Unconventional Warfare', Radio Free Europe/Radio Liberty, 15 March 2004. http://www.rferl.org/featuresarticle/2004/03/941e41ab-25ea-48b5-9090-3d3d35006bb8.html
7. Rashid (2008), pp. 242–5.
8. British Agencies Afghanistan Group (BAAG) Monthly Report November 2003.
9. Ibid.
10. Doughlas Jehl, 'Afghan front heats up, and Rumsfeld urges patience', *New York Times*, 8 September 2003. Rashid (2008), p. 247 dates similar reports to mid-2002.
11. Steven R. Weisman, 'Resurgent Taliban threatens Afghan Stability, U.S. Says', *New York Times*, 19 November 2003.
12. Cited in Karen DeYoung, *Soldier. The Life of Colin Powell* (New York: Alfred A. Knopf, 2006), p. 515.
13. The US Congressional Research Service, which usually tracks figures carefully, uses 8–9000 for force levels in its 2002 and 2003 reports. In its next

report of December 2004, the number has almost doubled to 18 000. Similar figures were reported in the media, although without much explanation for the jump.

14. Eric Schmitt, 'Up to 2000 Marines to go to Afghanistan from Gulf', *New York Times*, 26 March 2004.

15. Lisa Burgess, 'U.S. troop presence in Afghanistan at 17,900, and expected to hold steady', *Stars and Stripes*, 9 July 2004 http://www.globalsecurity.org/org/news/2004/040709-afghan-presence.htm

16. Alex Mundt and Susanne Schmeidl, 'The Failure to Protect: Battle-Affected IDPs in Southern Afghanistan', (Washington DC: The Brookings-Bern Project on Internal Displacement. The Brookings Institution, 2009).

17. Cited in Paddy Ashdown, 'We are failing in Afghanistan', *The Guardian*, 19 July 2007, referring to Richard's statement the previous year.

18. Interview with *Der Spiegel*, 10 August 2006.

19. James Fergusson, *A Million Bullets. The Real Story of the British Army in Afghanistan* (London: Transworld, 2008), Chp 3.

20. Memorandum from General Barry R. McCaffrey to Colonel Mike Meese, Department Head, Department of Social Sciences, United States Military Academy, 3 June 2006, 'Academic Report—Trip to Afghanistan and Pakistan, Friday 19 May through Friday 26 May'.

21. NATO and UNAMA, *Suicide Attacks in Afghanistan*, 9 September 2007, http://hsrp.typepad.com/afghanistan/UNAMA_suicideattacks200107.pdf

22. Afghan Conflict Monitor, Human Security Project, http://www.afghanconflictmonitor.org/hsrp/ and http://www.icasualities.org/oef.

23. 'Slouching Towards Riga', *New York Times*, 28 November 2006.

24. Finn Stepputat, 'Integrated National Approaches to International Operations: The Case of Denmark, the UK and the Netherlands' (Copenhagen: DIIS, 2009), p. 9.

25. Peter Viggo Jakobsen, 'Nato's Comprehensive Approach to Crisis Response Operations' (Copenhagen: DIIS, 2008).

26. www.nato.int/docu/pr/p06–150e.htm

27. David S. Yost, *Nato Transformed: The Alliance's New Role in International Security* (Washington, DC: United States Institute of Peace Press, 1998).

28. Speech by Secretary of Defense Robert M. Gates, 25 October 2007 http://www.defenselink.mil/speeches/speech.aspx?speechid=1188

29. Carlotta Gall, 'Blair, in Kabul, warns that fight against the Taliban will take decades', *New York Times*, 21 November 2006.

30. Cited in *Sunday Times*, 9 July 2006.

31. The Study Group report is on http://www.usip.org/isg

32. See e.g. Rashid (2008) and Maley (2009).

33. Anand Gopal, 'The Battle for Afghanistan. Militancy and Conflict in Kandahar' (Washington, DC: New America Foundation, 2010), p. 5.

34. Gopal (2010). Similarly, Sarah Chayes, who worked closely with the American forces in Kandahar, concluded that Karzai set aside his old ally, Mullah Naqib, in favour of the controversial strongman Gul Aga Sherzai to rule in Kandahar after the invasion because he feared US suspicions of Naqib's previous ties with the Taliban. Chayes (2006), pp. 60–61.

35. Thomas Ruttig, 'How Tribal Are the Taliban?' (Kabul: Afghan Analysts Network, 2010), p. 21. Ruttig cites Giustozzi on the initial limited response to Mullah Omar. Antonio Giustozzi, *Koran, Kalashnikov and Laptop. The Neo-Taliban Insurgency in Afghanistan* (London: Hurst & Co., 2007), p. 37.

36. Giustozzi (2007). Ruttig (2010) questions the importance of the novel elements.

37. Alia Brahimi, 'The Taliban's Evolving Ideology' (London: LSE Global Governance, 2010), p. 19.

38. Foreign fighters who joined the Taliban were often resented by local Afghans and local commanders, and the use of suicide bombings introduced by international fighters deeply divided the Taliban. The so-called purists opposed it for being against Islam and tactically unwise by alienating the population. Ruttig (2010), p. 17.

39. Cited in Steve Coll, 'War by Other Means', *The New Yorker*, 24 May 2010, p. 44.

40. Glatzer, cited in Robert D. Crews, 'Moderate Taliban?' in Robert D. Crews and Amin Tarzi, eds, *The Taliban and the Crisis of Afghanistan* (Cambridge, Mass.: Harvard University Press, 2008), p. 242.

41. Antonio Giustozzi, ed., *Decoding the New Taliban: Insights from the Afghan Field* (London: Hurst & Co, 2009).

42. Author's discussion with villagers in Sayedabad, Wardak, 2003.

43. Chayes (2006).

44. Christoph Reuter and Borhan Younus, 'The Return of the Taliban in Andar District, Ghazni', in Giustozzi (2009), pp. 101–118.

45. Tribal Liaison Office, 'Zabul Provincial Assessment' (Kabul: Tribal Liaison Office, 2008).

46. David McKiernan, 'Speech to the Atlantic Council 18 November 2008' (2008). Ruttig (2010) likewise describes the movement as network-based.

47. Martine van Bijlert, 'Unruly Commanders and Violent Power Struggles: Taliban Networks in Uruzgan', in Giustozzi (2009), p. 160.

48. The autobiography of Mullah Zaeef gives a fascinating glimpse into the role of Islam in the daily lives and struggles of the 'old' Taliban movement: Abdul Salam Zaeef, *My Life with the Taliban*, ed. Alex Strick von Linschoten and Felix Kuhn (London Hurst & Co., 2010). Giustozzi (2007) found that conservative and traditionalist clergy formed the core of the 'new' Taliban.

49. Graeme Smith of the Toronto *Globe & Mail*, based in Kandahar in 2006–8.

See his online report Graeme Smith, *Talking to the Taliban* (Toronto Globe and Mail, 2008); available from http://v1.theglobeandmail.com/talkingtothetaliban/. A study carried out for the UN in 2007 found that the most dedicated (or fanatical) fighters cited Islam as well as national or family honour as reasons for making the ultimate sacrifice. A study of would-be suicide bombers who failed in the task found that they were motivated by 'a sense of [foreign] occupation, anger over civilian causalities, and affronts to their national, family and personal senses of honour and dignity that are perpetrated in the conduct of counterinsurgency operations. Some attackers were also motivated by religious rewards and duties'. UNAMA, 'Suicide Attacks in Afghanistan' (Kabul: 2007), p. 6.

50. Olivier Roy, *Islam and Resistance in Afghanistan* (Cambridge University Press, 1990), p. 62, cited in Brahimi (2010), p. 5.

51. Agence France Presse, 8 July 2006.

52. M. Cherif Bassiouni, 'Report of the Independent Expert on the Situation of Human Rights in Afghanistan' (New York: United Nations. UN E/CN.4/2005/122, 2005). The Bush Administration reacted to the report by forcing the UN to dismiss Bassiouni, a prominent professor of law at DePaul University.

53. Antonio Donini et al., 'Mapping the Security Environment. Understanding the Perception of Local Communities, Peace Support Operations and Assistance Agencies. Afghanistan Case Study' (Boston: Feinstein International Center, 2005), p. 32.

54. The events in Uruzgan on the night of 1 July 2002 were closely covered by the international press and are not in dispute. A US air patrol flying over an area that had been a Taliban stronghold registered gunfire noise, which the pilot claimed was directed at the plane, but in fact was celebratory gunfire at a wedding. An AC-130 gunship fired rockets and swiped the area with machine gun fire. A B-52 was called in and dropped a bomb. On the ground, the wedding guests tried to run for cover, but an estimated 50 persons were killed and over 100 wounded. Early next morning, American soldiers entered the village, bound the hands of the survivors with plastic handcuffs, also the women. Outraged villagers told foreign journalists the soldiers also had photographed the dead bodies, including bodies of women whose clothing had been torn away.

55. Agence France Presse, 1 May 2005.

56. Jason Straziuso, 'Karzai: Nato Bombs; Terrorists Kill Kids', Associated Press, December 2006.

57. Press conference, Kabul, 22 June 2006, cited in Tom Regan, 'Karzai questions US, NATO tactics in Afghanistan', *Christian Science Monitor*, 23 June 2006. (Emphasis added).

58. See e.g. Rubin (2007); Jones (2006, 2009); William Maley, *Rescuing Afghanistan* (London: Hurst & Co, 2006) and Maley (2009) and Rashid (2008) (Rashid of course is not Western in a nationality sense).

59. David Kilcullen, *The Accidental Guerrilla: Fighting Small Wars in the Midst of a Big One* (London: Hurst & Co, 2009).The annual US Department of Defense reports to the Congress towards the end of the decade likewise make little reference to ideology as motivating factor for the insurgency. Department of Defense (2009 and 2010).

60. For an overview of initiatives, see Astri Suhrke et al., 'Conciliatory Approaches to the Insurgency in Afghanistan' (Bergen: Chr. Michelsen Institute, 2009). A detailed proposal for buy-back and integration of Taliban soldiers is presented by Michael Semple, *Reconciliation in Afghanistan* (Washington, DC: U.S. Institute of Peace, 2009).

61. For a list of publications resulting from the project, see https://wikis.uit. tufts.edu/confluence/pages/viewpage.action?pageId=19270958

62. *Restrepo*. A film by Tim Hetherington and Sebastian Junger.

63. My own work started to explore the historical parallels around mid-decade. See Astri Suhrke, 'When More Is Less: Aiding Statebuilding in Afghanistan', Report in External Series (Bergen: Chr. Michelsen Institute, 2006), co-published in Spanish as 'Cuando mas es Menos: Contribuir a la Construcción del Estado en Afganistan' by FRIDE Institute (Madrid), 2006.

64. Thomas Ruttig, 'The Other Side. Dimensions of the Afghan Insurgency: Causes, Actors and Approaches to "Talks"'. Afghan Analysts Network, July 2009, p. 2. See also Ruttig (2010) and Brahimi (2010).

65. Elizabeth Bumiller, 'In Afghanistan, Gates to talk of troop increases', *New York Times*, 12 December 2008.

66. *Progress toward Security and Stability in Afghanistan*. Report to Congress. Washington, DC; US Department of Defense, January 2009, p. 3.

67. Bobby Ghosh, 'Obama Afghanistan Plan Breaks Old Ground', *Time*, 28 March 2009.

68. Cited inTuchman (1985), p. 303.

69. Garry Wills, 'One-Term President?' *New York Review Blog*, 3 November 2009. http://www.nybooks.com/blogs/nyrblog/2009/nov/03/one-term-president/

70. Bob Woodward, *Obama's War* (New York: Simon & Schuster, 2010).

71. Victor Sebestyen, 'Transcripts of defeat', *New York Times*, 29 October 2009.

72. ISAF, 'COMISAF's Initial Assessment', International Security Assistance Force Headquarters, Kabul, Afghanistan, 30 August 2009, pp. 1–1.

73. Ibid., pp. 1–2.

74. US Army Colonel Collins in interview with a US army publication, Jim Garmarone, 'World Cannot Give up on Afghanistan, Coalition Officials Say', *American Forces Press Service*, 28 July 2006.

75. Jakobsen (2008), p. 15.

76. Department of Defense (2009), p. 17.

77. Ibid., p. 29.

78. David W. Barno, 'Fighting "the Other War". Counterinsurgency Strategy in Afghanistan. 2003–2005', *Military Review*, September-October 2007, pp. 32–44.
79. *Progress toward Security and Stability in Afghanistan*. Report to Congress. (Washington, DC: US Department of Defense, 2010), pp. 21–2.
80. Personal communication to author, 23 July 2010.
81. Rajiv Chandrasekaran, 'War the old-fashioned way'. *Washington Post*, 20 February 2010. See also Brett Van Ess, 'The Fight for Marjah: Recent Counterinsurgency Operations in Southern Afghanistan', *Small Wars Journal*, September, 2010. http://smallwarsjournal.com/blog/journal/docs-temp/563-vaness.pdf
82. http://www.army.mil/-news/2010/03/25/36324-a-historical-basis-for-force-requirements-in-counterinsurgency/index.html
83. The International Council on Security and Development (formerly the Senlis Council), *The Relationship Gap*. July 2010, pp. 9–10. Available at http://www.icosgroup.net/documents/afghanistan_relationship_gap.pdf. The organization's forerunner was expelled from Afghanistan for its critical reporting of the government and for advocating decriminalization of poppy production.
84. Data on ethnic composition in the ANA are difficult to obtain and not fully reliable, but it is clear that Pashtuns are underrepresented, particularly in the officer corps. Antonio Giustozzi, 'The Afghan National Army. Unwarranted Hope?' *The RUSI Journal* 154, no. 6 (2009). According to Ahmed Rashid, writing in early 2011, the Tajiks and Hazaras 'dominate the upper officer class in the army and the police', Pashtun representation in the army is 'lower than its proportion of the population' and 'only 3 per cent of recruits are from the volatile south'. Ahmed Rashid, 'The Way out of Afghanistan', *New York Review of Books*, 13 January 2011, p. 19.
85. Gareth Porter, 'Doubling of SOF Night Raids Backfired in Kandahar', IPS, 15 September 2010. http://ipsnews.net/news.asp?idnews=52842
86. Phil Stewart, 'Kandahar campaign's fate not clear until June: NATO', Reuters, 28 October 2010.
87. Army Sgt Tony J. Spain, *82nd Airborne Goes 'all the Way' During Operation Achilles*, 7 June 2007, http://192.31.19.143/sites/uscentcom2/Front-Page%20Stories/82nd%20Airborne%20Goes%20all%20the%20Way%20During%20Operation%20Achilles.aspx
88. Peter Graff, 'Promises and threats for Afghans to rid Taliban', Reuters 7 June 2007, http://uk.reuters.com/article/worldNews/idUKB79616920070607 (Emphasis added).
89. http://www.wired.com/dangerroom/2011/02/i-flattened-afghan-villages/
90. Ibid.
91. NATO/ISAF. HQ, Kabul, Afghanistan, *Tactical Directive*, 6 July 2008.
92. COMISAF/CDR USFOR-A 27 July 2010.
93. UN (2010), p. 13.

94. R.A. Oppel Jr and T. Shah, 'Afghans and NATO differ on civilian deaths', *New York Times*, 26 July 2010.

95. Spencer Ackerman, *Drones Surge, Special Ops Strike in Petraeus Campaign Plan*, 2010 (posted 31 August 2010); available from http://www. wired.com/dangerroom/2010/08/petraeus-campaign-plan/#ixzz0yCFa F0H2.

96. Local knowledge is particularly important in counterinsurgency campaigns. John A. Nagl, *Learning to Eat Soup with a Knife: Counterinsurgency Lessons from Malaya and Vietnam*, (Chicago: University of Chicago Press, 2005).

97. Michael T. Flynn, Matt Pottinger, and Paul D. Batchelor, 'Fixing Intel: A Blueprint for Making Intelligence Relevant in Afghanistan' (Washington, DC: Center for a New American Security, 2010), p. 4.

98. Barnett R. Rubin, *Informed Comment Blog*, posted 15 January 2008, available from http://icga.blogspot.com/2008/01/new-york-times-on-isi-serena-hotel

99. Rashid (2008), p. 244.

100. Jack Crowley, 'A million dollar militia', Al-Jazeera International, 2 September 2010; Mathieu Lefèvre, 'Local Defence in Afghanistan. A Review of Government-Backed Initiatives' (Kabul: Afghan Analysts Network, 2010), p. 18.

101. Martine van Bijlert, 'Counterinsurgency in Kandahar: What Happened to the Fence?' (Kabul: Afghan Analysts Network, 2010).

102. ICOS (2010), pp. 22–5.

103. Pamela Constable, 'The end of the Kabul Spring', *Washington Post*, 11 June 2006.

4. PROVIDING SECURITY ASSISTANCE

1. J. Alexander Thier, 'The Politics of Peacebuilding—Year One: From Bonn to Kabul', in Antonio Donini, Norah Niland and Karin Wermester, eds, *Nation-Building Unraveled Aid, Peace and Justice in Afghanistan*, (Bloomfield: Kumarian Press, 2004), pp. 53–6.

2. Scott Baldauf, 'Afghan campaign trail barely trod by Karzai', *The Christian Science Monitor*, 31 October 2003.

3. UN, *The Situation in Afghanistan and its Implications for International Peace and Security. Report of the Secretary-General*. 18 March 2002 (S/2002/278), p. 9.

4. Ibid., and http://webarchive.nationalarchives.gov.uk/+/http://www.opera-tions.mod.uk/fingal/index.htm

5. Author's interview with UN official, Kabul, March 2003.

6. Michael Ignatieff, 'Nation-building lite', *New York Times Sunday Magazine*, 28 July 2002.

7. Michael Ignatieff, *Empire Lite: Nation-Building in Bosnia, Kosovo and Afghanistan* (Toronto: Penguin, 2003).
8. Michael Barnett and Christopher Zürcher, 'The Peacebuilder's Contract: How External Statebuilding Reinforces Weak Statehood', in Paris and Sisk (2009).
9. *Washington Post*, 26 March 2002.
10. 'Security Concerns Mount in Afghanistan as Country Enters Critical Reconstruction Phase', Eurasianet.org, 13 March 2002. www.eurasianet. org/departments/insight/articles/eav031402.shtml
11. Speech to the International Conference on Reconstruction Assistance to Afghanistan, Tokyo, 21 January 2002. Copy on file with author.
12. UN (2002/278).
13. UN, *The Situation in Afghanistan and its Implications for International Peace and Security. Report of the Secretary-General.* 11 July 2002. S/2002/737, p. 1.
14. UN (2002/737), p. 4.
15. Renata Dwan, Thomas Papworth and Sharon Wiharta, 'Multilateral Peace Missions, 2001', in *Yearbook 2002*, ed. SIPRI (Stockholm: SIPRI, 2002), p. 126.
16. Human Rights Watch, 'Paying for the Taliban's Crimes', April 2002, p. 49.
17. Ibid.
18. Committee on Foreign Relations US Senate, 'Afghanistan: Building Stability, Avoiding Chaos. Hearing', (U.S. GPO, 2002), p. 25.
19. Dwan et al. (2002), loc. cit.
20. Agence France-Presse, cited in Human Rights Watch (2002), p. 48.
21. GlobalSecurity.org, 'Operation Enduring Freedom—Deployments'. http://www.globalsecurity.org/military/ops/enduring-freedom_deploy-col.htm
22. Jones (2009), pp. 114–15.
23. US Senate (2002). p. 12.
24. Ibid., p. 28.
25. http://www.isaf.nato.int/troop-numbers-and-contributions/index.php. valid as of 14 December 2010.
26. Vincent Morelli and Paul Belkin, 'Nato in Afghanistan: A Test of the Transatlantic Alliance' (Congressional Research Service, 2009). http://www.fas.org/sgp/crs/row/RL33627.pdf
27. http://www.nato.int/isaf/topics/mandate/index.html
28. Author's interview with US Col. Michael Stout, Washington, DC, 14 May 2010.
29. Robert M. Perito, 'The U.S. Experience with Provincial Reconstruction Teams in Afghanistan: Lessons Identified', in *Special Report* (Washington, DC: United States Institute of Peace, 2005).
30. Barbara J. Stapleton, 'A Means to What End? Why PRTs Are Peripheral to the Bigger Political Challenges in Afghanistan', *Journal of Military and Strategic Studies*, 10, no. 1 (2007).

31. Timo Noetzel and Thomas Rid, 'Germany's Options in Afghanistan', *Survival*, 51, no. 5 (2009). Peter Schmidt, 'Stability Operation and Alliance Management: The German View', National Institute for Defence Studies (Tokyo), 2008. www.nids.gov.jp

32. Janice Gross Stein and J. Eugene Lang, *The Unexpected War: Canada in Kandahar* (Toronto: Viking Canada, 2007).

33. James Fergusson, *A Million Bullets. The Real Story of the British Army in Afghanistan* (London: Transworld, 2008).

34. In Uruzgan, for instance, the local population clearly distinguished between the Dutch and the American troops in the province, according to a report prepared for the Dutch government. TLO, 'The Dutch Engagement in Uruzgan' (Kabul: The Liaison Office, 2010).

35. Anders Sømme Hammer, *Drømmekrigen. Hjerter og sinn i Afghanistan og Norge* (Oslo: Aschehoug, 2010), p. 308.

36. Arne Strand and Organisation for Sustainable Development and Research, 'Faryab Survey. Comparison of Findings from Maymane, 2006 and 2009', in *CMI Report* (Bergen: Chr. Michelsen Institute, 2009).

37. Bob Woodward, *Obama's War* (New York: Simon & Schuster, 2010), p. 42.

38. For example, Germany agreed to take command of ISAF in February 2003, and increased its forces in Kabul, while denying that it was to pre-empt requests from Washington to contribute to the intervention in Iraq.

39. This section draws on research for a joint project with Kristian Berg Harpviken and Øyvind Ofstad of the Peace Research Institute Oslo, hereafter cited as the PRIO/CMI project. The analysis also draws on discussions with Ståle Ulrichsen at the Norwegian Institute of International Affairs (NUPI).

40. Stolenberg-regjeringens tiltredelseserklæring, 19 October 2005.

41. Antonio Giustozzi, *Empires of Mud* (London: Hurst & Co., 2008). Antonio Giustozzi, 'Armed Politics in Afghanistan', in *The Peace in Between. Post-War Violence and Peacebuilding*, ed. Astri Suhrke and Mats Berdal (London: Routledge, 2011) forthcoming.

42. Interview with author, 11 September 2010.

43. Interview with author, 3 September 2010.

44. This section draws on recollections of Norwegian officials central to the process in interviews with the author, September 2010.

45. British Agencies Afghanistan Group, monthly reports 2007.

46. Giustozzi (2007).

47. Peter Marsden and Josh Arnold-Forster, 'An Assessment of the Security of Asian Development Bank Projects in Afghanistan' (Asian Development Bank, 2007), p. 38.

48. Author's interview with Norwegian military official, 19 April 2010.

49. Internal memo, Embassy of Norway, Kabul, 12 November 2007.

50. PRIO/CMI project, interview with Norwegian military official, 24 August

2010. Giustozzi (2007) writes that Taliban 'allegedly' used Badghis to infiltrate Faryab (p. 66).

51. PRIO/CMI project, interview with Norwegian military official, 11 September 2010.

52. Eystein Røssum, 'Norsk plan ramma fattige sivile', *Bergens Tidende*, 12 May 2010.

53. *Tagesspiegel*, 5 December 2008, http://www.tagesspiegel.de/politik/ausweitung-der-kampfzone/1388038.html

54. Interview with Norwegian official, 9 September 2010.

55. *Spiegel Online International* http://www.spiegel.de/politik/ausland/0,1518, 601284,00.html

56. *Spiegel Online International*, 12 January 2011. http://www.spiegel.de/international/germany/0,1518,739140,00.html

57. Internal memo, Embassy of Norway, Kabul, 12 November 2007.

58. Interview with author, 8 September 2010.

59. Hammer (2010).

60. Lt. Col. Øglænd, Aftenposten, 'Norske soldater har tatt liv i Afghanistan', *Aftenposten*, 6 november 2007.

61. Eystein Røssum, 'Eldreråd i nord stiller seg bak Taliban', *Bergens Tidende*, 10 May 2010.

62. Per Anders Johansen, 'Under ild nesten hver dag', *Aftenposten*, 17 August 2010. http://www.aftenposten.no/nyheter/iriks/article3772619.ece

63. Col. Gjermund Eide, cited in ibid.

64. Theo Farrell and Stuart Gordon, 'Coin Machine: The British Military in Afghanistan', *RUSI Journal* 154, no. 3 (2009), p. 19.

65. Tom Coghlan, 'The Taliban in Helmand. An Oral History', in Giustozzi (2009), pp. 125–6.

66. Cited in Fergusson (2008), p. 209.

67. Declan Walsh, 'Welcome to Helmand', *Guardian Weekly*, 10–16 February 2006, p. 16.

68. Zaeef (2010).

69. 'Hopes and fears as NATO takes command in south Afghanistan', Agence France-Presse, 27 July 2006. Available on: http://www.e-ariana.com/ariana/eariana.nsf/allDocs/8EFCCF35E298F3A1872571B8003FC5CE?OpenDocument.

70. Ibid.

71. Anatol Lieven, 'Insights From the Afghan Field', Review Article, *Current Intelligence* 6 September 2010. http://www.currentintelligence.net/reviews/2010/9/6/insights-from-the-afghan-field.html

72. Cited in Fergusson (2008), p. 22.

73. Tom Coghlan et al., 'Cut off, outnumbered and short of kit: how the Army came close to collapse', *The Times*, 9 June 2010.

74. Phil Sherwood, 'Reconstruction and Development in Afghanistan: A Royal

Engineer Regiment's Experiences', *RUSI Defence Systems*, October (2007), p. 91.
75. Farrell and Gordon (2009).
76. Coghland (2009), p. 129.
77. Leo Docherty, *Desert of Death. A Soldier's Journey from Iraq to Afghanistan* (London: Faber and Faber Limited, 2007), p. 68. The author was the aide-de-camp to the Helmand-based Task Force Commander. He later resigned from the army in protest against the British engagement in Afghanistan.
78. Fergusson (2008), p. 207.
79. Daniel Marston, 'British Operations in Helmand, Afghanistan', *Small Wars Journal* (2008), p. 2.
80. Anthony King, 'Understanding the Helmand Campaign: British Military Operations in Afghanistan', *International Affairs*, 86, no. 2 (2010), p. 312.
81. Ibid.
82. Fergusson (2008).
83. Antonio Giustozzi and Noor Ullah, '"Tribes" and Warlordism in Southern Afghanistan, 1980–2005' (Crisis States Research Centre LSE, 2008). CSI, 'Afghanistan: Helmand's Deadly Provincial Politics—Competition and Corruption' (Courage Services Inc. Produced for the US Marine Corps Intelligence Activity, 2008).
84. Kim Sengupta, 'Sacked for 'Corruption and Drug-Dealing', but Warlord Seeks Return to Power in Helmand', *The Independent*, 9 October 2007.
85. Cited in 'Helmand Ex-Governor Joins Karzai Blame Game', *IWPR*, 3 March 2008.
86. Coghlan (2009), p. 128.
87. Ibid.
88. Nick Carter, 'Briefing from Kandahar by Commander of Nato's Regional Command (South), Major General Nick Carter, 7 January 2010' (UK MOD Afghanistan Briefing, 2010).
89. Badie (2000).
90. Jeremy Page, 'It's called peace support at home. The troops here know it is a war', *The Sunday Times*, 5 August 2006.
91. Marston (2008), p. 2 (htpl version).
92. Farrell and Gordon (2009), p. 23.
93. Richard Norton-Taylor, 'Army Strategy in Helmand under fire from former top diplomat', *The Guardian*, 13 January 2011. By this time Sir Sherard Cowper-Coles had resigned from the Foreign Office and publicly criticized the US actions in Afghanistan.
94. Patrick Bishop, *3 Para* (London: HarperCollins, 2007).
95. Background paper on Musa Qala, written by Aziz Hakimi for Astri Suhrke et al., 'Conciliatory Approaches to the Insurgency in Afghanistan' (Bergen: Chr. Michelsen Institute, 2009).
96. The transfer of command was on 1 February 2007.

97. Syed Saleem Shahzad, 'Rough Justice and Blooming Poppies', *Asia Times on Line*, 7 December 2007.

98. Blair's statement to the Foreign Affairs Committee, House of Commons on 4 October 2001, cited in House of Commons, Foreign Affairs Committee, *Global Security: Afghanistan and Pakistan*, Eighth Report, sess. 2008–09 para. 215. http://www.publications.parliament.uk/pa/cm2008 09/cmselect/cmfaff/302/30209.htm#a44

99. Foreign Affairs Committee (2008–09), para. 221–5.

100. Ibid., para. 222.

101. Theo Farrell, 'Improving in War: Military Adaptation and the British in Helmand, 2006–2009', *The Journal of Strategic Studies*, 33, no. 4 (2010).

102. Peter Dahl Thruelsen, 'Counterinsurgency and a Comprehensive Approach: Helmand Province, Afghanistan', *Small Wars Journal* (2008), p. 7. http://smallwarsjournal.com

103. Farrell and Gordon (2009), p. 21.

104. Cited in Foreign Affairs Committee (2008–09), para. 231.

5. BUILDING THE STATE

1. Francis Fukuyama, *State-Building: Governance and World Order in the 21st Century* (Ithaca, NY: Cornell University Press, 2004).

2. Julia Taft, head of the UNDP's Crisis Prevention and Recovery Bureau. Author's notes from meeting, New York, January 2002.

3. Charles Tilly, *Coercion, Capital, and European States, A.D. 990–1990, Studies in Social Discontinuity* (Cambridge, Mass.: B. Blackwell, 1990).

4. For a recent assessment, see Mats Berdal, *Building Peace after War* (London: International Institute of Strategic Studies, 2009).

5. Barnett R. Rubin, 'Constructing Sovereignty for Security', *Survival* 47, no. 4 (2005), pp. 93–106.

6. Caplan (2002).

7. Paris and Sisk (2009).

8. International Monetary Fund, 'Islamic Republic of Afghanistan: Sixth Review Under the Arrangement Under the Poverty Reduction and Growth Facility, Request for Waiver of Nonobservance of a Performance Criterion, Modification and Performance Criteria, and Rephasing and Extension of the Arrangement': January 2010, IMF *Country Report* No. 10/22, Table 2, p. 19. (Sum of grants/public finances [11.8] and external budget grants [37.7])

9. United States Government Accountability Office, *Afghanistan. Key Issues for Congressional Oversight*, Washington, DC, April 2009, GAO 2009 (473SP), Table 1, p. 4, includes economic and military assistance, but not the cost of American troops in Afghanistan.

10. UNODC and the World Bank, *Afghanistan's Drug Industry: Structure,*

Functioning, Dynamics and Implications for Counter-Narcotics Policy, Washington, DC and New York, 2006, Chp 7.

11. Jonathan Goodhand, 'Frontiers and Wars: The Opium Economy in Afghanistan', *Journal of Agrarian Change*, 5, no. 2 (2005).

12. See chapter 1, notes 35 and 36. For a critical review of this literature, see Jonathan Di John, 'Oil Abundance and Violent Political Conflict: A Critical Assessment', *Journal of Development Studies*, 43, no. 6 (2007), pp. 961–86.

13. Deborah Bräutigam, 'Introduction: Taxation and State-Building in Developing Countries', in Deborah Bräutigam, Odd Helge Fjeldstad, and Mick Moore, eds, *Taxation and State-Building in Developing Countries* (Cambridge University Press, 2008), p. 19.

14. World Bank, *Afghanistan. State Building, Sustaining Growth, and Reducing Poverty. A Country Economic Report*, Grey cover, 9 September 2004 ed. (Washington, DC: World Bank, 2004), p. 40.

15. Government of Afghanistan, Ministry of Finance, *Donor Financial Review*, Report 1388 November, 2009, p. 15.

16. GAO (2009), Table 1, p. 4.

17. Ibid., p. 9. Aid figures differ according to source owing to different procedures for registration and accumulation. The figures used here are official GoA figures prepared for donors in 2009.

18. Zlatko Hurtic, Amela Sapcanin and Susan L. Woodward, 'Bosnia and Herzegovina', in Shephard Forman and Stewart Patrick, eds, *Good Intentions: Pledges of Aid for Postconflict Recovery* (Boulder, CO: Lynne Rienner, 2000), p. 325.

19. Arve Ofstad et al., 'Assessing Needs and Vulnerability in Afghanistan', (Bergen: Chr. Michelsen Institute, 2001).

20. CARE International in Afghanistan, 'Rebuilding Afghanistan: A Little Less Talk, a Lot More Action', Policy brief, 1 October 2002, cited in Barnett R. Rubin, Humayun Hamidzada and Abby Stoddard, 'Through the Fog of Peacebuilding: Evaluating the Reconstruction of Afghanistan' (New York: Center on International Cooperation, 2003), pp. 4–5.

21. *Securing Afghanistan's Future. A Government/International Agency Report*, March 2004. http://www.effectivestates.org/Papers/Securing%20 Afghanistan's%20Future.pdf

22. Jean-François Bayart, 'Africa in the World: A History of Extraversion', *African Affairs*, 99 (2000), pp. 217–67.

23. The text of the Compact is available on http://www.nato.int/isaf/docu/ epub/pdf/afghanistan_compact.pdf

24. See also Astri Suhrke, Kristian Berg Harpviken and Arne Strand (2004).

25. Barnett R. Rubin, *The Fragmentation of Afghanistan: State Formation and Collapse in the International System* (New Haven, CT: Yale University Press, 1995). The 2nd edition (2002) is in this respect identical.

26. GAO (2009), p. 4. The cost of US trainers is not included in this figure.

27. Rubin (1995), p. 113.
28. Martin Kipping, 'Two Interventions. Comparing Soviet and U S-Led State-Building in Afghanistan' (Kabul: Afghan Analysts Network, 2010).
29. The Russian General Staff, with Michael A Gress and Lester W. Gau, *The Soviet-Afghan War: How a Superpower Fought and Lost* (Lawrence: University Press of Kansas, 2002).
30. Astri Suhrke, 'The Dangers of a Tight Embrace: Externally Assisted State-building in Afghanistan', in Paris and Sisk (2009), p. 113.
31. Calculated on the basis of the IMF Sixth Review (2010), and World Bank, 'Interim Strategy Note for Islamic Republic of Afghanistan' (Washington, DC: World Bank, 2009). In the Ministry of Finance report to donors for 2009 the estimate of the external budget has suddenly shrunk to under half of total expenditure (45 per cent and was projected at 41 per cent for 2010: Ministry of Finance (2009), p. 8. Even allowing for increased revenue in 2009, that is certainly a major underestimate. US aid authorization for 2009 alone was $9.6 billion (GAO-2009, p. 4), or about three times the size of the entire external budget as per the Ministry report.
32. Stephen D. Krasner, 'Sharing Sovereignty: New Institutions for Collapsed and Failing States', *International Security*, vol. 29, no. 2 (2004), pp. 85–120. Another version was formal parallel structures of external audits of national administrations, most stringently imposed in Liberia after the civil wars (GEMAP), but in various forms also instituted in Afghanistan. In the World Bank, some officials spoke of 'economic peacekeeping'.
33. The domestic-funded proportion of the core budget had increased partly because key foreign-funded items, including some support items for the army, had been shifted from the core budget to the 'external budget'.
34. SIGAR, 'Actions Needed to Mitigate Inconsistencies in and Lack of Safeguards over U.S. Salary Support to Afghan Government Employees and Technical Advisors' (Washington, DC: Office of the Special Inspector General for Afghanistan Reconstruction [SIGAR], 2010), p. 3. This does not include salaries for Afghan security forces.
35. MoF (2009), IMF (2010).
36. World Bank, *Afghanistan. Builiding an Effective State. Priorities for Public Administration Reform* (Washington, DC: World Bank, 2008), p. xvii.
37. World Bank, *Afghanistan. Managing Public Finances for Development. Main Report* (Washington, DC: World Bank, 2005), p. viii.
38. World Bank (2009), p. 6. The ratio is from IMF (2010), p. 19, revised prognosis for 2009/10.
39. Vartan Gregorian, *The Emergence of Modern Afghanistan. Politics of Reform and Modernization, 1880–1946* (Stanford University Press, 1969), p. 142.
40. ANA forces were airlifted in aboard US aircraft.
41. Dipali Mukhophadyay, 'The Neo-Khan of Nangarhar', Unpublished paper, December 2010.

42. World Bank (2005).

43. Anne Tully and Richard Hogg, 'Scaling up Technical Assistance and Capacity Development in Afghanistan' (Kabul: World Bank Office, 2009).

44. SIGAR (2010), p. 8.

45. Ibid., pp. 13–14.

46. Tully and Hogg (2009) and Sarah Parkinson, *Means to What End? Policymaking and State-Building in Afghanistan* (Kabul: AREU, 2010).

47. Tully and Hogg (2009), p. 14.

48. Ibid, p. 8.

49. SIGAR (2010), p. 8.

50. Carl-Johan Dalgaard and Ola Olsson, 'Windfall Gains, Political Economy and Economic Development', *Journal of African Economies*, 17, no. AERC Supplement 1 (2008).

51. USAID/Afghanistan, 'Assessment of Corruption in Afghanistan (Kabul: USAID, 2009), p. 4.

52. USAID (2009), UNODC, *Corruption in Afghanistan. Bribery as Reported by the Victims* (New York: United Nations Office on Drugs and Crime, 2010); World Bank, *Fighting Corruption in Afghanistan. Summaries of Vulnerabilities to Corruption Assessments* (Washington, DC: World Bank, 2009), Integrity Watch/Afghanistan, *Afghan Perceptions and Experiences of Corruption. A National Survey 2010* (Kabul: Integrity Watch Afghanistan, 2010).

53. Cable from US embassy, Kabul, cited in Wikileaks report, The New York Times, 29 November 2010.

54. Ivar Kolstad, Verena Fritz and Tam O'Neill, *Corruption, Anti-Corruption Efforts and Aid: Do Donors Have the Right Approach?* Report prepared for Irish Aid (Bergen: Chr. Michelsen Institute, 2008).

55. World Bank (2009), 'Fighting Corruption', p. 2.

56. SIGAR, 'DOD, State and USAID Obligated Over 17.7 Billion to about 7,000 Contractors and Other Entities for Afghanistan Reconstruction During Fiscal Years 2007–2009', Special Inspector General for Afghanistan Reconstruction, Washington, DC, 27 October 2010.

57. Wikileaks cable, cited in *New York Times*, 3 December 2010.

58. World Bank (2009), 'Fighting Corruption'.

59. Ibid., p. 62. The president appoints the commissioner who heads the Afghan Reform and Civil Service Commission and its board.

60. The combined cost of the Commanders Emergency Response Programme (CERP) and project money for the PRTs was budgeted at $1.5 billion. Both are discretionary funds used by the US military in Afghanistan. Data provided by CENTCOM and reported on http://publicintelligence.info/afghanistan-commanders-emergency-response-program-cerp-spending-data-2010-2011/.

61. GAO, 'Afghanistan Development. USAID Continues to Face Challenges in Managing and Overseeing U.S. Development Assistance Programs'

(Washington, DC: United States Government Accountability Office, 2010), p. 5.

62. Susanne Schmeidl, 'The Good, the Bad and the Ugly—the Privatized Security Sector in Afghanistan', in Alex Dowling and Eden Cole, eds, *Security Sector Governance in Afghanistan* (Geneva: Geneva Center for the Democratic Control of Armed Forces, forthcoming).

63. Cited in Matthieu Aikins, 'Last Stand in Kandahar', *The Walrus (Canada)*, December 2010. http://www.walrusmagazine.com/archives/2010.12/

64. See note 60 above.

65. See e.g. Asia Foundation polls which provide longitudinal data. http://www.asiafoundation.org/news/2010/11/asia-foundation-releases-2010-afghan-public-opinion-poll/

66. Report from meeting with (US) senior civilian representative to NATO, Frank Ruggiero, cable from US Embassy Kabul, 25 February 2010, Wikileaks, reproduced in *The New York Times*, 29 November 2010.

67. E-mail to author from Clare Lockhart, associate of Ashraf Ghani, 5 February 2007.

68. Susanne Schmeidl, 'The Man Who Would Be King: The Challenges to Strengthen Governance in Uruzgan' (Kabul: The Liaison Office, 2010).

69. Parkinson (2010), sec. 5.

70. Joshua Partlow, 'Karzai calls on U.S. to lighten troop pressure', *Washington Post*, 14 November 2010.

71. Ahmed Rashid, 'It is time to rethink the West's Afghan Strategy', *Financial Times*, 24 June 2010.

72. Najibullah survived under protection of the UN in Kabul until 1996, when the Taliban entered the city and murdered him.

73. Statement by Sultan Aziz. UNAMA/ReliefWeb. Press briefing by Manoel de Almeida e Silva, UNAMA Spokesman, 21 September 2003, UN Assistance Mission in Afghanistan. Distributed by AFGHANDEV Digest—22–23 September 2003—Special issue (#2003–356).

74. Mark Sedra, 'The Four Pillars of Demilitarization in Afghanistan', in Michael Bhatia and Mark Sedra, eds, *Afghanistan, Arms and Conflict. Armed Groups,Disarmament, and Security in a Post-War Society* (London and New York: Routledge, 2008), p. 128.

75. Ibid., p. 140.

76. UN/S/2008/159, 6 March 2008, p. 9, and UN, *Report of the Secretary-General on the Situation in Afghanistan and Its Implications for International Peace and Security*' UN S/2008/695, 10 November 2008, p. 5. Sedra (2008), pp. 135–6 uses figures in the same order: 1,870 armed groups with 129,000 men when the programme started, claiming they are conservative estimates.

77. *US Army Times*, 3 June 2010.

78. The joint target for the ANA and the national police (ANP) was increased to 378,000, to be met by October the following year. Ray Rivera, 'Support

expected for plan to beef up Afghan forces', *The New York Times*, 16 January 2011.

79. Giustozzi (2009), 'The Afghan national Army'; Helge Lurås, 'Build-up of Afghan Security Forces Ill Advised', *Noref Policy Briefs*, 22 January 2010. http://www.peacebuilding.no/eng/Publications/Noref-Policy-Briefs/Build-up-of-Afghan-security-forces-ill-advised

80. Astri Suhrke, 'When More Is Less: Aiding Statebuilding in Afghanistan', in *Report in External Series* (Bergen: Chr. Michelsen Institute, 2006).

81. Aid then rose sharply: DoD and other agencies requested a total of $7.5 billion for 2010 to build the ANA. U.S. Government Accountability Office, 'Afghanistan Security: Afghan Army Growing, but Additional Trainers Needed; Long-term Costs Not Determined'. 27 January 2011. 2011http://www.gao.gov/products/GAO-11–66

82. LOTFA had a budget of $613 million for 2008–10. UNDP, 'Law and Order Trust Fund for Afghanistan (LOTFA) Phase V'. http://www.undp. org.af/whoweare/undpinafghanistan/Projects/sbgs/prj_lotfa.htm. By comparison, the US budget for support to the ANP for fiscal year 2009 was $1.5 billion. GAO (2009), p. 4.

83. World Bank (2004), and William Byrd and Stephanie Guimbert, *Public Finance, Security, and Development. A Framework and an Application to Afghanistan* (Washington, DC: World Bank. Policy Research Working Paper, 2009).

84. United Nations, *Report of the Secretary-General on the Situation in Afghanistan and its Implications for International Peace and Security*. S/2005/183, 18 March 2005, p. 14.

85. Mathieu Lefèvre, 'Local Defence in Afghanistan. A Review of Government-Backed Initiatives' (Kabul: Afghan Analysts Network, 2010), p. 1. The following discussion draws heavily from this report.

86. Ibid., p. 15.

87. Carlotta Gall and Ruhullah Khapalwak, 'Nato seeks Afghan police in the South', *New York Times*, 13 November 2010.

88. For a fuller discussion, see Astri Suhrke, 'Exogenous State-Building', in Whit Mason, ed., *The Rule of Law in Afghanistan* (Cambridge University Press, 2011) pp. 225–48.

89. Amin Tarzi, 'The Judicial State: Evolution and Centralization of the Courts in Afghanistan, 1883–1896' (New York University PhD thesis, 2003), p. 145, referencing similar findings by Ashraf Ghani, 'Disputes in a Court of Sharia, Kunar Valley, Afghanistan 1885–1890', *International Journal of Middle East Studies* 15 (1983); and Asta Olesen, *Islam and Politics in Afghanistan* (Richmond: Curzon, 1995).

90. Abdul Rahman Khan's chronicler, cited in Gregorian (1969), pp. 129–30.

91. Amin Saikal, *Modern Afghanistan: A History of Struggle and Survival* (London: I.B. Tauris, 2004), p. 80.

92. Ibid., p. 86.
93. Agreement on provisional arrangements in Afghanistan pending the re-establishment of permanent government institutions. http://www.afghang-overnment.com/AfghanAgreementBonn.htm
94. Abdulkader H. Sinno, *Organizations at War in Afghanistan and Beyond* (Ithaca, NY: Cornell University Press, 2008).
95. Ibid., p. 273.

6. DESIGNING A DEMOCRATIC TRANSITION

1. Gregorian (1969), p. 165. See also Vartan Gregorian, 'Mahmud Tarzi and Saraj-ol-Akhbar: Ideology of Nationalism and Modernisation in Afghanistan', *The Middle East Journal*, 21(3), summer 1967.
2. Text of this and the other constitutions are available on http://www.idlo.int/AfghanLaws/Laws%201921_todate.htm
3. Nazif M. Shahrani, 'Statebuilding and Social Fragmentation in Afghanistan: A Historical Perspective', in A. Banuazizi and Myron Weiner, eds, *The State, Religion, and Ethnic Politics: Afghanistan, Iran and Pakistan* (Syracuse University Press), 1986; Rubin (2002), p. 62; Saikal (2004), p. 106.
4. Richard S. Newell, *The Politics of Afghanistan* (Ithaca, NY: Cornell University Press, 1972), p. 98.
5. Cited in Saikal (2004), p. 116.
6. Thomas Ruttig, *Islamists, Leftists—and a Void in the Center. Afghanistan's Political Parties and Where They Came From (1902–2006)* (Kabul, Konrad Adenauer Stiftung, 2006).
7. Rubin (2002).
8. Saikal (2004).
9. Hasan M. Kakar, 'The Fall of the Afghan Monarchy in 1973', *International Journal of Middle East Studies*, vol. 9, no. 2, 1978, pp. 195–214.
10. George Reid Andrews and Herrick Chapman, eds, *The Social Construction of Democracy* (New York University Press, 1995).
11. Gilles Dorronsoro, *Revolution Unending. Afghanistan: 1979 to the Present* (New York: Columbia University Press, 2005); Kristian Berg Harpviken, 'Warlordism: Three Biographies from Southeastern Afghanistan', in Suhrke and Berdal (2011).
12. Paris and Sisk (2009), pp. 1–20.
13. Giustozzi (2008 and 2011) argues there was little overt violence; rather, underlying popular fear, and the transformation of warlords into politicians and of their movements into more conventional political parties explain the electoral results. An AREU analyst found that in the run-up to the 2005 elections, incumbents used force to dissuade other candidates from running, while the latter used violence to show that the incumbents

could not prevent disorder. Noah Coburn, *Parliamentarians and Local Politics in Afghanistan. Elections and Instability II* (Kabul: AREU, 2010).

14. The point was noted at the time. A state without power over its budgets and the military 'hardly merits the term democracy', Barnett Ruben wrote: Rubin (2005), p. 66. Ashraf Ghani referred to 'the sovereignty gap'. Ashraf Ghani, Clare Lockhart, and Michael Carnahan, 'Closing the Sovereignty Gap: An Approach to State-Building' (London: ODI, 2005). Ironically, both were influential voices arguing for increasing foreign aid, although this would sharpen the rentier character of Afghanistan and further weaken both sovereignty and democracy.

15. Håvard Hegre et al., 'Towards a Democratic Civil Peace? Opportunity, Grievance and Civil War 1816–1992', *American Political Science Review* 95, no. 1 (2001); Edward Mansfield and Jack Snyder, *Electing to Fight: Why Emerging Democracies Go to War* (Boston: MIT Press, 2005).

16. Chris Johnson et al. *Afghanistan's political and constitutional development*. Report prepared for DFID, London, ODI, January 2003, p. 12.

17. Author's interviews with Afghan human rights and civil society representatives, September 2002.

18. Suhrke, Leslie, and Strand (2003), p. 22.

19. ICG, 'The Afghan Transitional Administration: Prospects and Perils' (Brussels/Kabul: International Crisis Group, September 2002), p. 5.

20. Interview with author, October 2002.

21. Ibid., p. 5.

22. Thier, cited in Cornelia Schneider, 'Striking a Balance in Post-Conflict Constitution-Making: Lessons from Afghanistan for the International Community', *Peace, Conflict and Development*, 7, no. July (2005), p. 187.

23. Barnett R. Rubin, 'Crafting a Constitution for Afghanistan', *Journal of Democracy*, 13, no. 3 (2004). International Crisis Group, *Afghanistan's Flawed Constitutional Process* (Brussels/Kabul, June 2003).

24. ICG (2003), p. 3.

25. As recollected by independent observers to the *loya jirga* in interviews with author, July and August 2007.

26. Rubin (2004), p. 12.

27. External experts elaborated this view, e.g. Rubin (2004). This author and two colleagues made similar recommendations in a report prepared for the Norwegian Ministry of Foreign Affairs in 2004: Suhrke, Harpviken and Strand (2004).

28. Amin Tarzi, 'Afghanistan: What Unites the "United Front"?' http://www.globalsecurity.org/military/library/news/2007/05/mil-070510-rferl01.htm

29. Richard Soudriette and Andrew Ellis, 'Electoral Systems Today. A Global Snapshot', *Journal of Democracy*, 17 (2), 2006, pp. 78–88.

30. Andrew Reynolds, 'The Curious Case of Afghanistan', *Journal of Democracy*, 17(2), 2006, pp. 104–117.

31. Ibid., p. 107. In this version, an episode involving a bungled presentation of the rival proportional representation system is given much weight.
32. Reynolds (2006), p. 107.
33. Maley (2006), pp. 48–49; International Crisis Group, *Political Parties in Afghanistan* (Brussels/Kabul, June 2005).
34. Ruttig (2006), p. 42.
35. The US government-supported Asia Foundation also argued that focus group discussions had shown the Afghan people were strongly against political parties. 'Formative Research for Civic Education Programs on Elections: Focus Group Discussions in the North, West, Southeast and South of Afghanistan' (Kabul, The Asia Foundation, 2005).
36. Arthur Kent, 'Cashing in on Karzai & Co', *Policy Options*, November 2007, p. 11.
37. Author's interview with former US official in Kabul, July 2007.
38. The legislature was bicameral, with an elected lower house and the upper house partly indirectly elected and partly appointed by the president.
39. Andrew Wilder, *A House Divided? Analysing the 2005 Afghan Elections*, Kabul: AREU, 2005, p. 1; Reynolds (2006), p. 116; Ruttig (2006), pp. 42–6. The main parties were: Ittihad of Abdul Sayyaf (under a new name: Dawat), Jamiat led by Burhanuddin Rabbani, Wahdat led by Mohammad Mohaqqeq, Junbish of Abdul Rashid Dostum, and Hezb-e Islami (led by supposed defectors from the old party of Gulbuddin Hekmatyar).
40. Wilder (2005), pp. 20–25.
41. Anna Larson, 'The Wolesi Jirga in Flux, 2010, Elections and Instability I' (Kabul: AREU, 2010).
42. HRW, 'Blood-Stained Hands: Past Atrocities in Kabul and Afghanistan's Legacy of Impunity' New York: Human Rights Watch, July 2005. http://www.hrw.org/en/reports/2005/07/06/blood-stained-hands-0
43. Cited in Wilder (2005), p. 14.
44. Hafizullah Gardesh, 'Afghan Government Divided Against Itself', Institute for War and Peace Reporting, hereafter IWPR, 27 June 2007.
45. Amin Tarzi, 'Afghanistan: Amnesty Bill Places Karzai in a Dilemma', http://www.rferl.org/featuresarticle/2007/02/85e5a401–6ce9–4424-bbdc-01a084f6c60b.html, and later reporting by Ron Synowitz, http://rfe.rferl.org/featuresarticle/2007/03/69572c45-d232–4fc4-b4be-a5de9f9fb97c.html
46. For instance, USAID funded a programme for the State University of New York (SUNY) to provide technical assistance to the *Wolesi Jirga*, which included the establishment of a Budget Office in 2007. The programme leaders in Kabul found that Afghan parliamentarians were not always receptive to their advice and rarely solicited it. Interviews with author, Kabul, November 2009.

47. Marvin Weinbaum, 'The Legislator as Intermediary: Integration of the Centre and Periphery in Afghanistan', in A.F. Eldridge, ed., *Legislatures in Plural Societies: The Search for Cohesion in National Development*, Durham, NC: Duke University Press, 1977, pp. 95–121.

48. Joel D. Barkan et al., *Emerging Legislatures: Institutions of Horizontal Accountability*, Report prepared for the World Bank Institute, 2004, p. 32. http://www-wds.worldbank.org/servlet/WDSContentServer /WDSP/IB/2004/11/03/000012009_20041103133057/Rendered/INDEX/302630 PAPER0Building0state0capacity.txt

49. English summary of a report of the Kabul Center for Strategic Studies, prepared by Waliullah Rahmani, distributed by e-mail 22 January 2011. A Dari version is posted on www.kabulcenter.org

50. Dorronsoro (2005), p. 44 notes that most writers use the 10 per cent estimate. In 1979, that amounted to a population of 1.5 million, a figure also used by both Bernt Glatzer, 'Is Afghanistan on the Brink of Ethnic and Tribal Disintegration', in Maley (1999), p. 170, and Barnett Rubin (2002), p. 26. Rubin sources the information to a table of ethnic populations prepared by Anthony Hyman, *Afghanistan under Soviet Domination, 1964–83* (London: Macmillan, 1984), p. 11, which relies on the 1979 census data. Afghanistan's total population in 1979 was given as 15.3 million. There is no reason why the proportion of Hazaras in relation to the population as a whole would have changed dramatically since then. Official US publications use a 9 per cent figure, or 2.6 million of a total population estimated to 29.1 million in 2011. CIA, *The World Factbook*, Updated 13 January 2001, https://www.cia.gov/library/publications/the-world-factbook/geos/af.html

51. Borzou Daraghi, 'A formerly persecuted minority gains clout in Afghanistan', *Los Angeles Times*, 16 December 2010. The term 'advanced minority' is from Donald L. Horowitz, *Ethnic Groups in Conflict* (Berkeley: University of California Press, 1985).

52. Thomas Ruttig, 'Ghazni's Election Drama—It's the System', AAN Blog, posted 2 December 2010. http://aan-afghanistan.com/index.asp?id=1361

53. 'Election Stalemate and the Revival of Old Fault Lines', AAN Blog, posted 23 December 2010. http://aan-afghanistan.com/index.asp?id=1406

54. 'In September 2002, nearly a year after an American-led coalition deposed the Taliban, the United States launched what would become an aggressive effort to build or refurbish as many as 1,000 schools and clinics by the end of 2004, documents show. However [...] the U.S. effort was poorly conceived in a rush to show results before the Afghan presidential election in late 2004'. Joe Stephens and David Ottaway, 'A Rebuilding Plan Full of Cracks', *Washington Post*, 20 November 2005.

55. HRW, 'Campaigning against Fear: Women's Participation in Afghanistan's 2005 Elections' (New York: Human Rights Watch, 2005).

56. Scott Worden, 'Afghanistan: An Election Gone Awry', *Journal of Democracy* 21, no. 3 (2010): 15.
57. Worden (2010), p. 20.
58. Worden (2010), p. 15.
59. Astri Suhrke, 'Electing to Fight in Afghanistan' (Oslo: Norwegian Peacebuilding Centre (NOREF), 2009).
60. Martine van Bijlert, 'Election Blog No. 23: How much are we expected to believe?' Afghan Analysts Network, posted 23 August 2009. http://www.aan-afghanistan.org/index.asp?id=265
61. Worden (2010), p. 23, citing a report by the U.S. Special Inspector General for Afghanistan Reconstruction (SIGAR).
62. Jeffrey A. Dressler, 'Securing Helmand. Understanding and Responding to the Enemy' (Washington, DC: Institute for the Study of War, 2009), pp. 34–8.

7. REFORMING THE LEGAL SYSTEM

1. *Justice for All. A Comprehensive Needs Analysis for Justice in Afghanistan.* Prepared by the Ministry of Justice in cooperation with The Justice Sector Consultative Group. Kabul, May 2005, p. 3. A similar phrase appeared in the group's October 2005 report.
2. In the language of the OECD and aid agencies working in post-conflict reconstruction and peacebuilding, justice sector reform is broadly defined to include the police and the prison system, the state institutions that administer justice, and informal or traditional mechanisms for resolving disputes.
3. Curt Tarnoff, *Afghanistan: U.S. Foreign Assistance* (Washington, DC: Congressional Research Service. Reports to Congress, 2010), p. 7.
4. UNDP and Center for Policy and Human Development, *Rule of Law and the Search for Justice. Afghanistan Human Development Report 2007* (Kabul: Center for Policy and Human Development, 2007). Hereafter cited as UNDP/AHDR (2007).
5. The Afghan Independent Human Rights Commission, 2005, *A Call for Justice*. http://www.aihrc.org.af/Rep_29_Eng/rep29_1_05call4justice.pdf
6. Suhrke, Leslie and Strand (2003).
7. UN, *Report of the independent expert on the situation of human rights in Afghanistan*, M. Cherif Bassiouni E/CN.4/2005/122,11 March 2005, http://daccess-dds-ny.un.org/doc/UNDOC/GEN/G05/128/24/PDF/G0512824.pdf?OpenElement.
8. Lisa Rimli and Susanne Schmeidl, *Private Security Companies and Local Populations. An Exploratory Study of Afghanistan and Angola* (Berne: Swisspeace, 2007). See also report of the US Senate Armed Services Committee hearings on private security contractors in Afghanistan, October

2010, available at http://levin.senate.gov/newsroom/supporting/2010/ SASC.PSCReport.100710.pdf

9. Olesen (1995), Tarzi (2003); Bruce Etling, *Legal Authorities in the Afghan Legal System (1964–1979)*, Afghan Legal History Program, Islamic Legal Studies Program, Harvard Law School, p. 2. http://www.law.harvard.edu/ programs/ilsp/research/alhp.php

10. Marvin Weinbaum, 'Legal Elites in Afghanistan', *International Journal of Middle East Studies* 12, no. 2 (1980).

11. The other lead-nations were the United Kingdom (counter-narcotics) and the US (rebuilding the armed forces). The British role had a tinge of irony given the country's colonial history of promoting narcotics, including the Opium Wars to open the China market for opium from British India.

12. Matteo Tondini, *Statebuilding and Justice Reform: Post-Conflict Reconstruction in Afghanistan* (London and New York: Routledge, 2010), p. 47.

13. USIP, *Establishing the Rule of Law in Afghanistan* (Washington, DC: United States Institute of Peace. Special Report, 2004).

14. *Justice for All* (May 2005), p. 7.

15. ICG, *Afghanistan: Judicial Reform and Transitional Justice* (Kabul/Brussels: International Crisis Group, 2003), pp. 8–9.

16. Tondini (2010), pp. 47–9.

17. Martin Lau, *Islamic Law and the Afghan Legal System*, Paper prepared for the International Commission of Jurists, Geneva, http://unpan1.un.org/ intradoc/groups/public/documents/APCITY/UNPAN018244.pdf (accessed 14 May 2008).

18. Michael E. Hartmann and Agnieszka Klonowiecka-Milart, 'Lost in Translation: Legal Transplants without Consensus-Based Adaptation', in Whit Mason, ed., *The Rule of Law in Afghanistan* (Cambridge University Press, 2011), pp. 275–6. The authors worked with the UN and US rule of law projects in Kabul from 2005 to 2010.

19. Ibid. Di Gennaro resigned in July 2004, shortly after the law had been gazetted, amid reports of friction with the Italian Ambassador.

20. Hartmann and Klonowiecka-Milart (2011).

21. Interview with author, 18 May 2007. Hartmann and Klonowiecka-Milart (2011) confirm the threat to withhold funding.

22. Hartmann and Klonowiecka-Milart (2011), pp. 275–82, Tondini (2010), pp. 54–5.

23. Hartmann and Klonowiecka-Milart (2011).

24. David Nelken, 'Comparing Criminal Justice', in M. Maguire, R. Morgan and R. Reiner, eds, *Oxford Handbook of Criminology* (Oxford: Oxford University Press, 2002).

25. As told to Michael Hartmann, then seconded by the US State Department to UNODC, Hartmann and Klonowiecka-Milart (2011), p. 278.

26. Recollections of a UN official close to the programme, in interview with author, 20 May 2007.

27. Hartmann and Klonowiecka-Milart (2011), p. 284.
28. Only the number of trainees is available from websites of the consultant, Checchi and Company, as well as USAID. A report to Congress (Tarnoff 2010) on the rule of law programme in Afghanistan likewise only cites numbers of persons who have passed through the training programme.
29. Thomas Carrothers, *Promoting the Rule of Law Abroad. The Problem of Knowledge* (Washington, DC: Carnegie Endowment for International Peace. Working Paper, Rule of Law Series, 2003), p. 12.
30. UNDP/AHDR (2007), pp. 69–70.
31. Weinbaum (1980).
32. The Ministry of Justice signed off on 188 laws in the 2002–06 period, i.e. most before Parliament's first session in early 2006. Session 4 of the Joint Monitoring and Coordination Board, http://www.moj.gov/af/news.html#3
33. ICG (2003), p. 9.
34. Abdul Rahim Karimi could be presented as both a Tajik and an Uzbek; for the purpose of this appointment his Uzbek identity was the relevant one.
35. ICG (2003), p. 10.
36. Astri Suhrke and Kaja Borchgrevink, 'Afghanistan: Justice Sector Reform', in Edward Newmann, Roland Paris, and Oliver P. Richmond, eds, *New Perspectives on Liberal Peacebuilding* (Tokyo: United Nations University Press, 2009).
37. Scott Baldauf, 'The West pushes to reform traditionalist Afghan courts', *The Christian Science Monitor*, 21 February 2006. http://www/csmonitor.com/2006/0221/p01s04-wosc.htm
38. Barnett R. Rubin, 'Afghanistan's Uncertain Transition from Turmoil to Normalcy' (New York: Council on Foreign Relations 2006), p. 24.
39. Suhrke and Borchgrevink (2009).
40. *The Afghanistan Compact*, p. 8.
41. Tondini (2010), p. 84.
42. The UNDP was said to have urged the Afghans to start developing a plan to 'get the Italians off their back'. Recollections of UN official in the rule of law programme: interview with author, 20 May 2007.
43. *Justice for All* (May 2005), p. 3.
44. In interview with Kaja Borchgrevink, cited in Suhrke and Borchgrevink (2009), note 10.
45. Tondini (2010), p. 88.
46. Ibid.
47. M. Cherif Bassiouni and Daniel Rothenberg, 'An Assessment of Justice Sector and Rule of Law Reform in Afghanistan and the Need for a Comprehensive Plan. Paper Prepared for the Rome Conference 'the Rule of Law in Afghanistan', 2–3 July 2007', p. 35.
48. *The Afghanistan Compact*, p. 3. (Emphasis added).
49. Bassiouni and Rothenberg (2007), p. 35.

50. Rubin (2006), p. 24.

51. Hartmann and Klonowiecka-Milart (2011), p. 16.

52. When not otherwise noted, the two case studies draw on research carried out in Kabul in 2009–10 by the author in cooperation with Torunn Wimpelmann Chaudhary and Orzala Ashraf Nemat for a study supported by the Norwegian Ministry of Foreign Affairs. A full report is included in Ole Jacob Sending, ed., *Learning to Build Sustainable Peace. Ownership and Everyday Peacebuilding.* CMI Report 2010:4. Available on http://www.cmi.no/publications/publication/?3732=learning-to-build-a-sustainable-peace.

53. Juan R.I. Cole, 'The Taliban, Women, and the Hegelian Private Sphere', in Robert D. Crews and Amin Tarzi, eds, *The Taliban and the Crisis of Afghanistan* (Cambridge, Mass.: Harvard University Press, 2008), p. 118.

54. Andrea Fleschenberg, *Afghanistan's Parliament in the Making* (Berlin: Heinrich Böll Stiftung, in collaboration with UNIFEM, 2009), p. 113. See also Anna Wordsworth, *A Matter of Interests: Gender and the Politics of Presence in Afghanistan's Wolesi Jirga* (Kabul: AREU, 2997).

55. Fleschenberg (2009), quoting Thomas Ruttig, see also Andrew Wilder (2005).

56. Lauryn Oates, A *Closer Look. The Policy and Law-Making Process Behind the Shiite Personal Status Law* (Kabul: AREU, 2009).

57. The government maintains that the law was finally passed on 22 February, but there is no record of the Upper House discussing it that day or any other day.

58. Ali Wardak, 'Building a Post-War Justice System in Afghanistan', *Crime, Law & Social Change* 41(2004), pp. 319–41.

59. UNDP/AHDR (2007), p. 126.

60. Surveys for the report were conducted by a UNDP-supported centre based at Kabul University, the Centre for Policy and Human Development.

61. UNDP/AHDR (2007), pp. 128–32.

62. Amin Tarzi (2003).

63. Internal UNDP memo, forwarded to the author, 26 September 2007.

64. Author's notes from conference, Nansenskolen, Lillehammer (Norway), 7–12 August 2007.

65. Bassiouni and Rothenberg (2007), p. 36.

66. World Bank (2008), 'Building an Effective State', p. xiii.

67. Tondini (2010), p. 73.

68. ISAF, 'COMISAF's Initial Assessment', Kabul, 30 August 2009. See Chp 3, note 70.

69. *U.S. Government Rule of Law Strategy for Afghanistan.* 2010, p. 3. Document on file with author. Hereafter referred to as RoL (2010).

70. US Department of State, 'Afghanistan and Pakistan Regional Stabilization Strategy' (Office of the Special Representative for Afghanistan and Pakistan. Updated February 2010), p. xviii.

71. Figure for 2002–07 from Tondini (2011), p. 84.
72. RoL (2010), p. 5.
73. Ibid.
74. RoL (2010), p. 2.
75. The Executive Board of the American Anthropological Association was sufficiently concerned to establish a commission to examine the ethical issues of the Human Terrain System. See its statement 31 October 2007. http://www.aaanet.org/pdf/EB_Resolution_110807.pdf
76. Noah Coburn and John Dempsey, *Informal Dispute Resolution in Afghanistan* (Washington, DC: United States Institute of Peace. Special Report, 2010), p. 5.
77. The World Bank, *Judicial Systems in Transition: Assessing the Past, Looking to the Future* (Washington, DC: The World Bank, 2005).
78. For a recent formulation, see Abdullah An-Nai'im, *Islam and the Secular State* (Cambridge, Mass.: Harvard University Press, 2008).
79. Hartmann and Klonowiecka-Milart (2011), p. 267.

8. CONCLUSIONS: SCALING DOWN

1. The term is here used to denote the tendency in American foreign policy to attack a problem with military rather than non-military means. The historical and sociological roots of this tendency, as well as its consequences, are developed in the recent work by Andrew Bacevich (2005).
2. See chapter 4.
3. It is symptomatic that the title of Larry Goodson's book, published on the eve of the 2001 intervention, was *Afghanistan's Endless Wars. State Failure, Regional Politics and the Rise of the Taliban* (Seattle: Washington University Press, 2001)
4. Tarnoff (2010), p. 3.
5. An article written by Vahid Brown, an instructor at the Combatting Terrorism Center at the US Military Academy at West Point, and published in its journal, attracted a great deal of attention when it stressed the mutual distrust between Mullah Omar and Osama Bin Laden. Mullah Omar, for instance, asked the Al Qaeda leader to hand over his satellite telephones when he visited Kandahar. 'The Façade of Allegiance: Bin Laden's Dubious Pledge to Mullah Omar', *The CTC Sentinel*, vol. 3 Issue 1, pp. 1–5. http://www.ctc.usma.edu/sentinel/CTCSentinel-Vol3Iss1.pdf. Soon after the invasion, the differences between the Taliban and Al Qaeda, and the possibility of avoiding a larger conflict by dividing them by approaching the Taliban, had been obvious to general observers (Mann 2003). By 2010, when the international engagement was reaching a fork in the road, more detailed analyses on the nationalist perspective of the Taliban appeared in the public realm, including Ruttig (2010*)*, Brahimi (2011), Mullah Zaeef (2010) and Alex Strick van Linschoten and Felix Kuehn, *Separating the Taliban*

from al-Qaeda: The Core of Success in Afghanistan. New York: Center for International Cooperation, 2011.

6. Ottaway and Lieven (2002), see chp. 1.

7. Bertrand Badie (2000). See chp. 5.

8. See e.g. Thomas Ruttig, 'Direct US-Taleban talks and Bonn 2 conference', Afghanistan Analysts Network, 18 May 2011. http://www.aan-afghanistan.org/index.asp?id=1726

9. Ahmed Rashid, 'The Way out of Afghanistan', *New York Review of Books*, 13 January 2011, p. 19.

10. Miller (2011), see chp 1. For a similar view, see Frederick W. Kagan, *Defining Success in Afghanistan*, Washington, DC: American Enterprise Institute, 7 January 2011. http://www.aei.org/paper/100184.

11. *Washington Times*, 6 January 2011.

12. Zabi Ullah (pseud.), 'A View from Kandahar', *Afghan Voices*, December, 2010. Lowy Institute (Sydney), http://www.lowyinstitute.org/Publication.asp?pid=1478.

13. Ray Rivera, 'Support expected for plan to beef up Afghan forces, '*New York Times*, 16 January 2011.

14. Government Accountability Office GAO-09-473SP(2009), p. 4.

15. In the interests of full disclosure, it should be noted that this author signed an open letter to President Obama dated 10 December 2010, calling on the United States to open unconditional talks with the Taliban. The letter was signed by sixty scholars, journalists and analysts. Available on http://www.afghanistancalltoreason.com/

16. A task force co-chaired by Lakhdar Brahmi and Thomas Pickering and hosted by the Century Fund in New York issued in March 2011 its report with signposts for eventual talks, entitled *Afghanistan: Negotiating Peace*. (available at http://tcf.org/publications/2011/3/afghanistan-negotiating-peace). Parallel research on possible talks was undertaken at the Peace Research Institute, Oslo in cooperation with the United States Institute of Peace and the Chr. Michelsen Institute. The first report of the report, entitled *Afghan Perspectives on Achieving Durable Peace* was issued in June 2011 (available at http://www.prio.no/News/NewsItem/?oid=772796)

BIBLIOGRAPHY

Ackerman, Spencer. 'Drones Surge, Special Ops Strike in Petraeus Campaign Plan', August 2010. http://www.wired.com/dangerroom/2010/08/petraeus-campaign-plan/#ixzz0yCFaF0H2. (Accessed 31 August 2010).

Afghan Independent Human Rights Commission. *A Call for Justice*. Kabul, 2005. http://www.aihrc.org.af/Rep_29_Eng/rep29_1_05call4justice.pdf.

Aikins, Matthieu. 'Last Stand in Kandahar'. *The Walrus (Canada)*, December 2010.

Andres, Richard B., Craig Wills and Thomas E. Griffith, Jr., 'Winning with Allies. The Strategic Value of the Afghan Model', *International Security* 30, no. 3 (Winter 2005/6): 124–60.

Andrews, George Reid and Herrick Chapman (eds.), *The Social Construction of Democracy*. New York University Press, 1995.

An-Nai'im, Abdullah. *Islam and the Secular State*. Cambridge, Mass.: Harvard University Press, 2008.

Bacevich, Andrew J. *The New American Militarism: How Americans Are Seduced by War*. New York: Oxford University Press, 2005.

Badie, Bertrand. *The Imported State: The Westernization of the Political Order*. Stanford University Press, 2000.

Baldauf, Scott. 'Afghan campaign trail barely trod by Karzai'. *The Christian Science Monitor*, 31 October 2003.

Barkan, Joel D. et al. *Emerging Legislatures: Institutions of Horizontal Accountability*, Report prepared for the World Bank Institute, 2004.

Barnett, Michael N. *Eyewitness to a Genocide: The United Nations and Rwanda*. Ithaca, NY: Cornell University Press, 2002.

Barnett, Michael N. and Christopher Zürcher. 'The Peacebuilder's Contract: How External Statebuilding Reinforces Weak Statehood', in Roland Paris and Timothy D. Sisk (eds.), *The Dilemmas of Statebuilding*, 23–52. New York: Routledge, 2009.

Barno, David W. 'Fighting 'the Other War'. Counterinsurgency Strategy in Afghanistan, 2003–2005'. *Military Review*, September-October 2007.

Bassiouni, M. Cherif and Daniel Rothenberg. 'An Assessment of Justice Sector and Rule of Law Reform in Afghanistan and the Need for a Comprehensive

Plan. Paper Prepared for the Rome Conference 'the Rule of Law in Afghanistan', 2–3 July 2007'. http://www.law.depaul.edu/centers_institutes/ihrli/pdf/rome_conference.pdf

Bates, Robert H. *Prosperity and Violence: The Political Economy of Development*. New York: W.W. Norton, 2001.

Bayart, Jean-François. 'Africa in the World: A History of Extraversion'. *African Affairs*, 99 (2000), pp. 217–67.

Berdal, Mats. *Building Peace after War*. London: International Institute of Strategic Studies, 2009.

Bergen, Peter. 'After the Taliban'. *Washington Post*, 13 March 2005.

Biddle, Stephen. *Afghanistan and the Future of Warfare*. Carlisle, Pennsylvania: Strategic Studies Institute, U.S. Army War College, 2002.

Bishop, Patrick. *3 Para*. London: HarperCollins, 2007.

Brahimi, Alia. 'The Taliban's Evolving Ideology'. London: London School of Economics Global Governance Program, Working Paper 02/2010.

Bräutigam, Deborah. 'Introduction: Taxation and State-Building in Developing Countries'. In Deborah Bräutigam, Odd Helge Fjeldstad and Mick Moore (eds.), *Taxation and State-Building in Developing Countries*, pp. 1–33. Cambridge University Press, 2008.

————. Odd-Helge Fjeldstad and Mick Moore (eds.), *Taxation and Statebuilding in Developing Countries*. Cambridge University Press, 2008.

Brown, Vahid. 'The Façade of Allegiance: Bin Ladin's Dubious Pledge to Mullah Omar'. *The CTC Sentinel* 3, no. 1 (January 2010), pp. 1–5.

Bumiller, Elizabeth. 'In Afghanistan, Gates to talk of troop increases'. *New York Times*, 12 December 2008.

Burgess, Lisa. 'U.S. troop presence in Afghanistan at 17,900, and expected to hold steady'. *Stars and Stripes*, 9 July 2004.

Byrd, William and Stephanie Guimbert. *Public Finance, Security, and Development. A Framework and an Application to Afghanistan*. Washington, DC: World Bank. Policy Research Working Paper, 2009.

Caplan, Richard. *A New Trusteeship? The International Administration of War-Torn Territories*. Oxford University Press for the International Institute for Strategic Studies, 2002.

Carrothers, Thomas. 'Promoting the Rule of Law Abroad. The Problem of Knowledge'. Washington, DC: Carnegie Endowment for International Peace. Working Paper, Rule of Law Series, 2003.

Carter, Nick. 'Briefing from Kandahar by Commander of Nato's Regional Command (South), Major General Nick Carter, 7 January 2010'. UK Ministry of Defence Afghanistan Briefing, 2010.

Chandler, David. *Empire in Denial: The Politics of State-Building*. London; Ann Arbor, MI: Pluto, 2006.

Chandrasekaran, Rajiv. 'War the old-fashioned way'. *Washington Post*, 20 February 2010.

Chayes, Sarah. *The Punishment of Virtue. Inside Afghanistan after the Taliban*. New York: The Penguin Press, 2006.

Chesterman, Simon. *You, the People: The United Nations, Transitional Administration, and State-building*. New York: Oxford University Press, 2004.

Coburn, Noah. 'Parliamentarians and Local Politics in Afghanistan. Elections and Instability II'. Kabul: AREU, 2010.

Coburn, Noah and John Dempsey. 'Informal Dispute Resolution in Afghanistan'. Washington, DC: United States Institute of Peace. Special Report, 2010.

Coghlan, Tom. 'The Taliban in Helmand. An Oral History'. In Antonio Giustozzi (ed.), *Decoding the New Taliban*, pp. 19–54. London: Hurst & Co., 2009.

Coghlan, Tom, Deborah Haynes, Anthony Loyd, Sam Kiley and Jerome Starkey. 'Cut off, outnumbered and short of kit: how the Army came close to collapse'. *The Times*, 9 June 2010.

Cole, Juan R.I. 'The Taliban, Women, and the Hegelian Private Sphere', in Robert D. Crews and Amin Tarzi (eds.), *The Taliban and the Crisis of Afghanistan*, pp. 118–54. Cambridge, Mass.: Harvard University Press, 2008.

Coll, Steve. 'War by Other Means'. *The New Yorker*, May 24, 2010

Collier, Paul et al. *Breaking the Conflict Trap*. New York: Oxford University Press, 2003.

Constable, Pamela. 'The end of the Kabul Spring'. *Washington Post*, 11 June 2006.

Cooper, Robert. *Re-Ordering the World: The Long-term Implications of September 11th*. London: Foreign Policy Centre, 2002.

Cordesman, Anthony H. and Nicholas B. Greenough. *The Afghan War. A Survey of 'Metrics'*. Washington, DC: Center for Strategic and International Studies, 2009.

Crews, Robert D. 'Moderate Taliban?' In Robert D. Crews and Amin Tarzi (eds.), *The Taliban and the Crisis of Afghanistan*, Cambridge, Mass.: Harvard University Press, 2008.

Crowley, Jack. 'A million dollar militia', *Al-Jazeera International*, 2 September 2010.

CSI. 'Afghanistan: Helmand's Deadly Provincial Politics—Competition and Corruption': Courage Services Inc. Produced for the US Marine Corps Intelligence Activity, 2008.

Dalgaard, Carl-Johan and Ola Olsson. 'Windfall Gains, Political Economy and Economic Development'. *Journal of African Economies*, 17, AERC Supplement 1 (2008), pp. 72–109.

Daraghi, Borzou. 'A formerly persecuted minority gains clout in Afghanistan'. *Los Angeles Times*, 16 December 2010.

Darbon, Dominique, Ole Jacob Sending, Severine Bellina and Stein Sundstøl Eriksen. *The Legitimacy of the State in Fragile Situations*. Oslo: NORAD Report for the OECD DAC International Network on Conflict and Fragility, 2009.

DeYoung, Karen. *Soldier. The Life of Colin Powell.* New York: Alfred A. Knopf, 2006.

Di John, Jonathan, 'Oil Abundance and Violent Political Conflict: A Critical Assessment'. *Journal of Development Studies*, 43, no. 6 (2007), pp. 961–86.

Dobbins, James. *America's Role in Nation-Building: From Germany to Iraq.* Santa Monica, CA: RAND, 2003.

———. *The Beginner's Guide to Nation-Building.* Santa Monica, CA: RAND National Security Research Division, 2007.

———. *The UN's Role in Nation-Building: From the Congo to Iraq.* Santa Monica, CA: RAND Corporation, 2005.

———. *After the Taliban:Nation-building in Afghanistan.* Washington, DC: Potomac Books, 2008.

Docherty, Leo. *Desert of Death. A Soldier's Journey from Iraq to Afghanistan.* London: Faber and Faber Limited, 2007.

Donini, Antonio et al. 'Mapping the Security Environment. Understanding the Perception of Local Communities, Peace Support Operations and Assistance Agencies. Afghanistan Case Study'. Boston: Feinstein International Center, 2005.

Dorronsoro, Gilles. *Revolution Unending. Afghanistan: 1979 to the Present.* London: Hurst & Co., 2005.

Doyle, Michael W. and Nicholas Sambanis. 'International Peacebuilding: A Theoretical and Quantitative Analysis'. *American Political Science Review*, 94, no. 4 (2000), pp. 779–801.

Dressler, Jeffrey A. 'Securing Helmand. Understanding and Responding to the Enemy'. Washington, DC: Institute for the Study of War, 2009.

Duffield, Mark R. *Development, Security and Unending War: Governing the World of Peoples.* Cambridge: Polity, 2007.

Dwan, Renata, Thomas Papworth and Sharon Wiharta. 'Multilateral Peace Missions, 2001'. In *Yearbook 2002*, pp. 124–50. Stockholm: SIPRI, 2002.

Etling, Bruce. *Legal Authorities in the Afghan Legal System (1964–1979)*, Afghan Legal History Program, Islamic Legal Studies Program, Harvard Law School. http://www.law.harvard.edu/programs/ilsp/research/alhp.php

Farrell, Theo. 'Improving in War: Military Adaptation and the British in Helmand, 2006–2009'. *The Journal of Strategic Studies*, 33, no. 4 (2010).

Farrell, Theo and Stuart Gordon. 'Coin Machine: The British Military in Afghanistan'. *RUSI Journal*, 154, no. 3 (2009), pp. 18–25.

Fearon, James D. and David D. Laitin. 'Neotrusteeship and the Problem of Weak States'. *International Security*, 28, no. 4 (2004): 5–43.

Ferguson, Niall. *Virtual History: Alternatives and Counterfactuals.* New York: Basic Books, 1999.

Fergusson, James. *A Million Bullets. The Real Story of the British Army in Afghanistan.* London: Transworld, 2008.

Fleschenberg, Andrea. *Afghanistan's Parliament in the Making.* Berlin: Heinrich Böll Stiftung, in collaboration with UNIFEM, 2009.

Flynn, Michael T., Matt Pottinger and Paul D. Batchelor. 'Fixing Intel: A Blueprint for Making Intelligence Relevant in Afghanistan'. Washington, DC: Center for a New American Security, 2010.

Franks, Tommy. *American Soldier*. New York: Regan Books, 2004.

Fukuyama, Francis. *State-Building: Governance and World Order in the 21st Century*. Ithaca, NY: Cornell University Press, 2004.

Gall, Carlotta. 'Blair, in Kabul, warns that fight against the Taliban will take decades'. *New York Times*, 21 November 2006.

Gall, Carlotta and Ruhullah Khapalwak. 'NATO seeks Afghan police in the south'. *New York Times*, 13 November 2010.

Gardesh, Hafizullah. 'Afghan Government Divided Against Itself'. Kabul: Institute for War and Peace Reporting, 27 June 2007.

Garmarone, Jim. 'World Cannot Give up on Afghanistan, Coalition Officials Say'. *American Forces Press Service*, 28 July 2006.

Gelb, Leslie. 'Vietnam: The System Worked'. *Foreign Policy*, no. 3 (1971), pp. 140–67.

Ghani, Ashraf. 'Disputes in a Court of Sharia, Kunar Valley, Afghanistan 1885–1890'. *International Journal of Middle East Studies*, 15 (1983), pp. 353–67.

Ghani, Ashraf, Clare Lockhart and Michael Carnahan. 'Closing the Sovereignty Gap: An Approach to State-Building'. London: ODI, 2005.

Ghosh, Bobby. 'Obama Afghanistan Plan Breaks Old Ground'. *Time*, 28 March 2009.

Giustozzi, Antonio. 'The Afghan National Army. Unwarranted Hope?' *The RUSI Journal*, 154, no. 6 (2009), pp. 36–42.

———. 'Armed Politics in Afghanistan'. In Astri Suhrke and Mats Berdal (eds.), *The Peace in Between. Post-War Violence and Peacebuilding*. London: Routledge. Forthcoming 2011.

———. *Empires of Mud*. London: Hurst & Co., 2008.

———. *Koran, Kalashnikov and Laptop. The Neo-Taliban Insurgency in Afghanistan*. London: Hurst & Co., 2007.

——— (ed.) *Decoding the New Taliban: Insights from the Afghan Field*. London: Hurst & Co., 2009.

Giustozzi, Antonio and Noor Ullah. '"Tribes" and Warlordism in Southern Afghanistan, 1980–2005'. Crisis States Research Centre LSE, 2008.

Goodhand, Jonathan. 'Frontiers and Wars: The Opium Economy in Afghanistan'. *Journal of Agrarian Change*, 5, no. 2 (2005), pp. 191–216.

Goodson, Larry. *Afghanistan's Endless Wars. State Failure, Regional Politics and the Rise of the Taliban*. Seattle: Washington University Press, 2001.

Gordon, Michael R. 'Afghans block British plan for brigade force'. *New York Times*, 20 November 2011.

Gopal, Anand. 'The Battle for Afghanistan. Militancy and Conflict in Kandahar'. Washington, DC: New America Foundation, 2010.

Gregorian, Vartan. *The Emergence of Modern Afghanistan. Politics of Reform and Modernization, 1880–1946*. Stanford University Press, 1969.

Hammer, Anders Sømme. *Drømmekrigen. Hjerter og sinn i Afghanistan og Norge*. Oslo: Aschehoug, 2010.

Harpviken, Kristian Berg. 'Warlordism: Three Biographies from Southeastern Afghanistan'. In Astri Suhrke and Mats Berdal (eds.), *The Peace in Between: Post-War Violence and Peacebuilding*. London: Routledge. Forthcoming 2011.

Hartmann, Michael E. and Agnieszka Klonowiecka-Milart. 'Lost in Translation: Legal Transplants without Consensus-Based Adaptation'. In Whit Mason (ed.), *The Rule of Law in Afghanistan*, pp. 266–98. Cambridge University Press, 2011.

Hegre, Håvard, Tanja Ellingsen, Scott Gates and Nils Petter Gleditsch. 'Towards a Democratic Civil Peace? Opportunity, Grievance and Civil War 1816–1992'. *American Political Science Review*, 95, no. 1 (2001), pp. 33–48.

Horowitz, Donald L. *Ethnic Groups in Conflict*. Berkeley: University of California Press, 1985.

Human Rights Watch. *Campaigning against Fear: Women's Participation in Afghanistan's 2005 Elections*. New York: Human Rights Watch, 2005.

———. *Paying for the Taliban's Crimes*. New York: Human Rights Watch, April 2002.

———. *Blood-Stained Hands: Past Atrocities in Kabul and Afghanistan's Legacy of Impunity*. New York: Human Rights Watch, July 2005.

Hurtic, Zlatko, Amela Sapcanin and Susan L. Woodward. 'Bosnia and Herzegovina'. In Shephard Forman and Stewart Patrick (eds.), *Good Intentions: Pledges of Aid for Postconflict Recovery*, pp. 315–66. Boulder, Colo.: Lynne Rienner, 2000.

Hyman, Anthony. *Afghanistan under Soviet Domination, 1964–83*. London: Macmillan, 1984.

Ignatieff, Michael. 'Nation-Building Lite', *New York Times Sunday Magazine*, 28 July 2002.

International Council on Security and Development (formerly the Senlis Council), *The Relationship Gap*. July 2010. http://www.icosgroup.net/documents/afghanistan_relationship_gap.pdf.

International Crisis Group. *The Afghan Transitional Administration: Prospects and Perils*. Kabul/Brussels: International Crisis Group, September 2002.

———. *Afghanistan: Judicial Reform and Transitional Justice*. Kabul/Brussels: International Crisis Group, January, 2003.

———. *Afghanistan's Flawed Constitutional Process*. Kabul/Brussels: International Crisis Group June, 2003.

International Monetary Fund, 'Islamic Republic of Afghanistan: Sixth Review Under the Arrangement Under the Poverty Reduction and Growth Facility, Request for Waiver of Nonobservance of a Performance Criterion, Modification and Performance Criteria, and Rephasing and Extension of the Arrangement'. Washington, DC: IMF, *Country Report* No. 10/22, January 2010.

BIBLIOGRAPHY

————. *Empire Lite: Nation-Building in Bosnia, Kosovo and Afghanistan.* Toronto: Penguin, 2003.

Integrity Watch/ Afghanistan. *Afghan Perceptions and Experiences of Corruption. A National Survey 2010.* Kabul: Integrity Watch Afghanistan, 2010.

ISAF. 'COMISAF's Initial Assessment'. International Security Assistance Force Headquarters, Kabul, Afghanistan, 30 August 2009.

Jakobsen, Peter Viggo. 'NATO's Comprehensive Approach to Crisis Response Operations'. Copenhagen: Danish Institute for International Studies, 2008.

Jehl, Doughlas. 'Afghan Front Heats Up, and Rumsfeld Urges Patience'. *New York Times,* 8 September 2003.

Jones, Seth G. 'Averting Failure in Afghanistan', *Survival* 48, no. 1 (March 2006), pp. 111–28.

————. *The Graveyard of Empires. America's War in Afghanistan.* New York: W.W. Norton.

Johansen, Per Anders. 'Under ild nesten hver dag', *Aftenposten,* 17 August 2010.

Johnson, Chris and Jolyon Leslie. *Afghanistan. The Mirage of Peace.* London: Zed, 2004.

Johnson, Chris et al. *Afghanistan's political and constitutional development.* London: ODI. Report prepared for DfID, January 2003.

Kagan, Frederick W. *Defining Success in Afghanistan,* Washington, DC: American Enterprise Institute, 7 January 2011. http://www.aei.org/paper/100184

Kakar, Hasan M. 'The Fall of the Afghan Monarchy in 1973', *International Journal of Middle East Studies* 9, no. 2 (1978), pp. 195–214.

Kent, Arthur. 'Cashing in on Karzai & Co'. *Policy Options,* November 2007.

Kilcullen, David. *The Accidental Guerrilla: Fighting Small Wars in the Midst of a Big One.* London: Hurst & Co., 2009.

King, Anthony. 'Understanding the Helmand Campaign: British Military Operations in Afghanistan'. *International Affairs,* 86, no. 2 (2010), pp. 311–32.

Kipping, Martin. 'Two Interventions.Comparing Soviet and U.S.-Led State-Building in Afghanistan'. Kabul: Afghan Analysts Network, 2010.

Kolstad, Ivar, Verena Fritz, and Tam O'Neill. *Corruption, Anti-Corruption Efforts and Aid: Do Donors Have the Right Approach?* Bergen: Chr. Michelsen Institute. Report prepared for Irish Aid, 2008.

Krasner, Stephen D. 'Sharing Sovereignty: New Institutions for Collapsed and Failing States'. *International Security,* 29, no 2 (2004), pp. 85–120.

Larson, Anna. 'The Wolesi Jirga in Flux. 2010, Elections and Instability I'. Kabul: AREU, 2010.

Lau, Martin. *Islamic Law and the Afghan Legal System,* Paper prepared for the International Commission of Jurists, Geneva, http://unpan1.un.org/intradoc/groups/public/documents/APCITY/UNPAN018244.pdf

Lefèvre, Mathieu. 'Local Defence in Afghanistan. A Review of Government-Backed Initiatives'. Kabul: Afghan Analysts Network, 2010.

Lieven, Anatol. 'Only a Muslim UN force can secure peace', *The Independent,* 14 October 2001.

275

————. 'Insights From the Afghan Field'. Review Article. *Current Intelligence*, 6 September 2010.

Lutz, Catherine. 'Introduction: Bases, Empire and Global Response'. In Catherine Lutz (ed.), *The Bases of Empire: The Global Struggle against US Military Posts*, pp. 1–46. New York : New York University Press, 2009.

Lynch, Colum. 'Envoy urges UN not to send peacekeepers', *Washington Post*, 17 October 2001.

MacAskill, Ewen. 'Special envoy arrives for talks in Pakistan'. *The Guardian*, 27 October 2001.

MacEachin, Doug and Janne E. Nolan, *The US and Soviet Proxy War in Afghanistan, 1989–1992: Prisoners of Our Preconceptions?* Working Group Report no IV, November 15, 2005 (Washington, DC: Georgetown University). http://www12.georgetown.edu/sfs/isd/Afghan_2_WR_report.pdf, 10.

MacGinty, Roger and Oliver Richmond. 'Myth or Reality: Opposing Views on the Liberal Peace and Post-War Reconstruction'. In Roger MacGinty and Oliver Richmond (eds.), *The Liberal Peace and Post-War Reconstruction*, pp. 1–7. London: Routledge, 2009.

Maley, William. *Rescuing Afghanistan*. London: Hurst & Co., 2006.

————. *The Afghanistan Wars*. 2nd ed. New York: Palgrave Macmillan, 2009.

Maloney, Sean M. 'Afghanistan: From Here to Eternity?' *Parameters* 4, no. 1 (Spring 2004), pp. 4–15.

Mann, Michael. *Incoherent Empire*. London: Verso, 2003.

Mansfield, Edward and Jack Snyder. *Electing to Fight: Why Emerging Democracies Go to War*. Boston: MIT Press, 2005.

March, James G. *The Pursuit of Organizational Intelligence*. London: Blackwell, 1999.

Marsden, Peter and Josh Arnold-Forster. *An Assessment of the Security of Asian Development Bank Projects in Afghanistan*. Asian Development Bank, 2007.

Marston, Daniel. 'British Operations in Helmand Afghanistan'. *Small Wars Journal*. Posted 13 September 2008. http://smallwarsjournal.com/blog/2008/09/british-operations-in-helmand/

McKiernan, David. 'Speech to the Atlantic Council 18 November 2008'. http://www.acus.org/event_blog/general-david-d-mckiernan-speaks-councils-commanders-series

Miller, Paul D. 'Finish the Job. How the War in Afghanistan Can Be Won'. *Foreign Affairs* 90, no. 1 (2011), pp. 51–65.

Ministry of Finance, Government of the Islamic Republic of Afghanistan. *Donor Financial Review*, Report 1388. Kabul, November 2009.

Ministry of Justice. Government of the Islamic Republic of Afghanistan. *Justice for All. A Comprehensive Needs Analysis for Justice in Afghanistan*. Kabul, May 2005.

Morelli, Vincent and Paul Belkin. *NATO in Afghanistan: A Test of the Transatlantic Alliance*. Washington, DC: Congressional Research Service, 2009.

Mukhophadyay, Dipali. 'The Neo-Khan of Nangarhar'. Unpublished paper, December 2010.

Mundt, Alex and Susanne Schmeidl. 'The Failure to Protect: Battle-Affected IDPs in Southern Afghanistan'. Washington, DC: The Brookings-Bern Project on Internal Displacement. The Brookings Institution, 2009.

Nagl, John A. *Learning to Eat Soup with a Knife: Counterinsurgency Lessons from Malaya and Vietnam*. University of Chicago Press, 2005.

Nelken, David. 'Comparing Criminal Justice'. *Oxford Handbook of Criminology*, Mike Maguire, Rod Morgan and Robert Reiner (eds.), pp. 175–202. Oxford University Press, 2002.

Newell, Richard S. *The Politics of Afghanistan*. Ithaca, NY: Cornell University Press, 1972.

Noetzel, Timo and Thomas Rid. 'Germany's Options in Afghanistan'. *Survival* 51, no. 5 (2009), pp. 71–90.

Norton-Taylor, Richard. 'Army strategy in Helmand under fire from former top diplomat'. *The Guardian*, 13 January 2011.

North, Douglass Cecil. *Institutions, Institutional Change, and Economic Performance, The Political Economy of Institutions and Decisions*. Cambridge and New York: Cambridge University Press, 1990.

Oates, Lauryn. A *Closer Look. The Policy and Law-Making Process Behind the Shiite Personal Status Law*. Kabul: AREU, 2009.

Ofstad, Arve et al. 'Assessing Needs and Vulnerability in Afghanistan'. Bergen: Chr. Michelsen Institute, 2001.

Olesen, Asta. *Islam and Politics in Afghanistan*. Richmond: Curzon, 1995.

Oppel, Richard A. Jr and Taimoor Shah, 'Afghans and NATO differ on civilian deaths', *New York Times*, 26 July 2010.

Ottaway, Marina, and Anatol Lieven. 'Rebuilding Afghanistan; Fantasy Versus Reality'. Washington, DC: Carnegie Endowment for International Peace, Policy Brief no. 12, January 2002.

Page, Jeremy. 'It's called peace support at home. The troops here know it is a war'. *The Sunday Times*, 5 August 2006.

Palmer, Diego A. Ruiz. 'Afghanistan's Transformational Challenge'. *NATO Review*, summer 2005.

Paris, Roland and Timothy D. Sisk. 'Introduction: Understanding the Contradictions of Postwar Statebuilding'. In Roland Paris and Timothy D. Sisk (eds.), *The Dilemmas of Statebuilding*, pp. 1–20. New York: Routledge, 2009.

Parkinson, Sarah. 'Means to What End? Policymaking and State-Building in Afghanistan'. Kabul: AREU, 2010.

Partlow, Joshua. 'Karzai calls on U.S. to lighten troop pressure'. *Washington Post*, 14 November 2010.

Perito, Robert M. 'The U.S. Experience with Provincial Reconstruction Teams in Afghanistan: Lessons Identified'. USIP *Special Report*. Washington DC: United States Institute of Peace, 2005.

Porter, Gareth. 'Doubling of SOF Night Raids Backfired in Kandahar'. IPS, 15 September 2010. http://ipsnews.net/news.asp?idnews=52842

Rashid, Ahmed. *Descent into Chaos*, London: Allen Lane, 2008.
————. 'It is time to rethink the West's Afghan strategy'. *Financial Times*, 24 June 2010.
————. 'The Way out of Afghanistan'. *New York Review of Books*, 13 January 2011.
Rimli, Lisa and Susanne Schmeidl. *Private Security Companies and Local Populations. An Exploratory Study of Afghanistan and Angola*. Berne: Swisspeace, 2007.
Rivera, Ray. 'Support expected for plan to beef up Afghan forces'. *The New York Times*, 16 January 2011.
Ross, Michael. 'Does Oil Hinder Democracy?' *World Politics*, 53, no. 3 (2001), pp. 325–61.
Roy, Olivier. *Islam and Resistance in Afghanistan*. Cambridge University Press, 1990.
Rubin, Barnett R. 'Afghanistan's Uncertain Transition from Turmoil to Normalcy'. New York: Council on Foreign Relations 2006.
————. 'Constructing Sovereignty for Security'. *Survival*, 47, no. 4 (2005), pp. 93–106.
————. 'Crafting a Constitution for Afghanistan'. *Journal of Democracy*, 13, no. 3 (2004), pp. 5–19.
————. *The Fragmentation of Afghanistan: State Formation and Collapse in the International System*. New Haven, CT: Yale University Press, 1995. 2nd edn, 2002.
————. Humayun Hamidzada and Abby Stoddard. 'Through the Fog of Peacebuilding: Evaluating the Reconstruction of Afghanistan'. New York: Center on International Cooperation, 2003.
Ruttig, Thomas. *Islamists, Leftists—and a Void in the Center. Afghanistan's Political Parties and Where They Came From (1902–2006)*. Kabul: Konrad Adenauer Stiftung, 2006.
————. 'How Tribal Are the Taliban?' Kabul: Afghan Analysts Network, 2010.
————. 'Ghazni's Election Drama—It's the System', AAN Blog, posted 2 December 2010. http://aan-afghanistan.com/index.asp?id=1361
Røssum, Eystein. 'Eldreråd i nord stiller seg bak Taliban'. *Bergens Tidende*, 10 May 2010.
————. 'Norsk plan ramma fattige sivile'. *Bergens Tidende*, 12 May 2010.
Russian General Staff, with Michael A. Gress and Lester W. Gau. *The Soviet-Afghan War: How a Superpower Fought and Lost*. Lawrence: University Press of Kansas, 2002.
Saikal, Amin. *Modern Afghanistan: A History of Struggle and Survival*. London: I.B. Tauris, 2004.
Schmemann, Serge. 'U.S. and partners quickly set sights on a post-Taliban Kabul'. *New York Times*, 13 November 2001.
Schmidt, Peter. 'Stability Operation and Alliance Management: The German View'. National Institute for Defence Studies (Tokyo). 2008. www.nids.gov.jp

BIBLIOGRAPHY

Schmitt, Eric. 'Up to 2000 Marines to go to Afghanistan from Gulf'. *New York Times*, 26 March 2004.

Schmeidl, Susanne. 'The Good, the Bad and the Ugly—the Privatized Security Sector in Afghanistan', in Alex Dowling and Eden Cole (eds.), *Security Sector Governance in Afghanistan*, Geneva: Geneva Center for the Democratic Control of Armed Forces. Forthcoming 2011.

———. 'The Man Who Would Be King: The Challenges to Strengthen Governance in Uruzgan'. Kabul: The Liaison Office, 2010.

Schneider, Cornelia. 'Striking a Balance in Post-Conflict Constitution-Making: Lessons from Afghanistan for the International Community'. *Peace, Conflict and Development* 7, no. July (2005), pp. 174–216.

Sebestyen, Victor. 'Transcripts of defeat'. *New York Times*, 29 October 2009.

Sedra, Mark. 'The Four Pillars of Demilitarization in Afghanistan'. In Michael Bhatia and Mark Sedra (eds.), *Afghanistan, Arms and Conflict. Armed Groups, Disarmament and Security in a Post-War Society*, pp. 119–57. London and New York: Routledge, 2008.

Semple, Michael. *Reconciliation in Afghanistan*. Washington, DC: U.S. Institute of Peace, 2009.

Sending, Ole Jacob (ed.), *Learning to Build Sustainable Peace. Ownership and Everyday Peacebuilding*. Bergen: Chr. Michelsen Institute, 2010.

Sengupta, Kim. 'Sacked for 'corruption and drug-dealing', but warlord seeks return to power in Helmand'. *The Independent*, 9 October 2007.

Shahrani, Nazif M. 'Statebuilding and Social Fragmentation in Afghanistan: A Historical Perspective', in A. Banuazizi and Myron Weiner (eds.), *The State, Religion, and Ethnic Politics: Afghanistan, Iran and Pakistan*. Syracuse University Press, 1986.

Shahzad, Syed Saleem. 'Rough Justice and Blooming Poppies'. *Asia Times Online*, 7 December 2007.

Sherwood, Phil. 'Reconstruction and Development in Afghanistan: A Royal Engineer Regiment's Experiences'. *RUSI Defence Systems*, October 2007.

SIGAR. *Actions Needed to Mitigate Inconsistencies in and Lack of Safeguards over U.S. Salary Support to Afghan Government Employees and Technical Advisors*. Washington, DC: Office of the Special Inspector General for Afghanistan Reconstruction (SIGAR), 29 October 2010. www.sigar.mil/pdf/audits/SIGAR%20Audit-11-5.pdf

———. *DOD, State and USAID Obligated Over 17.7 Billion to about 7,000 Contractors and Other Entities for Afghanistan Reconstruction During Fiscal Years 2007–2009*. Washington, DC: Office of the Special Inspector General for Afghanistan Reconstruction (SIGAR), 27 October 2010. www.sigar.mil/pdf/audits/SIGAR%20Audit-11-4.pdf

Sinno, Abdulkader H. *Organizations at War in Afghanistan and Beyond*. Ithaca, NY: Cornell University Press, 2008.

Smith, Graeme. 'Talking to the Taliban'. *Toronto Globe and Mail*, 22 March 2008. http://v1.theglobeandmail.com/talkingtothetaliban/

BIBLIOGRAPHY

Smith, Justine. 'War on Terror. Bush's pledge: smoke'em out'. *The Mirror*, 26 September 2001.

Soudriette, Richard and Andrew Ellis. 'Electoral Systems Today. A Global Snapshot'. *Journal of Democracy* 17, no 2 (2006), pp. 78–88.

Stapleton, Barbara J. 'A Means to What End? Why PRTs Are Peripheral to the Bigger Political Challenges in Afghanistan'. *Journal of Military and Strategic Studies*, 10, no. 1 (2007).

Stedman, Stephen John, D. Rotschild and Elizabeth Cousens (eds.), *Ending Civil Wars: The Implementation of Peace Agreements*. Boulder, Colo.: Lynne Rienner, 2002.

Stein, Janice Gross and J. Eugene Lang. *The Unexpected War: Canada in Kandahar*. Toronto: Viking Canada, 2007.

Stephens, John and David Ottaway. 'A rebuilding plan full of cracks'. *Washington Post*, 20 November 2005.

Stepputat, Finn. 'Integrated National Approaches to International Operations: The Case of Denmark, the UK and the Netherlands'. Copenhagen: Danish Institute for International Studies, 2009.

Stewart, Rory. 'Where less is more'. *New York Times*, 23 July 2007, op-ed.

Strand, Arne and Organisation for Sustainable Development and Research. 'Faryab Survey. Comparison of Findings from Maymane, 2006 and 2009'. Bergen: Chr. Michelsen Institute, 2009.

Strick von Linschoten, Alex and Felix Kuehn. *Separating the Taliban from al-Qaeda: The Core of Success in Afghanistan*. New York: Center for International Cooperation, 2011.

Steele, Jonathan. 'Turkey asked to lead Islamic peace troops'. *The Guardian*, 18 October 2001.

Suhrke, Astri. 'The Dangers of a Tight Embrace: Externally Assisted State-building in Afghanistan'. In Roland Paris and Timothy D. Sisk (eds.), *The Dilemmas of Statebuilding. Confronting the Contradictions of Postwar Peace Operations*, pp. 226–51. London: Routledge, 2009.

———. 'Electing to Fight in Afghanistan'. Oslo: Norwegian Peacebuilding Centre (NOREF), 2009.

———. 'Exogenous State-Building'. In Whit Mason (ed.), *The Rule of Law in Afghanistan*, pp. 225–48. Cambridge University Press, 2011.

———. 'Reconstruction as Modernisation: The 'Post-Conflict' Project in Afghanistan'. *Third World Quarterly*, 28, no. 7 (2007): 1291–1308

———. 'When More is Less: Aiding Statebuilding in Afghanistan'. Bergen: Chr. Michelsen Institute, 2006.

Suhrke, Astri, and Kaja Borchgrevink. 'Afghanistan: Justice Sector Reform'. In Edward Newmann, Roland Paris and Oliver P. Richmond (eds.), *New Perspectives on Liberal Peacebuilding*, pp. 178–200. Tokyo: United Nations University Press, 2009.

Suhrke, Astri et al. 'Conciliatory Approaches to the Insurgency in Afghanistan'. Bergen: Chr. Michelsen Institute, 2009.

BIBLIOGRAPHY

Suhrke, Astri, Jolyon Leslie and Arne Strand, 'Afghanistan. A Snapshot Study'. In Nicola Dahrendorf (ed.), *A Review of Peace Operations: A Case for Change*, pp. 325–368. London: King's College, 2003. http://ipi.sspp.kcl. ac.uk/index.html

Suhrke, Astri, Kristian Berg Harpviken and Arne Strand. *Conflictual Peacebuilding: Afghanistan Two Years after Bonn*. Bergen: Chr. Michelsen Institute. Report prepared for the Norwegian Ministry of Foreign Affairs, 2004.

Tarnoff, Curt. *Afghanistan: U.S. Foreign Assistance*. Washington, DC: Congressional Research Service. Report to Congress, July 2010.

Tarzi, Amin. 'The Judicial State: Evolution and Centralization of the Courts in Afghanistan, 1883–1896'. New York University. PhD thesis, 2003.

———. 'Afghanistan: What Unites the 'United Front'?' http://www.globalsecurity.org/military/library/news/2007/05/mil-070510-rferl01.htm

———. 'Afghanistan: Amnesty Bill Places Karzai in a Dilemma', http://www. rferl.org/featuresarticle/2007/02/85e5a401–6ce9–4424-bbdc-01a084f6c60b. html,

Thier, J. Alexander. 'The Politics of Peacebuilding—Year One: From Bonn to Kabul'. In Antonio Donini, Norah Niland and Karin Wermester (eds.), *Nation-Building Unraveled? Aid, Peace and Justice in Afghanistan*, pp. 39–60. Bloomfield: Kumarian Press, 2004.

Thruelsen, Peter Dahl. 'Counterinsurgency and a Comprehensive Approach: Helmand Province, Afghanistan'. *Small Wars Journal* (2008). http://smallwarsjournal.com/blog/journal/docs-temp/100-thruelsen.pdf

Tilly, Charles. *Coercion, Capital, and European States, A.D. 990–1990*. Cambridge, Mass.: B. Blackwell, 1990.

Tondini, Matteo. *Statebuilding and Justice Reform: Post-Conflict Reconstruction in Afghanistan*. London and New York: Routledge, 2010.

Traub, James. *The Best Intentions: Kofi Annan and the UN in the Era of American World Power*. New York: Farrar, Straus and Giroux, 2006.

Tribal Liaison Office. 'Zabul Provincial Assessment'. Kabul: Tribal Liaison Office, 2008.

———. 'The Dutch Engagement in Uruzgan'. Kabul: The Liaison Office (formerly the Tribal Liaison Office), 2010.

Tuchman, Barbara. *The March of Folly: From Troy to Vietnam*. New York: Ballantine Books, 1985.

Tully, Anne, and Richard Hogg. 'Scaling up Technical Assistance and Capacity Development in Afghanistan'. Kabul: World Bank Office, 2009.

UK. House of Commons, Foreign Affairs Committee, *Global Security: Afghanistan and Pakistan*, Eight Report, sess.2008–09, http://www.publications. parliament.uk/pa/cm200809/cmselect/cmfaff/302/30209.htm#a4

UN. *Report of the Secretary-General on the Situation in Afghanistan and its Implications for International Peace and Security*. S/2002/278. 18 March 2002.

———. *Report of the Secretary-General on the Situation in Afghanistan and its Implications for International Peace and Security*. S/2002/737. 11 July 2002.

BIBLIOGRAPHY

————. *Report of the Secretary-General on the Situation in Afghanistan and its Implications for International Peace and Security.* S/2005/183, 18 March 2005.

————. *Report of the Secretary-General on the Situation in Afghanistan and its Implications for International Peace and Security.* S/2008/159, 6 March 2008.

————. *Report of the Secretary-General on the Situation in Afghanistan and its Implications for International Peace and Security.* S/2008/697, 10 November 2008.

————. *Report of the Secretary-General on the Situation in Afghanistan and its Implications for International Peace and Security.* S/2011/120, 9 March 2011.

————. *Report of the Panel on United Nations Peace Operations.* New York: United Nations, 2000.

————. *A More Secure World: Our Shared Responsibility.* Report of the Secretary-General's High-Level Panel on Threats, Challenges and Change. New York: United Nations, 2004.

————. *Report of the Independent Expert on the Situation of Human Rights in Afghanistan, M. Cherif Bassiouni* E/CN.4/2005/122, 11 March 2005.

UNAMA. 'Suicide Attacks in Afghanistan'. Kabul, 2007.

UNDP and Center for Policy and Human Development. *Rule of Law and the Search for Justice. Afghanistan Human Development Report 2007.* Kabul: Center for Policy and Human Development, 2007.

UNODC. *Corruption in Afghanistan. Bribery as Reported by the Victims.* New York: United Nations Office on Drugs and Crime, 2010.

UNODC and the World Bank. *Afghanistan's Drug Industry: Structure, Functioning, Dynamics and Impliations for Counter-Narcotics Policy*, Washington, DC and New York, 2006.

USAID/Afghanistan. *Assessment of Corruption in Afghanistan.* Kabul: USAID, 2009.

US Department of Defense. *Progress toward Security and Stability in Afghanistan.* Report to Congress. Washington, DC, January 2009.

————. *Progress toward Security and Stability in Afghanistan.* Report to Congress. Washington, DC, April 2010.

US Department of State. *Afghanistan and Pakistan Regional Stabilization Strategy.* Office of the Special Representative for Afghanistan and Pakistan. February, 2010. http://www.state.gov/documents/organization/135728.pdf

US Government Accountability Office, *Afghanistan. Key Issues for Congressional Oversight*, Washington, DC, April 2009.

————. *Afghanistan Development. USAID Continues to Face Challenges in Managing and Overseeing U.S. Development Assistance Programs.* Washington, DC, 2010.

————. *Afghanistan Security: Afghan Army Growing, but Additional Trainers Needed; Long-term Costs Not Determined.* Washington, DC, 2011.

BIBLIOGRAPHY

US Senate, Committee on Foreign Relations. *Afghanistan: Building Stability, Avoiding Chaos. Hearing.* June 26, 2002. Washington, DC; Government Printing Office, 2002.

USIP. *Establishing the Rule of Law in Afghanistan.* Washington DC: United States Institute of Peace. Special Report, 2004.

Van Bijlert, Martine. 'Unruly Commanders and Violent Power Struggles: Taliban Networks in Uruzgan'. In Antonio Giustozzi (ed.), *Decoding the New Taliban. Insights from the Afghan Field*, pp. 155–78. London: Hurst & Co., 2009.

————: 'Election Blog No. 23: How much are we expected to believe?' Afghan Analysts Network (AAN), posted 23 August 2009. http://www.aan-afghanistan.org/index.asp?id=265.

————. 'Election Stalemate and the Revival of Old Fault Lines', AAN Blog, posted 23 December 2010. http://aan-afghanistan.com/index.asp?id=1406

————. 'Counterinsurgency in Kandahar: What Happened to the Fence?' AAN Blog, posted 22 April 2010. http://www.aan-afghanistan.org/index.asp?id=730.

Van Ess, Brett. 'The Fight for Marjah: Recent Counterinsurgency Operations in Southern Afghanistan'. *Small Wars Journal*, September 2010. http://smallwarsjournal.com/blog/journal/docs-temp/563-vaness.pdf

Wardak, Ali. 'Building a Post-War Justice System in Afghanistan'. *Crime, Law & Social Change*, 41 (2004), pp. 319–41.

Weisman, Steven R. 'Resurgent Taliban threatens Afghan stability, U.S. says'. *New York Times*, 19 November 2003.

Weinbaum, Marvin. 'Legal Elites in Afghanistan'. *International Journal of Middle East Studies* 12, no. 2 (1980), pp. 39–57.

————. 'The Legislator as Intermediary: Integration of the Centre and Periphery in Afghanistan'. In A.F. Eldridge (ed.), *Legislatures in Plural Societies: The Search for Cohesion in National Development*, pp. 95–121. Durham, NC: Duke University Press, 1977.

Wilder, Andrew. *A House Divided? Analysing the 2005 Afghan Elections.* Kabul: AREU, 2005.

Witschi-Cestari, Alfredo, Paula Newberg and Michael Keating, *Coping with Complexity: Reforming International Assistance to Afghanistan, 1996–98.* UNCO, Islamabad, October, 1998.

Woodward, Bob. *Bush at War.* New York: Simon & Schuster, 2002.

————. *Obama's War.* New York: Simon & Schuster, 2010.

Worden, Scott. 'Afghanistan: An Election Gone Awry'. *Journal of Democracy* 21, no. 3 (2010), pp. 11–25.

Wordsworth, Anna. *Matter of Interests: Gender and the Politics of Presence in Afghanistan's Wolesi Jirga.* Kabul: AREU, 2007.

World Bank. *Afghanistan. State Building, Sustaining Growth, and Reducing Poverty. A Country Economic Report.* Grey cover edn. 9 September 2004. Washington, DC: The World Bank, 2004.

————. *Afghanistan. Managing Public Finances for Development. Main Report.* Washington, DC: The World Bank, 2005.

————. *Judicial Systems in Transition: Assessing the Past, Looking to the Future.* Washington, DC: The World Bank, 2005.

————. *Building an Effective State. Priorities for Public Administration Reform in Afghanistan.* Washington, DC: The World Bank, 2008.

————. *Interim Strategy Note for The Islamic Republic of Afghanistan.* Washington, DC: The World Bank, 2009.

————. *Fighting Corruption in Afghanistan. Summaries of Vulnerabilities to Corruption Assessments.* Washington, DC: The World Bank, 2009.

Yost, David S. *NATO Transformed: The Alliance's New Role in International Security.* Washington, DC: United States Institute of Peace Press, 1998.

Zabi Ullah (pseud.), 'A View from Kandahar', *Afghan Voices*, December, 2010. Lowy Institute (Sydney), http://www.lowyinstitute.org/Publication.asp?pid=1478

Zaeef, Abdul Salam. *My Life with the Taliban.* Alex Strick von Linschoten and Felix Kuhn (eds.). London: Hurst & Co., 2010.

INDEX

285